From Gutenberg to the Global Information Infrastructure

Digital Libraries and Electronic Publishing
series editor: William Y. Arms

Digital Libraries, William Y. Arms

From Gutenberg to the Global Information Infrastructure: Access to Information in the Networked World, Christine L. Borgman

From Gutenberg to the Global Information Infrastructure

Access to Information in the Networked World

Christine L. Borgman

The MIT Press
Cambridge, Massachusetts
London, England

First MIT Press paperback edition, 2003
© 2000 Christine L. Borgman

Set in Sabon by The MIT Press.
Printed and bound in the United States of America.

Library of Congress Cataloging-in-Publication Data

Borgman, Christine L., 1951–
From Gutenberg to the global information infrastructure : access to information in the networked world / Christine L. Borgman.
p. cm. — (Digital libraries and electronic publishing)
Includes bibliographical references and index.
ISBN 0-262-02473-X (hc : alk. paper), 0-262-52345-0 (pb)
1. Information superhighway. 2. Digital libraries. 3. Libraries—Special collections—Electronic information resources. 4. Information superhighway—United States. 5. Digital libraries—United States. 6. Libraries—United States—Special collections—Electronic information resources. I. Title. II. Series.
ZA3225. B67 2000
025.5'24—dc21   99-039906

10 9 8 7 6 5 4 3

Contents

Series Foreword

Since 1990, digital libraries and electronic publishing have moved from esoteric interests of a few visionaries to activities that are beginning to rival traditional libraries and traditional publishing. The catalysts have been technical (personal computers, the Internet, the World Wide Web), but contributions have come from every discipline that values the dissemination of high-quality information. Many of the challenges associated with building the new libraries are social, economic, or legal rather than technical.

Digital libraries are being implemented by people who work within conventional libraries, but also by people who do not consider themselves librarians or publishers. The World Wide Web has created new professions. Research in digital libraries has become a vibrant academic subdiscipline, with computer scientists working alongside economists, sociologists, lawyers, and librarians. An interdisciplinary body of expertise is emerging.

To write books about digital libraries may seem a contradiction. Most researchers in this field rely heavily on the Internet for current information, but these same people are very conscious of the strengths of conventional publications. Innovation and current research are widely reported in articles and papers published in journals and magazines and presented at conferences; much of this detailed material is openly available online. A book provides an opportunity to be more contemplative and to give perspective to a field. The aim of The MIT Press's series on Digital Libraries and Electronic Publishing is to provide a context. The hope is to have created a series that is valuable to both specialists and nonspecialists. The specialists will see how other leaders in the field view the state of the art, recent research, and longer-term trends. The non-specialists will be introduced to the initiatives that are leading to the new generation of libraries and publishing.

William Y. Arms

Preface

Amidst the enthusiasm surrounding the emerging global information infrastructure are claims that computer networks are the greatest advance in human communication since Gutenberg invented printing. Many contend that printed books and journals will soon be replaced by electronic documents that are malleable, mutable, and mobile. Physical libraries will be replaced by digital libraries, and librarians by cybrarians. Paper archives will be replaced by digital archives, and the appraisal role of archivists will no longer be needed because saving everything will be easier and cheaper. Commerce will be conducted online, and the neighborhood shopping mall will fade away. Political jurisdictions will cease to matter, as cyberspace respects few boundaries. Freedom of speech will become absolute, as people communicate across borders over a populist, decentralized medium devoid of central authority.

We are in the early stages of birthing a global information infrastructure (GII) and already the hyperbole of such statements is apparent. In the first place, Johannes Gutenberg did not invent either printing or movable type. Both originated in Asia centuries before his birth. Gutenberg's accomplishment was to perfect printing with movable type. To do so, he drew upon his knowledge of metalwork and jewelry making and experimented with inks, molds for letters, and presses. It was his holistic approach that enabled him to perfect each step of the process (Berger 1998), thereby contributing significantly to the technology of human communication.

This book does not claim to invent the ideas of a global information infrastructure or access to information, or any of the component parts, including computer networks, digital libraries, digital preservation, electronic publishing, information retrieval, human-computer interface design, telecommunications, information-related behavior, or information policy. Rather, following Gutenberg's example, the goal is a holistic approach to addressing access to information in a networked world. This book discusses all of these issues and more, drawing upon research and practice in computer science, communication, library and information science, psychology, law, information policy, sociology, history, political science, economics, education, business, archives, and museum studies. Domestic and international issues are explored, and my empirical research is complemented by extensive literature reviews and analyses. Considerable attention is devoted to defining terminology, given the many perspectives on issues related to access to information.

Providing access to information is only one of many reasons for constructing a GII, but an essential one. The success of applications such as electronic commerce, education, entertainment, and interpersonal communication depends upon the ability to discover and locate information, whether about products, services, people, places, facts, or ideas of interest. None of these applications are new. What is new is the process by which they are conducted. Activities associated with familiar physical spaces for working, shopping, browsing through bookshelves, wandering through galleries, playing games, or meeting friends for coffee are occurring in virtual spaces. Many activities associated with separate places are converging, all conducted from a single computer console. Yet other activities that were associated with a single place are now diverging, conducted over mobile and tetherless information appliances.

How will these new information technologies change the way that people lead their lives? History shows that, time and again, new technologies have supplemented, rather than supplanted, old ways of doing things. Most of the exaggerated promises for information technology arise from attempts to reinvent commerce, education, entertainment, communication, publishing, and libraries as though no lessons from the past carried over to this new environment. Much experience will carry forward, however. People know how to work, how to shop, how to learn, how to play, and how to talk to others. They will adopt new technologies for these activities when the technologies offer some perceived benefits, at a cost in time, money, and effort that they deem reasonable. They will adapt these technologies to suit their interests and needs. Technologies that are not perceived as useful, that are not compatible with the behavior and activities of their intended audience, or that are simply too hard to use will not be adopted. Technologies can and do fail in the marketplace. Thus, it is unwise to assume that if a global information infrastructure is built, people necessarily will come.

Most of the efforts in building a GII are being devoted to the technology and to policy, with relatively little attention to human behavior. Efforts are underway to scale up the Internet of today to support orders of magnitude more users, devices, and traffic on a GII. Information policy is actively concerned with issues such as copyright, fair use, privacy, filtering, cryptography, and trans-border data flows. But where do individuals and institutions fit in this picture? What technologies will they choose to adopt? How will individuals adapt technologies to suit their interests and needs, and how will institutions adapt them to their mission, their goals, and their managerial styles? What policies are viable, in view of the ways people create, use, and seek information? And what technologies and policies are portable across countries and cultures?

The success of a global information infrastructure will depend upon how well it fits into people's daily lives. To be attractive, it should be easy to use, available, and affordable, and it should fill perceived needs. But what do these terms mean, and to whom? What is known about information-related behavior, and how can that knowledge be applied to designing a GII that will achieve its promise of improving access to information? Therein lies the focus of this book. Much is known about the information-related behavior of individuals and institutions, yet relatively little of that knowledge is being applied to the design of digital libraries, national and global information infrastructures, or information policy. This book draws upon that body of research and practice to identify ways it can be employed in constructing a GII that is useful and usable to a broad audience.

Chapter 1 introduces the premise and the promise of a global information infrastructure, exploring concepts of technology adoption and adaptation, infrastructure, and the co-evolution of technology and behavior. Chapter 2 examines concepts of digital libraries that arise from multiple and competing perspectives. The term "library" is taking on new meanings, some narrower and some broader than before. I propose the construct of a global digital library as a way to explore behavioral, technical, and policy issues in information access. Chapter 3 is devoted to defining what is meant by "access to information," drawing upon ideas from libraries, telecommunications, law, and other arenas. The concepts of access and information are examined separately and together. Chapter 4 addresses the cycle of creating, using, and seeking information. Chapters 5 and 6 identify the difficulties in using digital libraries and ways to make them easier to use in the future.

The next two chapters draw together issues of communities, collections, and content. Chapter 7 assesses the role of libraries as institutions and how they are adapting to an age of distributed computer networks. Many lessons about moving from print to electronic environments can be learned from the experiences of libraries. Chapter 8 examines the tradeoffs in acting locally in the design of information systems and services while thinking globally. This chapter draws together issues of standards, data exchange, portability, interoperability, language, linguistics, and institutional practices.

In the concluding chapter, I reexamine the concept of a global digital library and the challenges inherent in scaling up from the Internet to a global information infrastructure. About half of the chapter is devoted to a case study of information infrastructure developments in Central and Eastern Europe after the end of the Cold War. This region entered the 1990s with minimal telecommunications and computing infrastructure and was immediately inundated with information technology. To explore the portability of information infrastructure across countries and cultures, I examine the choices that were made and the institutional and social changes that were wrought.

These are but the early days of constructing a global information infrastructure. As far as we have come, the penetration of personal computers into homes did not reach 50 percent in the United States until 1998 (Fox 1999), and the levels are much lower in most other countries. The promise of ubiquitous computing, ubiquitous networks, and ubiquitous information has yet to be achieved, and it may never be. Whether such an environment is desirable remains to be determined too.

This book raises more questions than it answers. But now is the time to be raising these questions. Individuals, institutions, businesses, and governments are making strategic decisions that will influence the design of information systems and services and associated applications in commerce, education, communication, entertainment, and government. The audience for this book includes scholars, practitioners, policy makers involved in making these decisions, students, and even users. I hope this book will stimulate discussion among all these players, because decisions made now will influence access to information, for everyone, for generations to come.

Acknowledgments

Behind the lonely process of writing a sole-authored book are the contributions of many colleagues, friends, and family. This book is no exception. First and foremost, credit is due to my husband, George M. Mood, who edited several drafts of the manuscript, as he has edited everything else I have published for more than 20 years. He also accompanied me on most of the journeys to collect data, living in England and Hungary and traveling in nearly 20 other countries over a decade. He shared not only in the agonies of writing, but in the joys of discovery. We were enlightened by conversations with colleagues at home and abroad, in offices and coffee shops, over desks and dinner tables, online and off.

The colleagues and friends who contributed time, effort, ideas, critiques, and materials are indeed too numerous to mention, but I will try, and apologize in advance to those I miss. Philip Agre of UCLA, Clifford Lynch of the Coalition for Networked Information, and Gary Marchionini of the University of North Carolina provided comprehensive reviews of the manuscript, completed in the summer of 1998. I substantially rewrote the manuscript based on their expert, thoughtful, and honest critiques. As a result, the book will appear six months later than planned, but is a far better product. Doug Sery, my editor at The MIT Press, has been remarkably, and thankfully, patient with my attempts at perfectionism.

My colleagues at UCLA have been generous with their time in helping me sort out ideas, in answering questions on fine points of technology, policy, practice, and history, and in referring me to useful information sources. These include Michele Cloonan, Jonathan Furner, Anne Gilliland-Swetland, Robert Hayes, Greg Leazer, Leah Lievrouw, and Mary Niles Maack in Information Studies; Aimee Dorr, Yasmin Kafai, and Ted Mitchell in

Education; Ivan Berend in the Center for European and Russian Studies; Leonard Kleinrock in Computer Science; Katalin Radics and Brian Schottlaender of the university libraries; Abdelmonem Afifi in Public Health; and Charles Kennel, who now heads the Scripps Institute of Oceanography. The students in my doctoral seminar on Information-Seeking Behavior in the fall term of 1998 read the penultimate manuscript and provided honest and valuable critiques. Appreciation is due to my fine colleagues, especially Margaret Evans, A. J. (Jack) Meadows, Ann O'Brien, and Cliff McKnight, at Loughborough University in England, where I have served as visiting professor since 1996. Many people at other institutions offered ideas, guidance, and resources for the work that resulted in this book. These include Dan Atkins of the University of Michigan; Micheline Beaulieu at Sheffield University; Michael Brittain of Victoria University (New Zealand); Michael Buckland and Peter Lyman of UC Berkeley; Wilma Minty at Oxford University; Jerry Campbell and Sandra Ball-Rokeach of the University of Southern California; Donald Case of the University of Kentucky; Blaise Cronin of Indiana University; Lorcan Dempsey of the UK Office for Library Networking; Ed Fox of Virginia Tech; Andrew Lass of Mt. Holyoke College; Michael Lesk of Bellcore and the National Science Foundation; Edward O'Neill and Liz Bishoff of the OCLC Online Computer Library Center; Roy Pea of SRI; Marc Rotenberg of the Electronic Privacy Information Center; Ben Shneiderman of the University of Maryland; Terry Smith of UC Santa Barbara; Leigh Star, Geoff Bowker, and Ann Bishop of the University of Illinois; Barbara Tillett of the Library of Congress; and Irene Wormell of the Royal Danish School of Librarianship. Clifford Lynch and Phil Agre have generously shared their technical expertise and vision on matters of information technology and policy, in many lengthy discussions. Sara Miller McCune, Chairman of Sage Publications, has been a rich source of knowledge about scholarly publishing, both print and electronic. William Paisley, my doctoral advisor at Stanford University, provided not only a solid grounding in scholarly communication but also continuing guidance in electronic publishing and related topics.

The Council on Library and Information Resources, on whose Board of Directors I serve, is a fountain of expertise about the challenges facing libraries and archives in these rapidly changing seas. Principals at CLIR include Deanna Marcum (president), Donald Waters (then head of the

Digital Library Federation), and W. David Penniman (past president). Y. T. Chien, Stephen Griffin, Su-Shing Chen, Les Gasser, and Michael Lesk, present and former staff of the National Science Foundation, provided me with many opportunities to participate in the Digital Libraries Initiatives. My three years of service on the board of the Regional Library Program (now the Networked Library Program) of the Soros Foundation Open Society Institute were invaluable for my research in Central and Eastern Europe, providing additional opportunities to travel in the region and to visit many institutions. Thanks are due to my insightful and dedicated colleagues on the board, Peter Burnett of Oxford University, Gvozden Flego of the University of Zagreb, Ekaterina Genieva of the Library for Foreign Literature in Moscow, Marianna Tax Choldin of the University of Illinois, and Winston Tabb of the Library of Congress, and the RLP staff, Melissa Hagemann and Rima Kupryte. Profound gratitude is due to the several hundred people in six countries in the region who responded to surveys and participated in interviews about information infrastructure. Public thanks can be given to a cadre of colleagues who have provided continuing consultation and guidance, however: Martin Svoboda of the Czech Republic; Zsolt Banhegyi, Sandor Daranyi, Andras Gabor, and Agnes Koreny of Hungary; and Predrag Pale, Nenad Prelog, Velimir Srica, and Mirna Willer of Croatia. Monika Klasnja and Vida Mocnik of Slovenia are inspirational and exemplify the energy of their small country.

The book was delayed while I wrote several journal articles based on empirical data, so that the data would appear more quickly and comprehensively and could be synthesized further here. Thanks are due to the journal editors who agreed to publish those articles under those conditions: Richard Kimber of the *Journal of Documentation,* John Richardson of *Library Quarterly,* and Tefko Saracevic of *Information Processing and Management.*

Support for the research reported here was provided by many sources over many years. The studies reported in chapter 5 on energy researchers and on the Science Library Catalog were funded by the US Department of Energy and the Sloan Foundation, respectively. Funding for the research in Central and Eastern Europe reported in chapter 9 was provided by the Office of International Studies and Overseas Programs, the Academic Senate, the Center for European and Russian Studies, and the Graduate

School of Education and Information Studies of UCLA; the Hungarian Ministry of Culture and Education, with funding from the World Bank; the Hungarian-American Fulbright Commission; the US Embassy in Slovenia; and the Ministry of Science, Technology, and Informatics of Croatia. The Mellon Foundation provided funding for additional research currently in progress by Nadia Caidi for her doctoral dissertation, under my supervision. Writing this book began in earnest at the Bellagio Study Center in Bellagio, Italy, in 1994 under a fellowship from the Rockefeller Foundation. I am eternally grateful for the rare opportunity of having a month of solitude to write, in the good care of the Bellagio staff, and the stimulating company of other scholars from around the world.

No major research project could be accomplished without able graduate students. Marianne Afifi, Nadia Caidi, Eva Fodor, Aniko Halverson, Agnes Koreny, and Katalin Radics provided superlative research assistance in multiple languages. Eva Fodor and Aniko Halverson assisted in the design and analysis of the mail survey of Central and Eastern European libraries. Nadia Caidi and Eun Park compiled the bibliography, checking and cross-checking a vast array of sources.

Many of those acknowledged will note that their names are misspelled because diacritics have been omitted. The same is true of bibliographic references, titles, and place names in the text. Diacritics and special characters frequently are omitted, changed, or incorrectly introduced through the processes associated with publishing and citing, and through storage, retrieval, and distribution in electronic forms. As a result, it is difficult to verify spellings of names and other words that contain diacritics. I made the pragmatic decision to be consistent by omitting diacritics and special characters. To keep them on the occasions where they could be found and verified would only suggest that words without diacritics are correct. The broader implications of this decision become apparent in chapter 8.

I am indebted to all of these and many others who guided, encouraged, and cajoled me throughout the writing process.

From Gutenberg to the Global Information Infrastructure

1

The Premise and the Promise of a Global Information Infrastructure

Let us build a global community in which the people of neighboring countries view each other not as potential enemies, but as potential partners, as members of the same family in the vast, increasingly interconnected human family.
—Vice-President Al Gore (1994a)

The information society has the potential to improve the quality of life of Europe's citizens, the efficiency of our social and economic organization and to reinforce cohesion.
—Bangemann Report (1994)

The premise of a global information infrastructure is that governments, businesses, communities, and individuals can cooperate to link the world's telecommunication and computer networks together into a vast constellation capable of carrying digital and analog signals in support of every conceivable information and communication application. The promise is that this constellation of networks will promote an information society that benefits all: peace, friendship, and cooperation through improved interpersonal communications; empowerment through access to information for education, business, and social good; more productive labor through technology-enriched work environments; and stronger economies through open competition in global markets.

The promise is exciting and the premise appears rational. Information technologies are advancing at a rapid pace and becoming ever more ubiquitous. Many scholars, policy makers, technologists, business people, and pundits contend that changes wrought by these new technologies are revolutionary and will result in profound transformations of society. Physical location will cease to matter. More and more human activities in working, learning, conducting commerce, and communicating will take place via information technologies. Online access to information resources will provide a depth and breadth of resources never before possible. Most print publication will cease; electronic publication and distribution will become the norm. Libraries, archives, museums, publishers, bookstores, schools, universities, and other institutions that rely on artifacts in physical form will be transformed radically or will cease to exist. Fundamental changes are predicted in the relationships between these institutions, with authors less dependent on publishers, information seekers less dependent on libraries, and universities less dependent on traditional models of publication to evaluate scholarship. Networks will grease the wheels of commerce, improve education, increase the amount of interpersonal communication, provide unprecedented access to information resources and to human expertise, and lead to greater economic equity.

In contrast, others argue that we are in the process of evolutionary, not revolutionary, social change toward an information-oriented society. People make social choices which lead to the development of desired technologies. Computer networks are continuations of earlier communication technologies such as the telegraph and telephone, radio and television, and similar devices that rely on networked infrastructures. All are dependent on institutions, and these evolve much more slowly than do technologies. Digital and digitized media are extensions of earlier media, and the institutions that manage them will adapt them to their practices as they have adapted many media before them. Electronic publishing will become ever more important, but only for certain materials that serve certain purposes. Print publishing will co-exist with other forms of distribution. Although relationships between institutions will evolve, publishers, libraries, and universities serve gatekeeping functions that will continue to be essential in the future. More activities will be conducted online, with the result that face-to-face relationships will become ever more valued and precious. Telecommuting, distance-independent learning, and electronic commerce will supplement, but not supplant, physical workplaces, classrooms, and shopping malls. Communication technologies often increase, rather than decrease, inequities, and we should be wary of the economic promises of a global information infrastructure.

Which of these scenarios is more likely to occur? Proponents of each offer historical precedent and argue rationally for their cases. Many other scenarios exist, some between those presented above and some at the far ends of the spectrum. The extremes include science-fiction-like scenarios in which technology controls all aspects of daily life, resulting in a police state where every activity is monitored, and survivalist scenarios in which some catastrophe destroys all technology, with the result that new societies are reinvented without it. The science fiction and survivalist scenarios are easily discounted because checks and balances are in place to prevent them. Choosing between the revolutionary, discontinuity scenario and the evolutionary, continuity scenario described above is more problematic. Each has merit and each is the subject of scholarly inquiry and informed public debate.

In view of the undisputed magnitude of some of these developments, it is reasonable to speak of a new world emerging. It is not reasonable, however, to conclude that these changes are absolute, that they will affect all people equally, or that no prior practices or institutions will carry over to a new world. Nor is it reasonable to assume that any individual institutions, whether libraries, archives, museums, universities, schools, governments, or businesses, will survive unscathed and unchanged into the next millennium. Strong claims in either direction are dangerous and misleading, as well as lacking in intellectual rigor. The arguments for these scenarios, the underlying assumptions, and the evidence offered must be examined. Upon close examination, it will often be found that strong claims about the effects of information technologies on society, and vice versa, are based on simplistic assumptions about technology, behavior, organizations, and economics. None of these factors exists in a vacuum; they interact in complex and often unpredictable ways.

I argue throughout this book that the most likely future scenario lies somewhere between the discontinuity and continuity scenarios. Information technology makes possible all sorts of new activities and new ways of doing old activities. But people do not discard all their old habits and practices with the advent of each new technology. Nor are new technologies created without some expectations of how they will be employed. The probable scenario is neither revolution nor evolution, but co-evolution of information technology, human behavior, and organizations. People select and implement technologies that are available and that suit their practices and goals. As they use them, they adapt them to suit their needs, often in ways not anticipated by their designers. Designers develop new technologies on the basis of technological advances, marketing data, available standards, human factors studies, and educated guesses about what will sell. Products evolve in parallel with the uses for which they are employed. To use a simplistic aphorism: Technology pushes, while demand pulls.

The central concern of this book is access to information in a networked world. Information access is among the primary arguments for constructing a global information infrastructure. Information resources are essential for all manner of human affairs, including commerce, education, research, participatory democracy, government policy, and leisure activities. Access to information for all these purposes is at the center of the discontinuity-continuity debates. Some argue that computer networks, digital libraries, electronic publishing, and similar developments will lead to radically different models of information access. The technologies of creation, distribution, and preservation will undergo dramatic transformation, as will information institutions such as libraries, archives, museums, schools, and universities. Relationships among these and other stakeholders, including authors, readers, users, and publishers, will evolve as well. Others argue that stakeholders, relationships, and practices are so firmly entrenched that structural changes will be slow and incremental because most new technologies are variations on those that came before. My view is that some degree of truth exists in each of these statements. These and other arguments are examined throughout the book.

Much has been written about technology, human behavior, and policy regarding access to information. Most of the writing, however, focuses on one of these three aspects with little attention to the other two. In this book I endeavor to bring all three together, drawing on themes, theories, results, and practices from multiple disciplines and perspectives to illustrate the complex challenges that we face in creating a global information infrastructure. Technical issues in digital libraries and information retrieval systems are addressed, but not in the depth provided in recent books by Lesk (1997a) and Korfhage (1997). Nor are design issues addressed to the degree covered by Winograd et al. (1996). Information-related behavior in electronic environments is covered, but in less depth than in Marchionini 1995. Institutional and organizational issues are treated more fully in Bishop and Star 1996, Bowker et al. 1996, and Sproull and Kiesler 1991. Policy issues of the Internet are addressed in more depth in Branscomb and Kahin 1995, Kahin and Abbate 1995, and Kahin and Keller 1995. In this book I draw on these and many other resources to weave a rich discussion of access to information in a networked world. In view of the early stages of these developments, more questions are raised than yet can be answered. My hope is to provoke informed discussion between the many interested parties around the world.

Converging Tasks and Technologies

People use computer networks for a vast array of activities, such as communicating with other individuals and groups, performing tasks requiring remote resources, exchanging resources, and entertainment (whether with interactive games or passive media such as videos). Among the few common threads in predictions of future technology (see, e.g., Next 50 Years 1997 and Pontin 1998) is that we will see more convergence of information and communication technologies, blurring the lines between tasks and activities and between work and play. We will have "ubiquitous computing" (Pontin 1998) and "pervasive information systems" (Birnbaum 1997). We will become "intimate with our technology" (Hillis 1997), and "information overload" (Berghel 1997a) will be more of a problem than ever.

An underlying theme of such predictions is "digital convergence," indicating that more and more information products will be created in digital form or will be digitized, allowing applications to be blended more easily. Digital technologies will co-exist with analog and other forms of information technologies yet to be invented. Analog technology is based on continuous flows, rather than the discrete bits of digital technology. Computer and communication networks are an example of the bridge between these technologies. The word "modem" was coined from "modulate" and "demodulate," which describe the device's function in converting digital data produced by computers into analog signals that could be sent over telephone lines designed for voice communication and vice versa. Predictions of ubiquitous computing are based on an increasing reliance on small communication devices and embedded systems such as those that control heating and lighting in homes and offices. Future computer networks are expected to link these devices just as they now link personal computers, data storage, printers, and other peripherals (Pontin 1998).

Modes of Communication

No matter what technologies gird the framework of the global information infrastructure, human activities involving the network will be intertwined. As the editors of *Wired* magazine (1997, p. 14) put it,

> . . . broader and deeper new interfaces for electronic media are being born. . . . What they share are ways to move seamlessly between media you steer (interactive) and media that steer you (passive). . . . These new interfaces work with existing media, such as TV, yet they also work on hyper-linked text. But most important, they work on the emerging universe of *networked* media that are spreading across the telecosm.

Despite the hyperbole, this quotation highlights a useful distinction between "pull" technology (which requires explicit action by the user) and "push" technology (which comes to the user without the user's explicit action). Some activities are easily categorized by this dichotomy, but others have characteristics of each. Composing and sending an email message and searching a database require explicit "pull" actions, for example. Although both the broadcast mass media and the emerging media services that deliver tailored selections of content to workstations during idle time can be classified as push technologies (editors of *Wired* 1997), the latter form also could be considered "pull," because the user presumably took action to subscribe to the service. Similarly, if composing and sending email is pull technology, then receiving mail can be viewed as a form of "push." Opening and reading messages requires explicit actions, but users can decide what to read, delete, or ignore. They also can sort desirable and undesirable messages by means of automatic filters. Because subscribing to desirable content and filtering out undesirable content require parallel actions, both can be viewed as forms of push technology if one accepts the *Wired* definitions of "push" and "pull."

Push and pull combine in other ways as well. People subscribe to distribution lists, which then send messages at regular or irregular intervals. They also subscribe to services that alert them when new resources are posted on a specific network site, but they must take explicit action to view or retrieve the resources from that site.

Truly interactive forms of communication are difficult to categorize as push or pull. People engage in conversations in "chat rooms," play roles in MUDS and MOOS, and hold conferences, meetings, and classes online in real time. All require explicit actions, but the characteristics of these two-way or multi-way conversations are far richer than the solo-action pull of searching a database or sending a message. Some of these are the "demassified" communication technologies that Rogers (1986) predicted, tailored to individual users and to small audiences. However, the "push" technologies of customized desktop news delivery touted by *Wired* in 1997, in which messages continually scroll across the subscriber's screen, have yet to become the commercial success that was predicted. Perhaps they were not sufficiently customized or "demassified." Perhaps people found them too disruptive, preferring "pull" modes in which they could acquire the desired content at their convenience.

The intertwining of communication modes in electronic environments adds new dimensions to information access. Although more study has been devoted to "active" than to "passive" information seeking, even these categories are problematic in this new environment. These are but a few of many communication definitions and concepts being reconsidered in the light of new information technologies.

Task Independence and Task Dependence

The more intertwined tasks and activities become, the more difficult it becomes to isolate any one task for study. In the past, most theory and research presumed that the human activities involved in access to information could be isolated sufficiently to be studied independently. This is particularly true of information-seeking behavior, a process often viewed as beginning when a person recognizes the need for information and ending when the person acquires some information resources that address the need. Such a narrow view of the process of seeking information simplifies the conduct of research. For example, information seekers' activities can be studied from the time they log onto an information retrieval system until they log off with results in hand. The process can be continued further by following subsequent activities to determine which resources discovered online were used, how, and for what purposes. Another approach is to constrain the scope of study to library-based information seeking. People can be interviewed when they first enter a library building to identify their needs as they understood them at that time. Researchers can follow users around the building (with permission, of course), and can interview the users again before departure to determine what they learned or accomplished.

Narrowly bounded studies such as these provide insights into detailed activities and are useful for evaluating specific systems, services, and buildings. However, their value and validity are declining for the purposes of studying the information environment of today and assessing the needs of the future. In the early days of information retrieval, people might reasonably conduct most or all of their searching on one retrieval system. Only a few systems existed, and each had a limited number of databases. These were complex systems requiring lengthy training. Information seekers, often with the assistance of skilled searchers, would devote considerable effort to constructing, executing, and iterating a search on a single system (Borgman, Moghdam, and Corbett 1984). A close analysis of user-system interaction could provide a rich record of negotiating a single search query. Even so, such studies provide little insight into the circumstances from which the information need arose or into the relationship between a particular system and the use of other information resources.

In today's environment, most people have access to a vast array of online resources via the Internet and online resources provided by libraries, archives, universities, businesses, and other organizations with which they are affiliated, as well as print and other hard-copy resources. They are much less dependent on any single system or database. Rather, they are grazing through a variety of resources, perhaps "berry picking" (Bates 1989) from multiple sources and systems. Studying any individual system is far less likely to provide a comprehensive view of information-seeking activities than it was in the past. Similarly, people have fewer reasons to spend time in library buildings, now that they can use many library resources from the convenience of home, office, dorm, coffee shop, or anywhere else with network access. And they can do so at hours of day or night when the buildings normally are closed. Thus, time spent in the library building may be for narrower and more specific purposes, and may occur only at critical stages in the search process. The use of physical libraries also reflects patterns that are influenced by age, generation, culture, discipline of study, and many other factors. Such research should yield insights into the design of future buildings and services, provided it is set in a larger context of overall information-use patterns.

Future research on access to information must consider the complex relationships between information-related activities and the context of work and leisure practices in which these activities are conducted. Although all scholarship is constrained by the necessity of studying that which can be studied, particular caution is necessary when studying tasks that tend to be interdependent.

Technology Adoption and Adaptation

Underlying the design of any information technology are assumptions about how and why people will use it. The assumptions are sometimes explicit and sometimes only implicit, whether for individual communication devices, for information systems, or for the design of a global information infrastructure. In identifying design criteria, and making implicit assumptions explicit, many methods and perspectives can be applied. We can evaluate which prior technologies were adopted and which were not, the processes by which they were adopted, how similar technologies are used, what features and functions are most popular and most effective, and how their users adapt them to new purposes.

I will highlight three perspectives on assessing how and why people use information technologies. Though many other perspectives and methods exist, these three are applicable to our concerns for access to information.

Adoption

Of the vast number of information technologies that are invented, only a few make it to the marketplace, and of these, even fewer are successful. The quality of the product is only one determinant of market success. Many products that receive critical acclaim fail to garner large market shares. The Beta video recording technology and the Macintosh computer are the best-known examples. In contrast, many products whose reviews range from skepticism to scorn achieve great market success. Business factors such as timing, marketing, and pricing are determinants of success. Other determinants are social factors involving how and why people choose to adopt any particular innovation. Rogers (1983, 1986) summarizes the results of a large number of adoption studies using a five-stage model. The first stage of adoption is knowledge, or becoming aware of the existence of a new technology that might be useful. This stage is influenced by factors such as previous practices, felt needs or problems, tendencies toward being innovative, and norms of the individual's social system. The second stage is persuasion, which in turn is influenced by the perceived characteristics of the innovation, how well it might work, how easy it is to try, and how easily the outcome can be observed. In the third stage, the adopter makes a tentative decision to accept or to reject the technology. Acceptance may lead to implementation (fourth stage) and, if the innovation is deemed sufficiently useful, to a confirmation to continue its use (fifth stage). If the innovation is rejected, the individual still may revisit the decision and adopt it later.

Electronic mail (email) provides an instructive example of the adoption process. A person may first become aware of its existence through news reports or through discussions with friends, family, or co-workers. Someone surrounded by email users will hear about it more quickly and frequently than someone whose acquaintances are nonusers. Even today, elderly Americans who have minimal contact with computer users may have at most a vague idea of what email is, for example. In countries with minimal telecommunications and computing penetration, only the elite may be aware of email as a potentially useful technology. In the persuasion stage, a person who has many potential email correspondents will find the technology more attractive than a person who knows no one else with an email address. Similarly, a person who already owns a computer with a modem will find it far easier to try email than one who must acquire the technology and the skills to use it. Once they have tried it, some people will find email sufficiently useful, affordable, and worth the time and effort to continue using it. Others will not. Thus, once people become aware of email, only some will consider trying it, a smaller number will make the effort to try it; of these, only some will acquire it and continuing using it, and they may abandon it later. Conversely, some who rejected email at any of these adoption stages may consider it again at some later time.

This adoption pattern also operates in the aggregate. The "early adopters" typically are risk takers who are willing to try unproven techniques, often at great expense. If they adopt the new technology, their successes may convince more risk-averse individuals to try it. Conversely, if the early adopters reject it, others may be more reluctant to try it. By the time the low-risk late adopters decide to implement a technology, the early adopters may have moved on to something yet newer and more innovative. Some technologies reach a critical mass of adoption in a short period of time and are great market successes. Others are unable to find a match with early adopters fast enough, and the entrepreneurs fail before finding their niche in the market. Others fail because they do not fill a perceived need. Yet others succeed because they are good enough, cheap enough, and at the right place at the right time, although not necessarily an optimal design. Though this explanation is a gross simplification of the adoption process, it illustrates a few of the many social variables that influence the success of new information technologies.

Again, email provides a useful case example. Email filled a perceived need early in the development of computer networks and reached a critical mass of computer users fairly quickly. Spreadsheets were a similarly attractive technology that contributed to the adoption of personal computers. Early adopters of both technologies were sophisticated computer users who tolerated complex user interfaces, often unreliable software, and minimal functionality because the technology was sufficiently valuable for their purposes. People who are early adopters of one technology tend to be early adopters of others, willing to tolerate immature technologies in return for their benefits, and often enjoy the challenge of working at the "bleeding edge" of technical frontiers.

Conversely, late adopters of one technology tend to be late adopters of others. These people are far less likely to appreciate technology for its own sake, preferring mature, easy-to-use technologies with a high perceived payoff relative to the effort required in learning to use them. They are happy to let others "work the bugs out" before spending the time, effort, and money to adopt them. This distinction between the personality characteristics and social context of early and late adopters is an important one to bear in mind when considering technologies intended for a mass market. If a global information infrastructure is to achieve wide acceptance, it must be attractive to late adopters.

Adaptation

Theories of diffusion and adoption are valuable in understanding the social processes involved in choosing to employ a particular technology. The "diffusion of innovations" theory originated in rural sociology to explain farmers' choices of agricultural innovations such as farming equipment, hybrid plants, pesticides, and techniques for planting, harvesting, and storing crops. The theory was later extended to study the adoption of a diverse array of innovations including solar energy during a fossil-fuels shortage and family planning methods in developing countries. One weakness of applying the "diffusion of innovations" theory to information technologies is the implicit assumption that the innovation is relatively static. Information technologies tend to be more dynamic and flexible than farming equipment, for example. Any communication device may be short-lived, making it difficult to compare the actions of someone who adopted the first crude implementation to those of someone who adopted a more sophisticated and less expensive version only months later. Moreover, information technologies are more malleable and adaptable to individual purposes than are most other technologies. Thus, we must look not just at the adoption of information technologies as a binary (adopt / not adopt) decision, but also at how technologies, once adopted, are adapted over time.

Books provide an early example of how people adapt information technologies to their purposes. Manuscripts (meaning, literally, hand-written) were the first form of written record. Manuscripts on sheepskin or parchment were easier to create and read than chiseled stone tablets, but still could be read only by one person in one place at a time. Manuscripts could be loaned for manual copying, which enabled duplication, however laborious. Gutenberg's improvements in movable type in the fifteenth century made multiple copies economically feasible for the first time. Early printed books retained the shape and size of manuscripts, following the earlier technology. Although the distribution of multiple copies meant that more people could own and read a work concurrently, books still were too bulky for portable use, except by the very rich. Greenberg (1998) recounts the oft-told story of Abdul Kassem Ismael, who was said to have had a library of 117,000 books in tenth-century Persia. Not only did he carry his library with him while he traveled, on the backs of 400 camels, he trained the camels to walk in alphabetical order. Later innovations led to publishing books in more portable sizes that fit not only in the saddlebags of yesteryear, but in the backpacks and briefcases of today.

We find similar adaptations in the use of computer networks. The ARPANET, precursor to the Internet, was created for remote access to scarce computing resources. Electronic mail was a feature intended to serve as an ancillary communication function. Email proved so useful for general communication that it became the dominant use of the network, much to the surprise of the ARPANET's designers (Licklider and Vezza 1978; Quarterman 1990). Email was the "killer application" that attracted most people to the Internet (Anderson et al. 1995; Quarterman 1990), and it remains the most important reason for becoming an Internet user (Katz and Aspden 1997).

Email is a far different application today than it was in the early days of the ARPANET, however. Early email consisted of very short plain text messages. Less than a decade ago, messages could take several days to arrive, with delays caused whenever a server in a store-and-forward network went down. Email was neither fast enough, reliable enough, nor functional enough to replace most other forms of communication. The technology advanced, as did users' perceived needs for more capabilities and better services. Today's email supports long messages of formatted text and is fast, reliable, convenient, and inexpensive (Berghel 1997b). Increasingly, email software allows people to send and receive file attachments that preserve the integrity of text, images, graphics, and sound. For many purposes, email is a suitable substitute for telephone, fax, post, or express mail.

Email now combines the features of word processors, file transfer (ftp), and multimedia file management. It also provides a bridge to the World Wide Web by embedding live links to web sites. By including a URL (uniform resource locator) address in an email message, a user can click on an address to launch a browser application and link to the web site. And the reverse is true. Once at the web site, a user can click on "email" and send a message to the web site.

Email has evolved from a simple application to one that combines a rich array of services. As users realized its value and its constraints, they identified further improvements that could be made. Yet today's complex email technology has too much functionality to be feasible for some purposes. Thus, we also find evidence of complex applications being stripped down to the bare elements that suit newly identified needs. An example is the convergence of email with pocket pagers, which themselves were initially a simple, single-function technology. Some of today's more elaborate pagers include a full, albeit tiny, QWERTY keyboard and alphanumeric display, on which people can send and receive terse messages. Other pagers include function keys for common responses to email-type messages: yes, no, time, date, etc. Such devices can convey cryptic but critical messages, such as

"When do you arrive?" (answer: "AA 75, 8:44pm LAX"), "Did we win the case?," "Running late, resched Tu at 3?" (answer: "no. Tu 2pm ok?")," "pls get milk," or "get KT @ school."

These are but a few examples of how people adapt information technologies by using them. People sometimes adopt only part of a technology, as illustrated by the example of stripped-down email. Other times they disable or circumvent features of a technology. Email file attachments are a case in point. They are extremely useful for exchanging files quickly between team members, co-authors, authors and editors, authors or publishers and readers, or teachers and students. But they are useful only when they work. When exchange partners have identical hardware and software platforms, fast connections, and (better yet) the ability to scan for viruses before receipt, file exchange may be seamless.

System designers, along with as those who send file attachments, often are unaware of the difficulties involved in receiving attachments intact and in a usable form, however. Despite considerable progress, the necessary platform independence and software independence required for reliable exchange of attachments over networks has yet to be achieved. File exchanges between different platforms (e.g., PC and Macintosh) and different operating systems (Windows 95, Windows 98, Windows NT, Macintosh OS 7.5, Macintosh OS 8.0, Unix, etc.) introduce compatibility problems. Files created with widely used word processing software such as Microsoft Word and Corel WordPerfect often fail to transfer intact. Text may transfer but formatting may be corrupted, and the likelihood of accurate transfer decreases with the inclusion of software-specific features such as tables, graphics, and macros. The more recent the version of the software used to create a file, the less likely that earlier versions of the same software or of competing software can open it intact. Exchanging files of graphics or sound is yet more problematic. Adding another layer of concern is the ability of attachments to carry computer viruses that can contaminate the receiver's computer.

Unsolicited file attachments containing job applications, advertisements, jokes, cartoons, greeting cards, and myriad other materials clog network and modem lines and fill disk space. Owing to problems with technical compatibility, viruses, and bandwidth, many people are making minimal use of file attachments, and some are setting their email parameters to reject them entirely. Local network managers are introducing delays in email delivery to scan all attachments for viruses, adding another layer of complexity. Sending faxes, or mailing paper and disks, can be faster, more reliable, and less labor intensive.

The email examples offer several lessons in the adoption and adaptation of information technologies. One lesson is that early adopters are willing to use an immature technology. As they use it, they will identify problems, recognize new possibilities, and demand improvements. Later adopters will identify yet more problems and more desirable capabilities as they integrate it into their practices, refining the technology further. Another lesson is that one simple technology may spawn so many features that it subdivides into component parts, as email has done. We also see that advanced features that are extremely useful in some situations may result in unintended and undesirable consequences in others, as is the present case with file attachments. When people have positive experiences with a technology, they often are more inclined to adopt another technology. Conversely, when they have negative experiences, they trust the technology less than before, and are less inclined to try something new. All these lessons argue for the importance of studying the use of information technologies in actual working situations. Though laboratory experiments are extremely valuable for improving technologies under ideal conditions, field studies are essential to determine how technologies are adopted and adapted.

Organizational Adaptation

Though some technology adoption and adaptation is attributable to individual choices by individual users, much of it takes place in the context of organizations. Organizations such as businesses, governments, universities, and schools make decisions about what hardware, software, and services to purchase for use by their constituencies. Individuals may have little choice in which computing platform, Internet provider, or services they use. Organizations usually set policies about how services such as email and information resources are used. Even in view of these constraints, individuals often have considerable latitude in how they employ these technologies in their work practices, however.

Sproull and Kiesler (1991) explain the unpredictable effects of introducing technology into organizations from a "two-level perspective." They argue that most inventors and early adopters of technology think primarily about efficiency of the technology. System designers, as well as early adopters, focus on the instrumental uses to which the technology is put, whether reducing "telephone tag" through the use of electronic mail or lowering secretarial costs by replacing typing with word processing. These are the "first-level effects" of a technology.

Users rarely implement a new technology in precisely the way that designers intend, however. Organizations find it difficult to determine accurate estimates of direct costs, much less to determine the first-level effects of technology on work practices, productivity, or profits.   Because technologies interact with routine work practices and policies, implementation leads to "long-term changes in how people work, treat one another, and structure their organizations" (Sproull and Kiesler 1991, p. 1). It is these "second-level effects" on the social system of interdependent people, events, and behaviors that are most pervasive and most important for organizations. These effects are also the most difficult to predict.

Again, email offers illustrations of first- and second-level effects of introducing an information technology into organizations. The instrumental uses of email are many: it offers rapid interpersonal communication within the organization and between the organization and the external world, whether clients, suppliers, members, customers, citizens, colleagues, friends, or family. Email is convenient and portable. Because it is asynchronous, it can improve time management by enabling people to send and receive messages at their convenience. It serves as a broadcast technology, allowing an organization to deliver the same message to a mass audience of its employees, students, or other groups simultaneously. Email has radically increased the speed and volume of communication for most people who use it.

We are finding many second-level effects of email that were not anticipated at the time of its initial development or adoption. Email is easily abused, whether by broadcasting messages that are of interest only to a few or by sending rude and inappropriate messages that are unlikely to be communicated by other means. Junk email can proliferate, resulting in inefficient use of staff time to sort through it, rather than the efficiency of communication intended. Once an organization adopts email, usually everyone who is provided access is expected to use it regularly. People are expected to respond to messages, and to do so quickly. As a result, memos and other communications that did not require a response in paper form now result in a flurry of acknowledgments and responses, adding another layer of communication activity.

Communications that once were oral, or confined to one or a few paper copies that were controlled by the individuals involved, are now captured in permanent form on an organization's email servers. As a result, organizations are faced with a difficult balance between controlling their resources and the rights of individuals to their privacy (Anderson et al. 1995; Berghel 1997b). Organizations that read employees' email may defend this practice on the grounds that email is organizational documentation and that it resides on computers owned by the organization. Individuals, particularly those who have lost jobs over the content of email messages, may contend that email is the equivalent of telephone or other oral communications and is subject to reasonable expectations of privacy.

Conversely, organizations are learning that email can have unexpected and adverse legal consequences. Conversations that once were oral and now are recorded can be treated as legal evidence. Among the evidence that convicted Oliver North in the Iran-Contra affair were email messages that he had deleted; they were recovered from backup storage as part of the legal discovery process. Similarly, email messages internal to the Microsoft Corporation were used by the US government as evidence in an antitrust case against the corporation. As a result of these and other cases, many organizations are expanding the scope of their email policies to limit the content of email messages and to minimize the archival storage of email transactions (Harmon 1998).

These are only a few of many examples of the positive and negative effects that email has had on organizational communication. (For more, see Anderson et al. 1995; Berghel 1997b; Markus 1994.) People's experiences with email and their perceptions of its role in an organization combine to determine how they will adapt it to their own practices.

As information technologies are more widely adopted, concern about their second-level effects is increasing. These concerns cross many disciplines, levels of analysis, and research methods. "Social informatics" is an emerging research area that brings together the concerns of information, computer, and social scientists with those in the domains of study (Bishop and Star 1996; Borgman et al. 1996; Bowker et al. 1996). Social informatics scholars are attempting to build upon research in the design and the use of information systems and upon social studies of science and technology. This book brings a social informatics perspective to bear on access to information in digital libraries and in a global information infrastructure, considering first-level effects when these are all that can be known and second-level effects where possible.

Creating a Global Information Infrastructure

The integration, interaction, and interdependence of information-related tasks and activities leads us to think in terms of an information infrastructure. Rather than relying on separate devices for producing text (e.g., typewriters and personal computers), producing images (e.g., personal computers, photocopy machines, drawing pads), communicating with individuals (e.g., telephones, telefacsimile (fax) machines, mailboxes and stamps), and searching for information resources (e.g., personal computers, local servers, print technologies), all these tasks can be accomplished via a personal computer connected to the Internet. Conversely, these tasks can be divided up in many new ways by means of specialized devices such as cell phones, pagers, palmtops, and other "information appliances" that can share information. Computer and communication networks enable the integration of tasks and activities involved in creating, seeking, and using information, increase the interaction between these activities, and make them ever more interdependent.

In considering the premise and the promise of a "global information infrastructure," we must determine what is meant by this phrase. Already it is used in a variety of contexts, with meanings that include a set of technologies, a set of principles for an international computing and communications network, and a loose aggregation of people, technology, and content.

What Is Infrastructure?

Terms such as "national information infrastructure" and "global information infrastructure" are being bandied about with minimal discussion of what is meant by "infrastructure." Social scientists and historians are beginning to take a research interest in this concept, particularly as it relates to organizational communication and work practices. Star and Ruhleder (1996, p. 111–112) describe infrastructure as follows:

It is both engine and barrier for change; both customizable and rigid; both inside and outside organizational practices. It is product and process. . . . With the rise of decentralized technologies used across wide geographical distance, both the need for common standards and the need for situated, tailorable and flexible technologies grow stronger.

Star and Ruhleder are among the first to describe infrastructure as a social and technical construct. Their eight dimensions (ibid., p. 113) can be paraphrased as follows: An infrastructure is *embedded* in other structures, social arrangements, and technologies. It is *transparent,* in that it invisibly supports tasks. Its *reach or scope* may be spatial or temporal, in that it reaches beyond a single event or a single site of practice. Infrastructure is *learned as part of membership* of an organization or group. It is *linked with conventions of practice* of day-to-day work. Infrastructure is the *embodiment of standards,* so that other tools and infrastructures can interconnect in a standardized way. It *builds upon an installed base,* inheriting both strengths and limitations from that base. And infrastructure *becomes visible upon breakdown,* in that we are most aware of it when it fails to work—when the server is down, the electrical power grid fails, or the highway bridge collapses.

As a means to explore the technical and public policy implications of information infrastructure, the Corporation for National Research Initiatives has sponsored a series of studies that address historical examples of large-scale infrastructure. These include studies of the growth of railroads, telephony and telegraphy, electricity and light, and banking (Friedlander 1995a,b, 1996a,b). In each case, the technologies involved took some time to be adopted, to stabilize, and to achieve the critical mass necessary to form an infrastructure. Railroads, telephones, power companies, and banks all provided local services for years, or even decades, before reaching nationwide connectivity. Each developed with some combination of public and private investment and government regulation. The means by which an integrated infrastructure evolved varied, and each involved experimentation with different forms of technology, regulation, and social arrangements.

Models of infrastructure for railroads, telephones, energy, and banking could have taken far different forms than they did. Indeed, with the possible exception of railroads, each of these infrastructures is still evolving actively. Telephony underwent extensive restructuring in the United States during the 1980s and the 1990s due to changes in regulatory structure, mergers and acquisitions, and technological advances. Similar regulatory restructuring is now underway in Europe and elsewhere. Meanwhile, technology advances and mergers and acquisitions continue apace. On the energy front, models for service provision are changing as energy companies are privatized and global power relationships shift with variations in supplies and prices of fossil fuels. On the financial front, models for banking infrastructure are under scrutiny as markets for stocks, commodities, currencies, and other financial instruments are becoming much more tightly coupled.

Each of these infrastructures is deeply embedded in our social fabric, relies on technical standards, and builds upon an installed base within the scope of its own and other infrastructures. A corollary to the notion that infrastructure becomes visible upon breakdown is that we rarely are aware of it when it is functioning adequately. We often fail to recognize these as essential infrastructures until telephone service becomes more complex and expensive, energy services change in cost and character, or the stock market takes a precipitous fall in value. And, although Americans make minimal use of railroads, railroads are an essential form of transportation in much of the world, where people are very aware of changes in schedules, routes, prices, and services.

Star and Ruhleder's (1996) set of eight infrastructure dimensions highlights the complex interaction of technology, social and work practices, and standards. They also emphasize social context by noting that infrastructure builds upon an installed base. An information infrastructure is built upon an installed base of telecommunications lines, electrical power grids, and computing technology, as well as on available information resources, organizational arrangements, and people's practices in using all these aspects. An installed base establishes a set of capabilities and a set of constraints that influence future developments. For example, mobile telecommunications must interoperate with land-based networks, and new computers should be able to read files that were created on the preceding generation of technology.

The concepts of embeddedness, transparency, and visibility are especially relevant to a discussion of a global information infrastructure. To be effective, a GII must be embedded in the technical and social infrastructure of the many nations and cultures it reaches—so much so that the infrastructure is invisible most of the time. Whether this degree of embeddedness is possible across countries and cultures is examined throughout this book. When an information infrastructure works well, people depend on it for critical work, education, and leisure tasks, taking its reliability for granted. When it breaks down (for example, when email cannot be sent or received, when transferred files cannot be read, or when online information stores cannot be reached), then the information infrastructure becomes very visible. People may resort to alternative means to complete the task, if those means exist; they may create redundant systems at considerable effort and expense; and they will trust the infrastructure a bit less each time it breaks down.

Infrastructure as Public Policy

Infrastructures of many kinds are subject to public policy. For example, the Clinton administration (1997, 1998) set forth a policy on "critical infrastructure protection" that is noteworthy for our concerns. The white paper on Presidential Decision Directive 63 (Clinton Administration 1998) defines "critical infrastructures" as "those physical and cyber-based systems essential to the minimum operations of the economy and government. They include, but are not limited to, telecommunications, energy, banking and finance, transportation, water systems, and emergency services, both governmental and private." In the past, these infrastructures were physically and functionally separate. However, with advances in information technology these systems are increasingly linked and interdependent. The significance of this interdependence is that critical systems are ever more vulnerable to "equipment failures, human error, weather and other natural causes, and physical and cyber attacks." PDD 63 has the goal of protecting critical infrastructure from intentional attack and minimizing service disruptions due to any other form of failure.

Information technologies link these critical infrastructures, making them interdependent, and thus all information technologies could be considered parts of an information infrastructure. Information infrastructure usually is more narrowly defined in public policy documents, however. Typically the scope includes computing and communications networks, associated information resources, and perhaps a set of regulations and policies governing use.

Metaphors for Information Infrastructure

Clever metaphors for information infrastructure have helped to capture public attention. The concept of information infrastructure is best known in common parlance as the "information superhighway" (Gore 1994b), or sometimes as the "I-way" or the "Infobahn." These metaphors for information infrastructure emphasize the roads or pipes over which data flow, whether telecommunications, broadcast, cable, or other channels. The highway metaphor captures only a narrow sense of infrastructure, as it does not encompass information content, communication processes, or the larger social, political, and economic context. The superhighway metaphor is misleading both because it skews public understanding toward a low-level infrastructure and because it suggests that the government would pay the direct costs of the highway's construction. The Internet was constructed with a combination of government and private funds. Current public policy, especially in the United States, is oriented toward private funding for further expansion (Branscomb and Kahin 1995; Kahin and Abbate 1995; Kahin and Keller 1995).

Though metaphors such as the information superhighway have been extremely effective in marshalling support for information infrastructure development, far more is involved than laying roads over which information will travel.

National and International Policies

Individual countries began plans for national information infrastructures in the early 1990s (see, e.g., Information Infrastructure Program 1992; Karnitas 1996). In the United States, there was the National Information Infrastructure Act of 1993. In Europe, there was the European Union's proposal for a European Information Infrastructure (Bangemann Report 1994). The installed base of technology on which these plans are predicated includes the Internet, which began in the late 1960s with the ARPANET (National Research Council 1994; Quarterman 1990), the "intelligent network" of telecommunications that followed the deregulation of telephony (Mansell 1993), and related technologies such as cable and satellite television networks.

In the mid 1990s, national information infrastructure plans began to converge. In 1994 the United States proposed formal principles for a global information infrastructure. The following principles were incorporated into the International Telecommunication Union's "Buenos Aires Declaration on Global Telecommunication Development for the 21st Century" (1994) and the United States' "Global Information Infrastructure: Agenda for Cooperation" (Brown et al. 1995):

- encouraging private sector investment
- promoting open competition
- providing open access to the network for all information providers and users
- creating a flexible regulatory environment that can keep pace with rapid technological and market changes
- ensuring universal service.

A few months later, the Group of Seven[1] (seven leading industrialized nations, known as "G-7") met to discuss these principles and agreed to collaborate "to realise their common vision of the Global Information Society" and to work cooperatively to construct a global information infrastructure (G-7 Ministerial Conference on the Information Society 1995a, pp. 1–2). These principles emerged from the 1995 G-7 meeting:

- promoting dynamic competition
- encouraging private investment
- defining an adaptable regulatory framework
- providing open access to networks

while

- promoting equality of opportunity to the citizen
- promoting diversity of content, including cultural and linguistic diversity
- recognizing the necessity of worldwide cooperation with particular attention to less developed countries.

The G-7 document also included the following.

These principles will apply to the Global Information Infrastructure by means of:

- promotion of interconnectivity and interoperability
- developing global markets for networks, services, and applications
- ensuring privacy and data security

1. The Group of Seven nations are Canada, France, Germany, Italy, Japan, the United States, and the United Kingdom. Russia has participated in some recent meetings. When Russia is involved, the press sometimes refers to these as meetings of "the G-7 plus Russia" or "the G-8."

- protecting intellectual property rights
- cooperating in R&D and in the development of new applications
- monitoring the social and societal implications of the information society.

The Buenos Aires and G-7 statements have much in common: they are concerned with technical capabilities ("interconnectivity," "interoperability," "open access"), promises of rights to provide network services ("open competition," "dynamic competition"), guarantees of network services ("universal service," "equality of opportunity"), a means of funding network development ("encouraging private investment"), and a means of regulating various aspects of its development and use ("flexible regulatory environment," "adaptable regulatory framework"). However, they vary on their treatment of content: the G-7 principles promote diversity of content and offer some general protections ("privacy," "data security," "intellectual property"), while the telecommunications principles do not mention content, addressing only the development and regulation of communication channels.

Implementing Global Policy

Statements by the G-7 and other multinational bodies such as the United Nations promote policy agendas of the countries involved, but they lack the force of law and they provide little if any funding for implementation. Some of the language offers more platitudes than policy, such as the claim in the European Information Infrastructure plan that, "as a strategic creation for the whole Union," it will lead to "a more caring European society with a significantly higher quality of life" (Bangemann Report 1994).

The G-7 policy statements that frame a global information infrastructure have raised considerable concern about human rights and social protections from adverse consequences of its use. Though the G-7 principles include a general statement about privacy and comment on the need to monitor the social implications of the information society, they do not ensure legal protection of rights such as privacy, free expression, and access to information. Despite requests by human rights groups, the G-7 principles omit references to assurances in the United Nations Declaration of Human Rights that were approved in 1948 (see United Nations 1998). Particularly relevant are articles 12 and 19:

Article 12: No one shall be subjected to arbitrary interference with his privacy, family, home or correspondence, nor to attacks upon his honor and reputation. Everyone has the right to the protection of the law against such interference or attacks.

Article 19: Everyone has the right to freedom of opinion and expression; this right includes freedom to hold opinions without interference and to seek, receive and impart information and ideas through any media and regardless of frontiers.

These principles are receiving renewed attention upon the fiftieth anniversary of their adoption (United Nations 1998). Computer networks offer unanticipated capabilities for free speech and access to information. Because transactions and interactions are easily trackable, computer networks also can create unanticipated intrusions into privacy (Kang 1998). Many privacy advocates promote an alternative design model, known as "privacy-enhancing technologies" (Burkert 1997), in which individuals can acquire access to most information services without revealing their identity if they so choose. Privacy, freedom of speech, and freedom of access to information are tenets of democracy (Dervin 1994; Lievrouw 1994a,b). People cannot speak freely or seek information freely if their movements are being tracked and if they cannot protect and control data about themselves (Agre and Rotenberg 1997; Diffie and Landau 1998; Information Freedom and Censorship 1988, 1991).

These are contentious issues in the United States. One example is that the federal policy on critical infrastructure protection, discussed above, is being challenged on the basis of its potential to erode civil liberties (Electronic Privacy Information Center 1998). Public policy on social aspects of information infrastructure is subject to the laws, the norms, and the practices of individual countries and jurisdictions, despite the global reach of computer networks. When local activities took place only locally, variances in policy and regulation were less apparent and jurisdiction was rarely an issue. Now that individual communications and information resources flow quickly and in vast quantities across borders, variances in policy and regulation can be highly visible and jurisdiction can be highly contentious. Privacy rights and regulations have become an international battlefield where many of these issues are being played out.

The European Union Data Directive, which took effect in late 1998, highlights fundamental differences in policy approaches to privacy protection. The United States long has taken a "sector approach," with specific laws governing credit reports, library borrowing records, videotape rentals, federal government databases, etc. In the new arena of computer networks, US policy has favored self-regulation by the private sector over government-imposed regulation. In contrast, European countries have favored generalized policies over the control of personal data, assigning stronger rights to individuals to control information about themselves than to organizations that collect and manage personal data. The EU Data Directive consolidates the policies of individual countries and regulates privacy protections throughout the European Union. In view of the extensive commerce between the United States and the European Union and the volumes of data about personnel, customers, clients, and suppliers that are subject to regulation, the policies of these jurisdictions often are in conflict.

For overviews of the rapidly evolving landscape of electronic privacy, see Agre and Rotenberg 1997, Diffie and Landau 1998, Kang 1998, Rotenberg 1998, and Schneier and Banisar 1997. Updates, including pointers to government documents and other primary sources, can be found at http://www.privacy.org and at http://www.epic.org.

Information Infrastructure as a Technical Framework

"Information infrastructure" can refer to a technical framework rather than to a public policy. As defined by the (US) National Research Council (1994, p. 22), an information infrastructure is "a framework in which communications networks support higher-level services for human communication and access to information. Such an infrastructure has an architectural aspect—a structure and design—that is manifested in standard interfaces and in standard objects (voice, video, files, email, and so on) transmitted over the interfaces."

One of the key components in defining an information infrastructure as a technical framework is for it to have an open architecture that will enable all parties to interconnect electronically and to exchange data. The "Open Data Network" concept (National Research Council 1994) follows both from the Internet (a successful open architecture for computing) and from established telecommunications policy principles (Mansell 1993; National Research Council 1994). Under the G-7 principles, closed networks can interconnect with the open network; closed service networks such as cable television are allowed under other communications regulations as well. As we move toward ubiquitous computing, a wider array of devices must interconnect; this makes open systems and interoperability much more essential.

The emerging global network that interconnects a wide variety of computing devices located around the world offers great utility for communication between individuals and organizations, whether for education, work, leisure, or commerce. The technical framework for such an information infrastructure is now expected to support a range of tasks and activities far wider than that for which it was originally designed, however. The original ARPANET and the early generations of the Internet were constructed by and for the research, development, and education communities (Quarterman 1990). Benign uses by a collegial community were presumed when its technical architecture was designed (Oppliger 1997).

Substantial enhancements are being made to the technical architecture of the Internet to support a vastly larger volume and variety of users, capabilities, and services than was anticipated in the original design. Two new network services illustrate the scope of the improvements that are under way (Lawton 1998; Lynch 1998). One is "quality of service": the ability to reserve a set amount of bandwidth, at a predetermined level of quality, in advance. Rather than the current model, which is largely "first come, first served" for bandwidth usage, mostly at flat pricing, the new model supports differential pricing for differential services. Many organizations are willing to pay a premium to guarantee adequate bandwidth at a specified time (for a teleconference or a distance-education course, for example). Conversely, many individuals are willing to tolerate delays in email delivery or Web access in return for lower costs. In view of the complexity of Internet architecture and the number of political and service-provider boundaries crossed by an individual transmission, guaranteeing quality of service will not be a simple accomplishment. Though quality of service is considered an essential capability of an information infrastructure, precise assessments of what can be guaranteed and how it can be measured have yet to be established (Lynch 1998).

Multicasting is another long-awaited service improvement for the technical framework of a global information infrastructure. At present, most communications are point-to-point ("unicasting"): copies of a message are sent individually to each intended recipient. The alternative is broadcasting, in which one message is sent to all users of the network, whether they want it or not. An intermediate model is "multicasting": one message is sent to a selected group of recipients, reducing the amount of bandwidth required. Technically, under multicasting, the originating server sends one message to each network router on which intended recipients are located and that router re-sends to its local subscribers (Lawton 1998). As with quality of service, the number of providers involved makes multicasting a complex process, but one that is necessary for efficient use of bandwidth on a global information infrastructure (Lynch 1998). A variety of economic and technical models for network service provision are under consideration for the next generation of network architecture (Shapiro and Varian 1998).

The Internet is already a "network of networks." A global information infrastructure will be even more so. Though we speak metaphorically of a single open network, in actuality the Internet links many layers of networks within organizations, within local geographic areas, within countries, and within larger geographical regions. These go by various names, including intranets, extranets, local-area networks (LANs), metropolitan-area networks (MANs), and even tiny-area networks (TANs). Suffice it to say that the information infrastructure topography is becoming increasingly complex, linking together internal organizational networks, closed networks such as cable TV, and the international Internet.

The boundaries of individual networks can be controlled to varying degrees. A common technique is to protect organizational or even national networks with "firewalls" that limit the abilities of authorized users to exit and of outsiders to enter. Some internal resources can be publicly accessible while others are restricted to internal use, for example. Similarly, firewalls and filtering techniques can be used to limit external sites that can be reached. Parents can limit their children's ability to connect to sites known to contain pornography or other undesirable material. The definition of "undesirable" varies by context. Companies can limit access to known sites containing games. Countries can limit access to sites known to provide undesirable political views. China, for example, currently attempts to control access to sites outside the country through a single gateway, so that specific sites deemed objectionable can be blocked. Chinese Internet users are required to register with the police to gain access to the network (Tan, Mueller, and Foster 1997). A key phrase here is "known sites." As the Internet proliferates, new sites appear daily, and sites change names, location, and content frequently. Reliable filtering software that can distinguish between acceptable and unacceptable materials is not yet feasible, and may never be.

For most businesses and governments, security and risk management are far greater concerns than is pornography. After connectivity, the most important enabling technology for electronic commerce is security (Dam and Lin 1996; Geer 1998; Oppliger 1997). One model being studied and implemented is "trust management," in which mechanisms such as cryptography are employed to verify the identities of all parties involved in electronic transactions. Such transactions include buying and selling goods or services, transferring secure data (such as financial transactions between banks and stock markets), and proprietary communications within organizations or between organizations and their clients, customers, and suppliers. Both retail transactions between individuals and companies and wholesale transactions between companies can be accommodated. An alternative model is "risk management," which focuses on the likelihood of losses and the size of potential losses from electronic commerce. Rather than assume that trust can be guaranteed in all transactions, parties try to determine the degree of risk exposure and to insure against it. Cryptography is essential to both models as a means of assuring the authenticity of transactions to the extent possible. The frontiers of electronic commerce are being tested in the financial markets today. In view of the size and volume of transactions among banks, stock markets, investors, and other parties, many technical and policy aspects of information infrastructure are likely to be tested first in this arena (Geer 1998).

Information Infrastructure as Technology, People, and Content

Among the broadest conceptualizations of an information infrastructure is that presented in National Information Infrastructure: Agenda for Action 1993, where an NII is defined as encompassing a nation's networks, computers, software, information resources, developers, and producers. This definition comes closer to capturing the larger sense of infrastructure as a complex set of interactions between people and technology than do most other public policy statements, technical definitions, or metaphors.

The above definition is compelling, if vague, because it recognizes that we are creating something new and something that is more than a sum of its parts. The information infrastructure is not a substitute for telephone, broadcast, or cable networks, for computer systems, for libraries, archives, or museums, for schools and universities, for banks, or for governments. Rather, it is a new entity that incorporates and supplements all these technologies and institutions but is not likely to replace any of them. However, a GII is likely to change each of these institutions, and how people use them, in profound ways.

The term "global information infrastructure" is used in this broad sense throughout the present book. A GII consists of a technical framework of computing and communications technologies, information content, services, and people, all of which interact in complex and often unpredictable ways. No single entity owns, manages, or controls the technical framework of a GII, although many governments, vast numbers of public and private organizations, and millions of people contribute to it and use it. The GII is perhaps best understood by the metaphor of the elephant being examined by a group of blind people—each one touches a different part of the beast, and thus senses a different entity. From this perspective, a global information infrastructure is a means for access to information. However, it can be viewed from many complementary perspectives that also are valid.

Summary

These are exciting times. Information technologies are increasing in speed, power, and sophistication, and they now can link together a vast array of devices into a network that spans the globe. They offer new ways of learning, working, and playing, as well as conducting global commerce. Some contend that these changes are revolutionary and will change the world; others argue that the changes are evolutionary, and that individuals and organizations will incorporate networked information technologies into their practices just as they incorporated many earlier media and technologies. In this book I take the view that these changes are neither revolutionary nor evolutionary but somewhere between: that they are co-evolutionary. New technologies are based on perceived needs and available capabilities. People adopt these new technologies if and when they deem the technologies useful and when they deem the effort and the costs appropriate. Sometimes individuals make these decisions; sometimes organizations make them. The result is that some technologies are adopted by some of the people some of the time. No matter how voluntary or involuntary the adoption process, individuals and organizations adapt technologies to their interests and practices, often in ways not anticipated by the designers of those technologies. Information technologies are more flexible and malleable to individual practices than are most other innovations, and this makes them especially adaptable. They also evolve more quickly than most other innovations, with new and improved versions appearing at a dizzying rate.

Adoption and adaptation of technology are difficult to predict, owing to the complex interactions between characteristics of information technologies, practices of individuals and organizations, economics, public policy, local cultures, and a host of other factors. Organizations acquiring new technologies find that estimates of first-level effects, such as those on productivity and profits, are unreliable. Reliable predictions of longer-term, second-level effects, such as those on organizational communication and structure, are nearly impossible. One reason is that external factors, such as changes in the legal status of electronic communications, can have profound effects on how individuals and organizations use information technologies.

We are in the process of creating a global information infrastructure that will interconnect computer networks and various forms of information technologies around the world. After a review of some of the many meanings of "information infrastructure," it was determined that the concept incorporates people, technology, and content and the interactions between them. This broad definition encompasses perspectives on information infrastructure as a set of public policies and as a technical framework. The broader definition is best suited to studying the co-evolution of technology and behavior as related to access to information, which is the primary concern of this book. An information infrastructure is only one of several infrastructures that are essential to a well-functioning society. Others include energy, transportation, telecommunications, banking and finance, transportation, water systems, and emergency services. Because each of these infrastructures is increasingly reliant on information technologies, they are more interconnected and interdependent. Their interdependence means that more and more aspects of daily life depend on the emerging global information infrastructure.

2

Is It Digital or Is It a Library? Digital Libraries and Information Infrastructure

If a global information infrastructure can link together electronic resources, whether public or private, large and small, located around the world, will it serve as a "global digital library"? Is a GII the library of the future? Is it a library of the future? If either, then who are its users, how will it be used, what capabilities and services will it offer, and who is responsible for funding and maintaining it? More fundamentally, is it a library at all?

Gross and Borgman (1995, p. 904) called for public discussion of visions for the library of the future:

A new conversation is necessary among librarians, library users, and officials responsible for funding libraries to insure that the library of the future serves the intellectual needs of diverse users and fields. Library literacy is as indispensable as computer literacy if the active scholar and the curious inquirer are to be empowered to seek and assess knowledge in any form or source. Even home shopping requires informed consumers.

These challenges are more urgent than ever, as we consider models for information institutions and services appropriate to a networked world. However, neither networks nor computers will be available to everyone. Some people never will have access to a GII, nor will all materials ever be in electronic formats. Multiple forms and hybrid forms of information institutions and services will be required. Thus, we must address not only questions of what is a library but also what "literacy" and "seek and assess knowledge" mean in this environment. These are but a few of the many questions to be discussed by policy makers and by those creating, designing, managing, and using information resources and systems.

Scholarly and professional interest in "digital libraries" grew rapidly in the 1990s. In the United States, digital libraries were designated a "national challenge application area" under the High Performance Computing and Communications Initiative (HPCC) and a key component of the National Information Infrastructure (Office of Science and Technology Policy 1994). The Digital Library Initiative (1994–1998) involved three federal agencies. Phase II of the Digital Libraries Initiative (1999–2004) involves eight agencies, indicating the expansion of interest and scope over this short period of time.[1] An international digital libraries program was announced by the National Science Foundation in 1998, extending the range of partnerships. The United Kingdom has the Electronic Libraries Programme (http://ukoln.bath.ac.uk/elib/), and many research projects having to do with digital libraries are underway in Europe, Asia, and elsewhere, some funded under initiatives specific to digital libraries and some with funding from other areas.

During the 1990s, multiple domestic and international digital libraries conferences were established and digital libraries topics were introduced at meetings in a variety of disciplines and professions. Several new print and online journals on digital libraries were founded. Online distribution lists with news of digital library projects proliferate. Libraries are undertaking projects in digital imaging, document management, and network services.

Why all this interest and activity? Did an urgent research and development problem lead to large amounts of grant funding? Did the availability of grant funding create opportunities for a new research area? Did successful research lead to practical developments? Did practical problems lead to research on solutions? Is digital library research and practice a definable area of interest, or has "digital library" merely become an umbrella term for a wide array of information and technology projects?

Causal relationships are notoriously difficult to establish. In view of the rate at which the trees of digital library research and practice are growing,

1. The Digital Library Initiative (1994–1998) was jointly funded by the National Science Foundation's Computer and Information Science and Engineering Directorate, the Advanced Research Projects Agency's Computing Systems Technology Office and Software and Intelligent Systems Technology Office, and the National Aeronautics and Space Administration. Phase II of the Digital Libraries Initiative (1998–2003) is funded by the above three agencies plus the National Library of Medicine, the Library of Congress, and the National Endowment for the Humanities, in partnership with the National Archives and Records Administration and the Smithsonian Institution.

it is difficult to grasp the shape and size of the forest. I expect the answers to these questions to become clearer in hindsight a few years from now. Yet actions we take now, and the perceptions that we form, may influence the shape of that forest profoundly.

Perspectives on Digital Libraries

A review of definitions reveals that the term "digital library" is being used to describe a variety of entities and concepts (Bishop and Star 1996; Fox 1993; Fox et al. 1995; Greenberg 1998; Lesk 1997a; Levy and Marshall 1995; Lucier 1995; Lyman 1996; Lynch and Garcia-Molina 1995; Schauble and Smeaton 1998; Waters 1998a; Zhao and Ramsden 1995). In general, researchers focus on digital libraries as content collected on behalf of user communities, while librarians focus on digital libraries as institutions or services. These communities are not mutually exclusive. Some researchers are focusing on practical problems related to institutions and services, and some practitioners are participating in research teams addressing issues of content, collections, and communities.

Research vs. Practice

Despite decades of research and practice in related areas, the term "digital library" is relatively new. The availability of research funding under this term has attracted scholars and practitioners from a variety of backgrounds, some of whom have minimal knowledge of related areas such as information retrieval, computer networks, cataloging and classification, library automation, archives, or publishing. Sometimes other research topics have simply been relabeled "digital libraries," adding to the confusion. Rapid growth of computer networks, of databases, and of public awareness has contributed to a bandwagon effect in hot topics such as digital libraries, digital archives, and electronic publishing. Only as an area matures do people give serious thought to rigorous definitions.

One reason for the confusion of terminology is that research and practice in digital libraries are being conducted concurrently at each stage of the continuum from basic research to implementation. Some people are working on fundamental enabling technologies and theoretical problems, others are working on applications, others are studying social aspects of digital libraries in experimental and field contexts, and yet others are deploying the results of earlier research. Their concerns and foci are understandably different.

The variety of concerns within the digital libraries research community reflects the interdisciplinary nature of the topic. Scholars based in computer science are largely concerned with enabling technologies and networks. Scholars based in library and information science are largely concerned with content, organization, user behavior, and publishing. Those based in sociology and in economics are more likely to concern themselves with social context and economic models, respectively. Topics such as human-computer interaction, interface design, and service delivery often cross all these disciplines and more. Scholars based in application areas such as education, geography, health, the arts, and the humanities may combine any of these areas with expertise in their problem domain. Many if not most digital libraries projects draw on the expertise and the research results of multiple disciplines.

Research and practice have a symbiotic relationship. Interesting research problems often arise from practice. Scholars attempt to isolate problems for research purposes and then provide solutions to practitioners for implementation. Partnerships between researchers and practitioners are fundamental to the design of current funding initiatives, encouraging such relationships. Universities are eager to establish partnerships between scholars and industry, in hopes of cross-fertilizing ideas and acquiring new funding sources.

Definitions can serve many purposes, one of which is to provide a focal point for a community. Research-oriented definitions are intended to highlight significant research problems and the relationships between them. They also are intended to attract other scholars, with the goal of achieving a critical mass of researchers to address a particular set of problems. Such definitions are more useful in directing attention to research problems than for drawing explicit boundaries.

Practice-oriented definitions are intended to highlight current and anticipated practical challenges. Research libraries in particular are focusing attention on the changing nature of the university, the evolution of libraries as institutions, the role that libraries play in serving the university community, and how that role is changing with the advent of digital collections and services. Librarians are faced with formulating visions for the future of their institutions and services while managing daily operations that may serve tens of thousands of users. The Digital Library Federation is a consortium of major research libraries whose purpose is to draw attention to these challenges. Their working definition (Waters 1998a) is a means of framing the practical, rather than research, problems they face as a community.

Community Building

Researchers and practitioners alike are engaged in deliberate efforts to build communities of interest around digital library issues. Funding agencies are building communities to address digital libraries research problems. They do so through workshops that bring together current and prospective grantees to identify research problems. The first US Digital Library Initiative also held semi-annual meetings of all the funded research teams, inviting selected observers from the research and practice communities as well. Proposals and collaborative efforts often evolve directly or indirectly from such meetings. Similarly, the Digital Library Federation is an intentional effort to build a community of librarians around practical issues. They do so by collaborating on projects, sharing expertise, and publicizing their initiatives and accomplishments.

The many digital libraries conferences play important roles in community building, as do journals and online news services. Early conferences were organized by individual universities and agencies. Later conference series were supported by professional societies, most notably the Association for Computing Machinery Digital Libraries conferences (Fox and Marchionini 1996) and the Advances in Digital Libraries conferences, first supported by the IEEE in 1998 (*Proceedings of the IEEE* 1998). The variety of regional meetings is expanding as well. In 1998 alone, European, Asian, Russian, and German conferences on digital libraries were held.[2] Sessions at related conferences assist in forming and extending communities of research and practice.

2. Announcements of digital library meetings and journals, documents, and pointers to related materials can be found on the site of the International Federation of Library Associations and Institutions (IFLA) (http://www.ifla.org/II/diglib.htm). Current articles and announcements also can be found in *D-lib Magazine* (http://www.dlib.org).

Framing the Issues

Digital libraries are attracting interest in many disciplines and professions. Though increased participation leads to the cross-fertilization of ideas, it also results in disputed territory and terminology. Lynch (1993a) was prescient in noting that the term "digital library" is problematic because it obscures the complex relationship between electronic information collections and libraries as institutions. Greenberg (1998, p. 106) comments that "the term 'digital library' may even be an oxymoron: that is, if a library is a library, it is not digital; if a library is digital, it is not a library." Battin (1998, p. 276–277) rejects the use of the term "digital library" on the grounds that it is "dangerously misleading."

Librarians tend to take a broad view of the concept of a library. In general terms, they see libraries as organizations that select, collect, organize, conserve, preserve, and provide access to information on behalf of a community of users. Libraries have existed for many centuries, and their social role and practices have evolved through many forms of civilization and many formats of media. With the advent of computer networks and digital media, libraries will employ yet another delivery system for yet another form of media. In this sense, the term "digital library" connotes "the future library," in which the institution is transformed to address the new environment in which it exists. A sense of continuity and the maintenance of information resources over time ("conserve," "preserve") is implicit as well.

Most of the definitions arising from the research community, especially those set forth by computer scientists, tend toward a narrower view of the concept of a library. Their emphasis is on databases and information retrieval and thus on collecting, organizing, and providing access to information resources. Much of the richer social and institutional context, services, and conservatorship are outside the scope of research-oriented definitions of digital libraries. The narrow scope of the term "library" follows from earlier uses in computer science research and practice in reference to any collection of similar materials. Rooms housing magnetic tapes are referred to as "tape libraries," and the clerks who check tapes in and out are referred to as "tape librarians," much to the dismay of professional librarians who hold graduate degrees in the field.

The term "digital library" serves as a convenient and familiar shorthand to refer to electronic collections, and it conveys a sense of richer content and fuller capabilities than do terms such as "database" or "information retrieval system." At the same time, such uses of the term convey a far narrower sense of a library than that of a full-service institution with long-term responsibilities. Computer scientists' predictions of a declining role for librarians in a digital age (e.g., Odlyzko 1995, 1997; Schatz 1997) are predicated on a constrained view of the present and future role of libraries.

Despite the tensions between these perspectives, the communities have not engaged in direct discussion to the extent that might be expected. Although US government digital libraries initiatives have shaped the direction of research activities, the practicing library community has made little mention of them or of their influence on conceptions of library services. A salient example is the widely cited *Books, Bricks, and Bytes: Libraries in the Twenty-First Century*, first published in 1996 as a special issue of *Daedalus* and then issued as a monograph (Graubard and LeClerc 1998). The only mention of the digital libraries initiatives is in a piece by the director of the German National Library (Lehmann 1996); Keller (1998) comments on this point too. Similarly, only one mention of the digital libraries initiatives can be found in a recent book on academic information resources for the twenty-first century published by the Council on Library and Information Resources and the Association of American Universities (Hawkins and Battin 1998), and that mention is by Waters (1998b), then head of the Digital Library Federation.

On the research front, some in library and information science (LIS) take computer scientists to task for reinventing their research on organization of information, information retrieval, user interfaces, and related topics; they are more likely to do so in conference discussion sessions or in private than in print, however. Computer science researchers sometimes counter that LIS researchers are bound by a narrow paradigm and pay insufficient attention to computer science's accomplishments. Such sniping increases tensions and is counterproductive to achieving common goals. Expertise in LIS, in computer science, and in related disciplines is essential to successful digital libraries research. It is to be hoped that increased collaboration will enhance mutual respect between computer scientists and LIS researchers.

Some encouraging signs of cooperation and engagement are evident. Digital libraries conferences, while dominated by researchers, also are drawing contributions and attendance from the practitioner community. The diversity of meanings of the term "digital library" continues to be apparent in conference programs, however, with odd juxtapositions of papers that bear more similarity in title than in content.

Defining Digital Libraries

Digital Libraries as Content, Collections, and Communities

Digital library research builds upon a long history of related work in information retrieval, databases, user interfaces, networks, information seeking, classification and organization, library automation, publishing, and other areas. It dates back several decades or several centuries, depending on what is included for consideration. I include in the research community scholars studying information-related problems that they or others have labeled "digital libraries." Most of these scholars are affiliated with academic departments or research groups in computer science, library and information science, or information studies, but some are located in related areas such as archives, sociology, psychology, communication, or economics, or in application areas such as education, geography, health sciences, or the arts and humanities.

Definitions of "digital libraries" arising from the computer and information science research community evolved in scope and content throughout the 1990s. The two initiatives funded by the multiple federal agencies (National Science Foundation 1993, 1998) were particularly influential in defining the boundaries of digital libraries research. The definitions were not established by the funding agencies alone. Rather, they arose from the many research workshops and conferences that took place before and during the initiatives, and from publications by researchers.

Evolution of Definitions

One of the first meetings to focus directly on digital libraries issues was a 1991 workshop on "Future Directions in Text Analysis, Retrieval and Understanding" (summarized in Fox 1993) and a white paper on electronic libraries that followed from it (Lesk, Fox, and McGill 1991). The resulting excitement led to more workshops that refined a research agenda and eventually led to the digital libraries initiatives.

The earliest research-oriented definition appears to be one proposed in 1992 for what were then called "electronic libraries" (Borgman 1992). It was included in a source book of materials for those preparing proposals to the Digital Library Initiative (Fox 1993). Summarizing from workshops conducted in 1991 and 1992, this definition states that a National Electronic Library is (1) a service; (2) an architecture; (3) a set of information resources, databases of text, numbers, graphics, sound, video, etc.; and (4) a set of tools and capabilities to locate, retrieve, and utilize the information resources available. The users of a national electronic library would include students, teachers, professors, researchers, scholars, librarians, authors, publishers, information providers, and practitioners. Contributors of information resources would include publishers, universities, professional societies, libraries, authors, editors, and compilers.

The above definition remains among the most comprehensive by including services, architecture, content, enabling technologies, users, and content. It provided a basis for further discussion and refinement. The Digital Library Initiative, announced in September 1993 and since dubbed DLI-1, defined the term only implicitly (National Science Foundation 1993), stating that "information sources accessed via the Internet are the ingredients of a digital library" and that "the problem for research and development is . . . to achieve an economically feasible capability to digitize massive corpora of extant and new information from heterogeneous and distributed sources; then store, search, process and retrieve information from them in a user friendly way." Note the use of the singular form, "digital library," which evolved from the goal of "a national electronic library."

The goals of DLI-1 were modest by today's standards. Research was supported in three areas:

• capturing data and metadata of all forms (text, images, sound, speech, etc.) and categorizing and organizing them
• advanced software and algorithms for browsing, searching, filtering, abstracting, summarizing and combining large volumes of data, imagery, and all kinds of information
• utilization of networked databases distributed around the [United States] and around the world.

The notion of a digital library and goals for research continue to be refined through workshops, conferences, and scholarly writing. A 1995 workshop that addressed scaling and interoperability issues in digital libraries resulted in several definitions, the most general of which defines a digital library as a system that provides "a community of users with coherent access to a large, organized repository of information and knowledge" (Lynch and Garcia-Molina 1995). Content, collection, and community all are included in this definition, as is the requirement that the content be organized.

One of the primary outcomes of the NSF-sponsored Social Aspects of Digital Libraries workshop was a definition of the term "digital libraries." In Borgman et al. 1996 the scope was broadened to encompass two complementary ideas:

1. Digital libraries are a set of electronic resources and associated technical capabilities for creating, searching, and using information. In this sense they are an extension and enhancement of information storage and retrieval systems that manipulate digital data in any medium (text, images, sounds; static or dynamic images) and exist in distributed networks. The content of digital libraries includes data, metadata that describe various aspects of the data (e.g., representation, creator, owner, reproduction rights), and metadata that consist of links or relationships to other data or metadata, whether internal or external to the digital library.

2. Digital libraries are constructed—collected and organized—by [and for] a community of users, and their functional capabilities support the information needs and uses of that community. They are a component of communities in which individuals and groups interact with each other, using data, information, and knowledge resources and systems. In this sense they are an extension, enhancement, and integration of a variety of information institutions as physical places where resources are selected, collected, organized, preserved, and accessed in support of a user community. These information institutions include, among others, libraries, museums, archives, and schools, but digital libraries also extend and serve other community settings, including classrooms, offices, laboratories, homes, and public spaces.

This two-part definition extends the scope of digital libraries in several directions, reflecting the contributions of scholars from a dozen disciplines. It moves beyond information retrieval to include the full cycle of creating, searching, and using information. Rather than simply collecting content on behalf of user communities, it embeds digital libraries in the activities of those communities, and it encompasses information-related activities of multiple information institutions.

Like the first initiative, the call for proposals for phase II of the Digital Libraries Initiative (National Science Foundation 1998) does not include an explicit definition of the term "digital library." Rather, the call notes that since the first initiative "the definition of a digital library has evolved." Compared to the first initiative, the DLI-2 call includes far more concern for social, behavioral, and economic aspects of digital libraries, and identifies research areas that encompass a broader range of academic disciplines, reflecting most of the issues raised in the definition from the Social Aspects of Digital Libraries workshop. Most of the call focuses on research, which is divided into human-centered research, content and collections-based research, and systems-centered research. The remainder addresses test beds and applications. Explicit in the call is a view of digital libraries as a component of a national and international information infrastructure. In addition, a sense of service to user communities is implicit in these new directions.

Other definitions require that digital libraries contain the full content of information resources in computer-readable form, and often assume that they contain more than text alone (Fox et al. 1995; Levy and Marshall 1995). In a book on "practical digital libraries," Lesk (1997a) defines a digital library simply as "a collection of information which is both digitized and organized." Summarizing a broad array of definitions of "digital library," Bishop and Star (1996) determine that three elements are necessary:

• some sense of a collection, with some kind of organization; the content may be partly physical and partly electronic, or entirely electronic

• a collection that is not entirely bibliographic or exclusively a set of pointers to other material—it must contain some "full-form online material" and may be in a variety of formats

• a goal of matching "audience, group, patron, or community with attributes of the collection," whether in the manner that physical collections are selected for an audience or in the sense of the virtual space that can be created around a community.

Defining Elements of Digital Libraries

Several aspects of the above definitions should be noted. One is that digital libraries are viewed as databases, albeit databases of rich content, whether full text, images, or combinations of media and representations. Much digital library research, particularly that conducted in departments of computer science, focuses on enabling technologies such as database structure, retrieval algorithms, filtering, intelligent agents, network architecture, and other necessary capabilities.

These definitions assume or require that content is collected on behalf of a user community. This aspect of the definition frames digital libraries in terms of their users, which also determines the tools and capabilities those users need to manipulate the content. Research on information needs and uses, users, usability, interface design, and social context derives from these aspects of the definitions. The one definition that mentions institutions indicates that digital libraries can be extensions of libraries, museums, archives, and schools, as well as extensions of work, education, and leisure environments in which information resources are used. The notion of "community" remains problematic, as none of these definitions provide criteria for identifying or determining the scope of a user community.

Another noteworthy assumption, particularly in definitions originating in the United States, is that digital libraries exist in distributed environments. This is not surprising, in view of the fact that the US digital libraries initiatives are closely related to information infrastructure development (National Science and Technology Council 1998; Office of Science and Technology Policy 1994). The call for proposals in DLI-1 (National Science Foundation 1993) begins by defining the Internet and setting the need for research in a network context. By the time DLI-2 was announced (National Science Foundation 1998), technical issues of operating digital libraries on computer networks had become core research concerns. These issues include interoperability, portability, data exchange, scalability, federation, extensibility, and open network architectures.

Digital Libraries as Institutions or Services
The terms "digital library," "electronic library," and "virtual library" have appeared in the professional literature of library and information science for some years, but rarely with explicit definitions. Lyman (1996), in an article entitled "What is a digital library? Technology, intellectual property, and the public interest," explores concepts he views to be prerequisite to defining the concept of a digital library, such as electronic publishing and digital documents. Young (1996, p. 122) lists characteristics of digital libraries, saying they "provide personalized or custom services for accessing, assembling, and analyzing information resources from a variety of diverse sources in many different formats."

Waters (1998a) provides the first succinct definition from a librarian's perspective. This is the working definition set forth by the Digital Library Federation (DLF):

Digital Libraries are organizations that provide the resources, including the specialized staff, to select, structure, offer intellectual access to, interpret, distribute, preserve the integrity of, and ensure the persistence over time of collections of digital works so that they are readily and economically available for use by a defined community or set of communities.

Waters acknowledges that the DLF statement is broad and is intended to comprehend other uses of the term, including those of the digital libraries initiatives. However, it is distinct from the research-oriented definitions in several respects. The focus of the DLF definition is on the digital library as an organization whose services include the provision of information resources in digital forms. The institutional focus also adds the element of conservatorship in preserving integrity and ensuring persistence of digital collections. The DLF definition thus captures a much broader sense of the term "library."

"Organization," as used by Waters, is a more general term than "institution," as used here. Librarians more commonly use the term "organization" in the sense of "knowledge organization," which implies imposing order on a collection through cataloging, classification, indexing, or other means. Lesk (1997a) uses the term in the latter sense when he defines a digital library as "a collection of information which is both digitized and organized." To avoid confusion, I will refer to libraries, archives, museums, and related entities as institutions rather than as organizations.

The DLF definition captures the senses and sentiments implicit in descriptions of digital libraries by other library agencies. The Library of Congress' American Memory project, for example, is part of a "national digital library." Note the singular form "digital library" in reference to an institution that provides many individual resources. American Memory (http://memory.loc.gov) is a project creating digital collections of historical texts, photographs, and sound recordings and providing public access via the Internet. It is similar to projects undertaken by other members of the DLF.[3]

The California Digital Library (http://www.cdlib.org) is a "tenth library" for the University of California, which has nine campuses. Again we find the sense of an institution that offers services: its web page announces that this digital library is "responsible for the design, creation, and implementation

3. See http://www.clir.org/programs/diglib/diglib.html.

of systems that support the shared collections of the University of California."

Funding for digital library projects in the United Kingdom is built upon a framework more similar to the DLF definition than to definitions arising from the US digital libraries initiatives. Primary funding in the United Kingdom is provided by the Electronic Libraries (eLib) Programme, which is a "program of collaborative partnerships between libraries, academic staff, publishers and others, to promote large scale pilot and demonstrator projects focusing on the components of a future electronic library service, and to provide stimulus to its creation" (Rusbridge 1998). The eLib program focuses on developing services rather than on basic research or enabling technologies. Libraries are the primary institutions involved, though eLib promotes partnerships with publishers, academic staff (university faculty in American parlance), and others.

Similarly, the summary report of the British Library's Initiatives for Access Programme, titled Towards the Digital Library, suggests a definition similar to that of the DLF (Carpenter, Shaw, and Prescott 1998). In an overview chapter (p. 11), Mahoney says "We were clear from the beginning that for The British Library, and probably for most libraries, being a digital library would emphatically not mean being an exclusively digital library." A few pages later (p. 17), Mahoney implies that a digital library is a service when he writes of "the issue of how one moves . . . towards a more integrated form of digital library provision."

The above statement from the British Library highlights another problem with using the term "digital library" to refer to an institution. Libraries collect content on the basis of the information needs of their user communities; the medium in which the content is captured is a secondary concern. Thus, defining an institution in terms of the format of materials (digital content) risks distinguishing among print libraries, digital libraries, film libraries, audio libraries, and so on. Librarians are not entirely comfortable with the use of the term "digital library" to describe some future form of the institution, but they have yet to propose a suitable alternative.

Digital Libraries as Databases

None of the definitions arising from the research or practice communities deal explicitly with the plethora of databases that exist on the Internet, on the World Wide Web, on CD-ROMs, and on proprietary services such as Dialog, Lexis/Nexis, Westlaw, STN, InfoAmerica, and CDB Infotek. Some of these databases and web sites identify themselves as digital libraries, whether for reasons of scholarship, for convenience as a recognizable term, or as a marketing ploy. In other cases, surveys of digital libraries include web-based, CD-ROM, and other databases within their scope.

These databases fall into a gray area between the definitions constructed by the research and library communities. The lack of fit is not surprising, as neither definition was intended to categorize electronic databases. We can say that electronic databases per se are not libraries as institutions or services, in the sense of the Digital Library Federation's definition. Griffiths (1998) confronts the question of "why the web is not a library." Her reasons include incompleteness of content, lack of standards and validation, minimal cataloging, and ineffective information retrieval. To this I add that the World Wide Web is not an institution and is not organized on behalf of a specifiable user community. However, one of the services that a digital library (in the DLF sense of the term) provides is access to electronic databases.

Some portion of electronic databases on the Internet, on proprietary systems, and on CD-ROMs are digital libraries as defined by the research community. On a case-by-case basis we can judge the degree to which databases are organized collections, whether they were created for a specified community, and whether their capabilities are sufficient to distinguish them from other forms of information retrieval systems, for example.

Working Definitions

For present purposes, it is essential to establish working definitions of the terms "digital library" and "global digital library." As was noted above, the term "digital library" is being used with two substantially different meanings. Taken together, the two definitions result in a tautology: A digital library is an institution that provides digital libraries. Both definitions are problematic because they confuse the boundaries between electronic collections and institutions. Underlying most of the research-oriented definitions is a constrained view of the nature of libraries. Yet using the term to imply the broader view favored by librarians constrains the institution by the type of content it collects.

The contrast between these two definitions is symptomatic of the tension between revolutionary and evolutionary views of information technologies. The revolutionary view is that digital libraries are databases linked by computing networks, and that, taken as a whole, they can provide an array of services that will supplant libraries. The evolutionary view is that digital libraries are institutions that will continue to provide content and services in many forms, just as their predecessor institutions have done, and that eventually they will supplement libraries as they exist today.

I prefer the middle ground of co-evolution, as expressed in the Social Aspects of Digital Libraries workshop report (Borgman et al. 1996). Digital libraries are an extension, enhancement, and integration both of information retrieval systems and of multiple information institutions, libraries being only one. The scope of digital libraries' capabilities includes not only information retrieval but also creating and using information. Thus, I take as a working definition of the term "digital libraries" the definition in Borgman et al. 1996, quoted in full above.

A "global digital library" is a useful construct that encompasses all the digital libraries that are connected to and accessible through a global information infrastructure. A global digital library would not be a single entity, nor would it be controlled by any single organization. Rather, it would consist of all the individual digital libraries; thus, it would involve many technologies, varieties of form and content, owners, and managers. Each digital library might be governed by different access privileges. Many political and organizational boundaries would be crossed. In principle, a user located at any point on a GII could search for content in any digital library located anywhere on the network. Also in principle, the owners or providers of each digital library would determine who has access to their resources, under what conditions, for what purposes, and at what price.

In some cases providers seek the widest possible audience for their digital libraries. Purveyors of retail products and services, from bookstores to mutual funds, advertise the availability of their digital information resources and promote their usage, for example. Governments provide free online public access to publications, to directories of services, and to some of the records they create or collect, such as census data. In contrast, private companies maintain proprietary online services for use by employees, with access privileges closely guarded. Online resources that are protected by firewalls or other security mechanisms may be visible on a GII only to authorized users. Other companies sell access to proprietary digital libraries. The existence of these resources is public, but only authorized paying customers can search and use them. Somewhere in between are libraries and other information institutions that provide a mix of public and private services. University and public libraries, for example, may provide free access to their catalogs and locally developed online resources, but because of contract requirements they may restrict access to purchased digital libraries to authorized members of their community (via passwords or by allowing access only from on-site computers, for example). All these online resources could be considered parts of a global digital library, but the array of digital libraries available to any individual user will vary widely.

A global digital library (GDL) is not the equivalent of a global information infrastructure. Rather, it is the component of a GII that supports access to information. Drawing boundaries between a GDL and a GII requires a definition of the concept of "information."

Whether or not it is possible or even useful to create a global digital library, the concept of a global digital library provides an opportunity for exploring aspects of digital libraries, access to information, information-related behavior, information infrastructure, international developments, and the transformation of information institutions such as libraries, archives, and museums.

Into the Digital Future

Despite the progress made to date, digital libraries are still in the early stages of research and practice under any of the above definitions. Where do we go from here? Many signs point to ever greater advancements and investments in networked information technologies (Lynch 1998). In the United States, the successful High Performance Computing and Communications program (HPCC), chartered by Congress, has been succeeded by the Executive Branch's Computing, Information, and Communications (CIC) research and development program (National Science and Technology Council 1998). Research areas include "high end computing and computation," "large scale networking, including the Next Generation Internet Initiative," "high confidence systems," "human centered systems," and "education, training, and human resources." Digital libraries research now falls under the human-centered systems program of CIC.

The United States is not alone in promoting the development of information and communication technologies. As was noted in chapter 1, the Group of Seven major industrialized nations supports the development of a global information infrastructure (G-7 Ministerial Conference on the Information Society 1995a,b). One of the G-7 policy statements is that the GII will provide access to culturally and linguistically diverse content. The European Union funds and promotes a wide range of information-related research and development under Directorate-General XIII, Telecommunications, Information Market and Exploitation of Research. Many other countries have established national information infrastructure programs and associated mechanisms for supporting research and development.

The continued expansion of information infrastructure and the penetration of information technology into more aspects of daily activities will require basic and applied research in many disciplines. Just as the frontiers of computing have moved from desktop to mobile computing to embedded systems, digital libraries are themselves becoming "enabling technologies" for many other applications. Contributing materials to digital libraries is a form of electronic publishing, and materials published electronically are collected, organized, preserved, and disseminated electronically. Distance-independent learning and tele-learning[4] require that content be associated with instruction; hence, digital libraries are an essential component. Software that supports computer-supported cooperative work must include a means to manage the associated work products, which is a digital library problem. And so on.

Many fundamental technical problems in digital libraries research remain to be solved. As digital libraries become more sophisticated, more practical, and more embedded in other applications, the challenges of understanding their uses and users become more urgent. These are inherently interdisciplinary problems, and they will require the contribution of researchers from many backgrounds. Some of those researchers have yet to hear the term "digital libraries."

---

4. The terms "distance learning" and (more correctly) "distance-independent learning" are widely used in the United States; the broader "tele-learning" is used in Europe.

Libraries as institutions stand to benefit from research on aspects of digital libraries. Research libraries and universities engaged in reinventing themselves for a digital age will need to draw on the best research, theory, and practice from a myriad of disciplines. Conversely, researchers studying many digital library problems will need partnerships with library institutions to study and test in operational settings. This is especially true of research on social, behavioral, and economic aspects of digital libraries. Partnerships with other information institutions, such as archives, museums, and schools, will also be essential.

Summary and Conclusions

Interest in digital libraries (both in research and in practice) expanded rapidly throughout the 1990s. Major funding initiatives in the United States, the United Kingdom, the European Union, and elsewhere have fueled research and development. Conferences, journals, and news services proliferate.

Upon closer examination, the term "digital library" has multiple meanings. These definitions cluster around two themes. From a research perspective, digital libraries are content collected and organized on behalf of user communities. From a library-practice perspective, digital libraries are institutions or organizations that provide information services in digital forms.

Definitions are formulated to serve specific purposes. The research community's definitions serve to identify and focus attention on research problems and to expand the community of interest around those problems. The library community's definitions focus on practical challenges involved in transforming library institutions and services. Databases available on the Internet, on proprietary services, and on CD-ROMs fall into a gray area. Neither the research community's nor the library community's definition provides a discrete categorization that can be applied to publicly available databases. Many such databases can be considered digital libraries, in the sense of research-oriented focus on content, collections, and communities. They are databases, rather than institutions, however, so they fall outside the scope of practice-oriented definitions.

In view of the rapid expansion of computer networks, distributed access to information resources, electronic publishing, tele-learning, distance-independent learning, electronic commerce, and related applications of information technologies, much more research on all aspects of digital libraries is needed. Practical challenges in creating content for digital libraries and in managing digital library services abound, as do the challenges of conceptualizing new forms of information institutions that will address future needs.

In exploring these definitions, we find that the research community's definitions have evolved from a narrow view emphasizing enabling technologies to a view that encompasses the social, behavioral, and economic contexts in which digital libraries are used. That view also has expanded from a primary emphasis on information retrieval to include the full life cycle of creating, seeking, using, preserving, and disposing of information resources. The library community has voiced the term "digital library" for some years, but only recently has it promulgated formal definitions. The working definition set forth by the Digital Libraries Federation appears to capture the sense in which practicing librarians intend the term.

Neither community is likely to surrender the term in favor of another. In view of this inherent conflict of interest, people using the term need to define what they mean in context. I employ the definition that originated from the Social Aspects of Digital Libraries workshop. It is a broad definition, viewing digital libraries as an extension, enhancement, and integration of information retrieval systems and of multiple information institutions, libraries being only one. Further, I propose "global digital library" as a construct to encompass digital libraries that are connected to, and accessible through, a global information infrastructure. A global digital library would not be a single entity, nor would it be controlled by any single organization.

The failure to define terms slows the development of theory, research, and practice. It also limits the ability to communicate the scope of the area or the nature of the research and practice problems to others. Confusions over terminology obscure deeper issues regarding the revolution, evolution, or co-evolution of information technologies and institutions and the behavior of individuals. Though all parties need not agree on one meaning, each can be more explicit in explaining choices of terminology. Sometimes we simply may need to agree to disagree. Words do matter, however, and they will influence the success of our ventures.

3

Access to Information

If knowledge indeed is power, then a global information infrastructure could empower people around the world by improving their access to information. Among the many promises of a GII is enhancing people's abilities to create, seek, and use information, regardless of their location or the location of the resources. These are laudable goals, but what does "access to information" mean? "Access" and "information" are ambiguous terms, with many meanings in many contexts.

Access

"Access" is a word with a variety of denotations and connotations. Most dictionary definitions focus on "freedom or ability to obtain or make use of," "permission, liberty, or ability to enter, approach, communicate with, or pass to and from" (Merriam-Webster 1993, p. 6), and "a means of approaching or nearing" or "passage" (Morris 1981). Roget's Thesaurus (1980) includes two less often used meanings of the word: "a sudden, violent expression, as of emotion (outburst)" and "a sudden and often acute manifestation of a disease (seizure)."

The sense of "freedom or ability" is seen in legal phrases such as "access to the property" and "access to the courts." This meaning also is present in library terminology that refers to loaning materials (e.g., "access services librarian") and to identifying and locating materials, whether owned by the institution (e.g., "improving access to our collection") or not (e.g., "access to that which one does not own") (Higginbotham and Bowdoin 1993, p. 3). Transportation usage, such as "freeway access" or "access road," implies the "passage" meaning.

Uses of "access" in information technology and policy contexts are consonant with the dictionary meanings noted above; the "outburst" and "seizure" senses are not encountered in this context.

Universal Service

"Universal service," a concept closely related to "access to information," reveals the complexity of defining "access." The concept of universal service was established by the Communications Act of 1934, in the early days of telephony in the United States (Baldwin, McVoy, and Steinfield 1996). The intent is that all households have access to the nation's telecommunications infrastructure. Basic connectivity should be universal, and thus economic and technical barriers to telephone service must be minimal. As a matter of public policy, telephone connectivity is viewed as a social necessity, and other services should be taxed to the extent necessary to subsidize basic telephone service for all households. The American concept of universal service, as it applies to telephony, was not universally applied in other countries (Mansell 1993). Views of the public interest in providing telecommunications services vary widely among nations, as do the means of regulation (Mansell 1993; Noam 1992).

In recent years, the concept of "universal service" has become yet more complex and contentious. In the United States, deregulation of telecommunications services has resulted in many more service providers, complicating the arrangements for cross-subsidies of basic services. The service environment also is more complex with the expansion of telecommunications from basic telephony to computer networks, mobile phones and pagers, cable, and other technologies. Nevertheless, the universal service concept is being carried over into information infrastructure policy. Note the specific assurances of universal service in the US policy statements on national information infrastructure and international statements quoted in chapter 1 (Gore 1994a; Brown et al. 1995). Those statements and the later ones by the G-7 nations on a global information infrastructure (G-7 Ministerial Conference on the Information Society 1995a) also ensured "open access to the network." The latter statements incorporate two senses of "open access," by further stating "for all information providers and users." Open access for users follows from the universal service concept. Open access for providers follows from an economic model of open markets.

The concepts of "universal service" and "access to information" were linked early in the public debates over information infrastructure (Kahin 1995). Universal service originally implied connectivity to essential telephony services. As with telephony, connectivity to a national or global information infrastructure is of little value unless accompanied by access to a set of services. Determining what services are essential, how they should be provided, and who should pay for them are matters of current public debate. Even the concept of connectivity is problematic, for access via a 5-year-old personal computer and a slow modem over antiquated phone lines is far different than access via a new, high-end machine with a fast network connection.

In the United States, access to information on computer networks is becoming the responsibility of public libraries. These services are partially subsidized by other telecommunications services (Federal Communications Commission 1996). "Universal access to email" is another service being promoted as a public good (Anderson et al. 1995). Neither "universal service" nor "open access to the network" is a universally accepted goal of public policy; these concepts and policies are likely to evolve for some years to come.

Computer Networks
Several instances of use of "access" occur in the context of computer networks and the information resources they support. Kahin (1995, pp. 6–7) compares universal service for telephony to universal service for a "general purpose information infrastructure." He asks: "How accessible is the new infrastructure in terms of ubiquity, affordability, and usability, and how is this accessibility paid for?" As Kahin notes, telecommunications carriers are not necessarily prepared to accept public responsibility for access to information. This role historically has fallen not only to public libraries, but also to other institutions such as archives and government printing offices, and by means such as copyright laws.

Keller (1995, pp. 34–35) defines public access in the context of information, adding another dimension by considering users as both sources and consumers of information:

By public access we mean not only establishing physical connections to the network, but also ensuring that those connections are easy to use, affordable, and provide access to a minimum set of information resources. In particular, network use should not be limited to the passive receipt of information. Instead, the environments should be open, distributed and easily navigable. Even the most basic connection should enable users to act as information sources as well as destinations.

Lynch (1993a, p. 3) focuses directly on access in the context of networked information:

The term "access" . . . is used in the broadest sense: not simply electronic connectivity to information resource providers through the network, but the ability for people to successfully locate, retrieve and use the information contained within various computer systems.

Both Keller and Lynch associate access to computer networks with usability. This relationship was the focus of a US National Research Council study, whose summary report states the following: "The concern of this study is that, even though the usability of systems has improved substantially over many years, current interfaces still exclude many people from effective NII access." (Computer Science and Telecommunications Board 1997a, p. 2)

Access to Information

Several elements of access are essential to defining "access to information" in the context of information infrastructure. One is connectivity, which is a prerequisite for using a computer network and the resources and services it supports. Connectivity arises from early notions of universal service and from access definitions specific to information infrastructure, such as those offered by Keller (1995) and Lynch (1993a). A second element is content and services, for connectivity is meaningless without them. Kahin (1995), Lynch (1993a), and Keller (1995) all distinguish between access to the network and access to the information it contains.

The third element of access is usability, which has three aspects. One is the usability of the computer network or information infrastructure itself, as indicated in the National Research Council report cited above. To be considered accessible, the network must be usable by "every citizen," rather than being designed primarily for technical specialists. (The report acknowledges that not everyone will be able to use all services; the goal is that everyone should be able to use basic services, at a minimum.) The second aspect is the set of skills or literacies that users bring to the system. Access is limited by people's abilities to use the technology and the information available. These usability aspects, which follow from the equity goals of universal service, are specifically mentioned in Keller's (1995) and Lynch's (1993a) definitions. A third aspect is implicit in Lynch's definition, and that is usability of content. To be considered "accessed," the information must be retrieved in some form in which it can be read, viewed, or otherwise employed constructively. A computer file or document that cannot be opened, displayed on a screen, run on available hardware and software, or read in a language one comprehends is not considered accessible.

Thus, for the purposes of this book, I define "access to information" as connectivity to a computer network and to available content, such that the technology is usable, the user has the requisite skills and knowledge, and the content itself is in a usable and useful form. Each of these factors has far-reaching implications for designing and deploying a global information infrastructure. Though a fairly broad definition, it excludes a number of factors that could be considered essential to access. Affordability is not included in defining access, although it is inherent in the concept of universal service. Nor are information providers' roles considered a definitional element, despite public policy statements on "open access to the network for all information providers and users." Providers fall on the supply side of the economic equation, whereas this book focuses on the demand side, or the users of a global information infrastructure. However, in line with Keller's (1995) definition of access (quoted above), users can be sources of information, and thus providers as well. When considering an information life cycle of creating, using, and seeking information, the line between using and providing information sometimes blurs. Thus, all these aspects are relevant to the concept of access to information. In the interest of simplifying the definition for the purposes of this book, I will view them as contextual matters rather than components of a definition.

Interpreting and applying the above definition of "access to information" depends on the definition of "information" applied.

Information

In discussions of the global information infrastructure and digital libraries, the word "information" is usually left undefined or else defined in general terms. For example, Fox et al. (1995, p. 23) define information as "what flows over the networks, what is presented to us by our consumer electronics devices, what is manipulated by our computers, and what is stored in our libraries." Such definitions are ambiguous, including any entity that could be digitized, from numeric facts to entertainment to conversations; information as symbols that can be manipulated; and can be interpreted to include information in the subjective or affective sense, such as human responses to what is presented by electronic devices.

Barlow (1993) proposes that in a global information infrastructure, "Freed of its containers, information is obviously not a thing;" rather, information is a phenomenon with three properties: an activity, a life form, and a relationship. Barlow's definition conflicts with that of Buckland (1991), who distinguishes three categories of information:

- information-as-process, or becoming informed
- information-as-knowledge, or that which is perceived in information as process
- information-as-thing, or an object such as a document that is informative or may impart knowledge.

In other contexts, information can be something large and amorphous, closely related to the concept of culture (Schiller 1994), or something very small and discrete, as in Shannon and Weaver's (1949) mathematical theory of communication, also known as information theory (Ritchie 1991). Definitions of information range widely between disciplines and contexts, as Losee (1997) notes in attempting a "discipline-independent" definition of information. The variety of definitions offered by these writers and many others indicates how difficult it is to think of "information" in any single sense. Philosophers have spent centuries explicating "information" and related concepts such as "knowledge" and "meaning;" I do not presume to resolve those debates here.

Digital Libraries and Documents

Our concern is with access to information that is available via a global information infrastructure; hence, we can constrain our search for a definition of "information" to this context. Buckland's (1991) classification of information definitions, noted above, is particularly relevant because his context is information systems. "Information-as-process" conveys the sense of the term in which information is the act of informing. When someone is informed, what he or she knows is changed. "Information-as-knowledge" refers to that which is perceived in "information-as-process." Knowledge is that which is being communicated. "Information-as-thing," according to Buckland, refers to objects such as data and documents that are informative or impart knowledge. Comparing the definitions, he determined that information systems such as digital libraries can deal directly with information only as "things." Mechanized systems operate on objects or representations, not on communicative processes or knowledge per se. Returning to the definition of digital libraries in chapter 2, we see that "things" can be collected and organized into digital libraries, while processes or knowledge cannot.

In later work, Buckland (1997) explores the concept of "document" in a similar vein. Digital libraries can manage many forms of documents, but the question arises of how far we can stretch the definition. Texts, photographs, music recordings, and feature-length movies, or digitized representations thereof, can be collected and organized into digital libraries, so all of them reasonably can be considered documents. Under some definitions, three-dimensional objects such as museum specimens are considered documents if people are informed by observing them (Buckland 1997; Otlet 1934). Yet other definitions include living beings as documents if they are objects of study, such as animals in a zoo (Briet 1951, translated in Buckland 1997). Buckland (ibid., p. 806) analyzes Briet's classifications to infer rules for when an object can be considered as a document:

(1) There is materiality: Physical objects and physical signs only;
(2) There is intentionality: It is intended that the object be treated as evidence;
(3) The objects have to be processed: They have to be made into documents; and, we think,
(4) There is a phenomenological position: The object is perceived to be a document.

Thus, whether something is a document depends on its function and its context. What may be a document for one person and one usage may not be for another. Considerations quickly cross over into matters of material culture and of semiotics, as Buckland acknowledges.

Digital documents are the subject of growing research and development interest. For example, a major conference on information systems began devoting a track to digital documents in 1995 (Sprague 1998). In the 1998 conference proceedings, 36 papers were divided into subtopics of "coping with information overload," "multimedia information systems," "genre in digital documents," "libraries for digital documents," "documents in organizations and the workplace," and "digital documents in context: organization and creation." Despite the lack of a specific definition of "digital document" for the conference, these subtopics suggest a definition by example. The organizers considered digital documents to be a topic lying at the "confluence of several traditional disciplines such as computer science, information systems, and library science, as well as law, sociology, linguistics, economics, and others" (Sprague 1998, p. ix). Elsewhere, Weibel (1995) largely avoids the definitional problem by referring to documents and "document-like objects."

In view of the vast array of formats and content that exists in a global information infrastructure, including forms yet to be invented, we will have to settle for a contextual definition of "document." What are documents to some people may be merely data to others, if they perceive them at all. The definition of a document can be constrained by imposing the definition of digital libraries stated in chapter 2. For the purposes of this book, "documents" are the things that are collected and organized in digital libraries on behalf of a community of users. Buckland (1991) views documents as one form of "things" that are informative or may impart knowledge. In this sense, documents are similar to Barlow's (1993) concept of containers or entities that carry some content that has meaning to its creators and users. Although documents or "document-like objects" (Weibel 1995) may be the unit that is collected and organized in digital libraries, people may need subunits of documents such as specific images, facts, or other data. Determining the appropriate unit for managing information remains problematic and may be the subject of philosophical debate. This issue can be addressed in practical terms as part of describing and organizing information.

Documents can exist outside digital libraries, of course, and thus another distinction is necessary. Only digital documents can exist in digital libraries. Almost any kind of object or living being can be represented by a digital document, however. Physical images can be photographed or otherwise captured and the results digitized and stored in electronic form. Text on paper can be scanned as images or keyed as electronic text. Music can be recorded and digitized. For some purposes, these representations are useful in themselves and will be considered documents. For other purposes, these representations are merely surrogates for entities that exist offline, such as people, pets, paintings, or places. I will expand on these distinctions in the following sections on digital and digitized documents, hybrid libraries, and metadata.

Various other forms of data that are transmitted over a global information infrastructure may be considered documents by some people, for some purposes. For example, television and radio broadcasts are continuous flows, whether carried by airwaves, cable, or computer networks. People do not perceive these signals without the appropriate receiving equipment to recognize and display them. Once received intact, a radio or television program could be considered a document, and it could become part of a digital library. In a related example, cellular phone networks continually poll their subscribers' mobile telephone devices to detect originating calls and to deliver incoming calls. These are continually broadcast signals, similar to the process of delivering radio and television signals. Most of the signals are transaction data to manage the communication process and do not cumulate to a document-like form such as a television show. The signals that carry conversations could be cumulated into a record of the conversation, which could be considered a document, and which could become part of a digital library. Such signals are rarely used for these purposes, however.

One can produce many examples of communications and transactions that take place over a global information infrastructure and whose status as a document depends on context. Electronic mail messages are easily considered documents, but may only rarely be collected and organized into digital libraries. Credit card verifications are discrete transactions for purposes of authentication, verification, and billing. Individual transactions are unlikely to stand alone as documents. However, when such transactions are aggregated with data that identify the goods or services purchased, and combined with personal identification data, they can be collected and organized into databases that contain rich profiles of individuals and resold as marketing data. These profiles of individuals thus become documents.

Forms and Genres

Many forms of documents will exist in a global information infrastructure, with all manner of content. Forms include text, graphics, moving images, sounds, and various multimedia combinations. Some electronic documents follow familiar conventions from the physical world, such as newspapers, journal articles, letters, photographs, and maps. They may appear on screen in a familiar way, with familiar features such as headlines, indexes, references, captions, salutations, and signatures. They may also take on new features that are specific to the capabilities of electronic form. Newspaper headlines may be grouped in "table of contents" form, enabling a faster scan than perusing the entire front page. Indexes may be active links, rather than static lists. References may be active links to other documents. Maps can be panned and zoomed in ways not possible in print form. Messages sent by email typically are shorter and less formal than letters transmitted by postal mail. Photographs are cropped and manipulated in ways not usually done with physical documents on paper.

Forms of physical documents such as letters, books, newspapers, and scholarly journal articles evolved over many generations before taking on the familiar characteristics of today. They changed in size, layout, and features. They diverged to take on many forms, such as evolution of business letters from their nineteenth-century forms to the email messages of today (Yates and Orlikowski 1992). Similarly, films have evolved from the early days of silent, black-and-white productions to today's sophisticated presentations of sound, color, and photographic and computer-generated images. The style and structure of films also have diverged, resulting in different formats for documentaries and feature films, and for films produced for audiences in North America, Central and South America, Europe, Asia, and other parts of the world.

These forms have adapted through usage and through changes in technology (Shepherd and Watters 1998). These forms are known as "genres," or stable and expected patterns of communication (Bazerman 1988). Though the concept of genre arises from the humanities, interest is growing as an approach to the design of digital libraries because genres can be reflected in documents (Sprague 1998). Among the first conclusions of a Library of Congress conference on "organizing the global digital library" was that "genre is a more useful organizing principle than format" (Library of Congress 1995, 1996). Agre (1996) offers research articles, subpoenas, menus, and interstate highway signs as examples of genres. Bishop and Star (1996) add fiction and nonfiction as useful document genre categories in digital libraries. These authors note that the genre cues so useful in physical artifacts, such as medium, format, and layout, often are lost in digital libraries and electronic publications.

Conversely, new genres can arise in electronic formats, as new communities incorporate electronic documents into their activities. Newspapers now can be customized to individual readers, for example, offering new ways of gathering, organizing, and presenting newspaper content (Morin 1998). These new forms are read and used differently than print forms, a topic long of interest in the field of communication (Dozier and Rice 1984). New genres specific to the World Wide Web are arising, such as personal home pages. Already, home pages are an object of study from the perspective of linguistics (Saint-Georges 1998), discourse analysis (Roberts 1998), and organization (Bates and Lu 1997).

Drawing Boundaries

In chapter 2, I proposed the term "global digital library" as a concept that encompasses digital libraries that are connected to, and accessible through, a global information infrastructure. For documents and the information they contain to be part of a global digital library, they must fall within the definition of a digital library, also established in chapter 2. The global digital library is a subset of a global information infrastructure, since a GII will provide capabilities and services other than digital libraries.

In defining documents, I offered examples of data and information that are not usually part of digital libraries, such as transactions in support of radio and television broadcasts, mobile communications, and credit card verifications. Others include the huge volume of financial transactions that take place electronically among banks, stock markets, commodity markets, mutual funds, brokers, other financial institutions, and their customers. Electronic commerce is a rapidly growing portion of online activity, although the largest growth is in wholesale transactions between companies, rather than retail transactions between individual consumers and companies (Geer 1998). These activities are essential aspects of a global information infrastructure. Few online transactions are inside the bounds of a global digital library, however.

Individuals conduct many activities online that are outside the bounds of a global digital library. They play interactive games, converse in chat rooms, conduct financial transactions, and compute mortgage payments, for example. The digital libraries in which they search for the best mutual funds or mortgages can be considered part of the global digital library, but not transactions executed by financial institutions in support of their purchases. Similarly, electronic mail, still the most popular use of computer networks (Katz and Aspden 1997), is outside the bounds of a global digital library unless it is collected and organized into a digital library. Email lies at the boundary of our concerns for access to information, however, for people frequently seek information by asking questions of others via email.

Digital and Digitized Documents

Although I refer generically in this book to "digital documents" and "digital information," the terms refers to two classes of items: "digital"—those that are created originally in digital form such as electronic text or video, and "digitized"—those that are copied or translated into digital form from some other medium such as paper or film. Digital documents are sometimes referred to as "born digital" to indicate that they originated in electronic form. An increasing portion of online materials are in this category, as text is written in word processors, images are captured by digital cameras, music is electronically synthesized, and content for many media are edited, manipulated, and composed in electronic forms. Many digital documents will exist only in that form, such as electronic publications and electronic mail. Others are "born digital" for the convenience of manipulating content, but ultimately transferred to some other medium. Publications such as newspapers and journals may be created, edited, and composed electronically, then printed on paper. Computer-generated movies, such as animation, are usually transferred to film for distribution.

Digitizing to Improve Access
Content created in other media can be digitized through scanning, keying text, photographing with digital cameras, or otherwise capturing in digital form. Materials are digitized for a number of purposes, one of which is to improve access. Instead of one physical copy of a document, a digital surrogate, or image of the document, can be distributed online, to multiple users. Already, the Library of Congress is finding that more people visit their "American Memory" site online than visit the library building on any given day (Smith 1999). Once digitized, documents can be manipulated easily. Deteriorating images can be enhanced, as can deteriorating sound

recordings. Graphical images can be panned and zoomed, and areas of interest enlarged. Documents can be edited, merged, or otherwise changed in ways not possible with physical forms.

Digital surrogates are adequate for many purposes, such as classroom teaching, some forms of scholarship, and a wide variety of commercial applications. Digital surrogates are particularly appropriate when they can enable access to content in rare or valuable documents that cannot otherwise be made widely available. Smith (1999) offers the example of the map of the District of Columbia prepared for George Washington in 1791 that "is so badly faded, discolored, and brittle that it resembles a potato chip." The digitized version of the map now yields information that was no longer apparent to the naked eye, such as subtle contours provided by the architect and annotations made by Thomas Jefferson. Students and scholars alike now have access to a surrogate of this precious document, very few of whom would have been allowed to view the original. Images of rare documents are also popular for commercial purposes, such as calendars, posters, greeting cards, and advertisements.

In other cases, only the original artifact is adequate. Rare and historical documents are of scholarly interest for their physical characteristics, such as the binding and paper, as well as for their content. Paintings and other art objects remain of great artistic and cultural significance, no matter how widely copies are disseminated. The familiarity of images of the Mona Lisa generates, rather than reduces, interest in traveling to Paris, and no computer display will substitute for the thrill of viewing the original painting. Nor would anyone conceive of destroying the few extant copies of the Gutenberg Bible on the grounds that an adequate number of printed and electronic bibles exist today. In routine work practices, original documents often are necessary as legal evidence to verify dates, signatures, inks, and other characteristics. As more documents are created and stored electronically, however, the question of what is an "original" becomes ever more problematic.

Digitizing Tradeoffs

As with any new technology, some things are gained and some are lost in digitization. Digitizing turns images and sounds into discrete bits that must be reconstructed to be viewed or played. Subtle shadings in images and subtle tonal changes in music can become sharp edges and contrasts.

Compared to paper and microfilm, digital formats have a very short life span. Documents printed on acid-free paper and kept in cool, low-humidity storage conditions can last for several hundred years. Moreover, paper remains "eye legible," requiring no special equipment. Preservation-quality microfilm, kept under appropriate storage conditions, has a long life, but requires special equipment (i.e., microfilm readers) to view it.

Magnetic tape, for which several decades of experience exists, has an estimated life span of 10–30 years (Van Bogart 1995). This life span for the physical medium can be obtained only under optimal storage and handling conditions, however. Maintaining the data on the tape requires regular refreshing, including transferring the data onto new tapes at regular intervals and adjusting the tension of the tape. Estimates for some other digital media are five years or less (Rothenberg 1995, 1997). The life expectancy of the physical medium may be irrelevant, considering how quickly the hardware and software necessary to interpret the contents of digital media become obsolete. Even if a 10-year-old tape or disk is in optimal condition, finding the appropriate combination of hardware and software to read it is a major problem. Digital information is not "eye legible." Without technical capabilities to run, display, or otherwise use the content, it is lost. Anyone with collections of 78-rpm records, 8-track tapes, 51/4-inch floppy disks, or Betamax videotapes has experienced the obsolescence of recording and reading devices.

Digital preservation looms as one of the greatest challenges of information technology management and policy. A number of solutions are being proposed, such as migration, emulation, and maintaining computer museums of all combinations of hardware and software. All the solutions proposed so far have serious drawbacks and all are likely to be expensive. At this stage in the discussion, I raise the issue to make the point that digitization is not preservation, at least not yet. Society is in greater danger of losing its records and artifacts in digital form than losing those in physical form.

Hybrid Libraries

The digital preservation problem is only one of many reasons that digitizing the print collections of libraries would not create a global digital library. Digitization also remains expensive, due largely to labor costs. Despite advances in technology, each item to be scanned must be handled, one page or image at a time, for example. Costs and handling increase depending on the condition, value, and complexity of the document and its intended uses. Digitization can be done only with the permission of the copyright owner. Owning a physical copy of a document and owning the rights to copy it are different matters. Even with older documents, the rights to copy and digitize may be unclear. Copyright and intellectual property issues are another thorny aspect of the digital age.

Research libraries and archives often hold many millions of physical documents, collected over decades or centuries. Only a small portion of these collections will be digitized, and those materials will be carefully selected. Criteria include the size of the audience for the materials, sources of funding, physical condition, value, appropriateness for wide distribution, and technical and legal constraints. While an increasing portion of new publishing is in electronic forms, print publishing continues unabated. Electronic publishing will replace print only in certain niches, and these remain to be determined. Similarly, only a small portion of the world's art, archives, and government and business records is likely to be digitized. We will have hybrid libraries, archives, and other information institutions for the indefinite future. New media will continue to be invented, and will supplement, rather than supplant, the old.

A global digital library is a hybrid library, containing digital documents and pointers to nondigital documents. Those pointers are a form of metadata. These metadata are collected into catalogs or indexes that refer to documents that may exist only offline, in physical form. Thus, people can search a global digital library to identify the existence and location of physical documents located in libraries, archives, museums, government offices, businesses, or elsewhere, in addition to obtaining the full content of digital documents that exist online.

Data and Metadata

Digital libraries are useful only to the extent that their existence can be discovered and that the content within them can be identified. A pile of books shorn of covers, title pages, and other identifying data is of little value, as is a magnetic disk containing files that lack names, types, dates, or hierarchical relationships. If the books are shredded or the files merged, the problem is only worse. Digital libraries and their contents need to be described and organized in some way to facilitate access. The description and organization of resources is an essential part of network architecture (Arms 1995; Kahn and Wilensky 1995; Dempsey and Heery 1998; Lynch et al. 1995; Metadata FAQ 1996; Metadata for Web Databases 1998; Schauble and Smeaton 1998; Weibel 1995).

Metadata, meaning "data about data," is a term that originated in the mid 1970s, incorporating concepts drawn from libraries, archives, records management, scientific data management, text markup, computer science, and related fields. By now, the term is so widely used as to be meaningless without qualification by context of use (Lynch et al. 1995). Our primary concern in this book is access to information; thus, a definition of metadata developed for the purpose of resource discovery is appropriate:

Metadata is data associated with objects which relieves their potential users of having to have full advance knowledge of their existence or characteristics. It supports a variety of operations. A user could be either a program or a person.

Dempsey and Heery (1998, p. 149) consider this to be a working definition, in view of the rapid evolution of types, forms, and applications of metadata for access to information. A more general definition, developed in the context of cultural heritage information, is offered by the Getty Information Institute (Baca 1998, p. 37):

Literally, "data about data," metadata includes data associated with either an information system or an information object for purposes of description, administration, legal requirements, technical functionality, use and usage, and preservation.

Resource Discovery

In networked environments, access to information involves identifying what exists, where, and in what form. Users need to discover resources, whether digital libraries, servers, files, documents, document-like objects, or metadata that act as surrogates for offline artifacts (Dempsey and Heery 1998; Gilliland-Swetland 1998; Lynch and Preston 1990, 1991; Lynch et al. 1995). Users (in this context either people or programs) may need to know any of a wide variety of things about resources, including their existence; history; custody; provenance; intellectual responsibility; integrity and authenticity; relation to other resources; intellectual property rights; tools required to use or manipulate them; genre, such as textbook, monograph, or geographic data set; terms and conditions of use; technical interfaces such as access protocols, searches and formats supported; and rating or score on some scale (Dempsey and Heery 1998). These are only a sampling of the metadata that could be valuable or essential to resource discovery.

Types of Metadata

Metadata formats arise from a wide variety of communities, and serve a wide variety of purposes. Conflicts exist between the need for specialized formats that serve specific purposes for specific communities and the need for generic formats that will enable resource discovery across domains. A starting point for addressing these conflicts is to assess the range of metadata formats that exist and group them by type.

Weibel and Iannella (1997) group metadata formats along a continuum of depth of description, ranging from full-text indexing to richly structured surrogates. At the low end, computers can automatically produce unstructured indexing of words in documents, capturing intrinsic data with minimal augmentation or interpretation. Web search engines and harvesters typically take this approach. At the high end, richly structured and elaborated records can serve as surrogates for the original document, usually requiring considerable manual effort, but providing intrinsic and extrinsic data and interpretation well beyond the capabilities of automatic indexing. In the middle of their continuum are unfielded surrogates, minimally fielded surrogates, and qualified surrogates.

Dempsey and Heery (1998) group metadata formats into three "bands," the first consisting of full-text indexes (e.g., global Internet search services, web indexing services), the second of simple structured generic formats (e.g., Dublin Core, IAFA/WHOIS++), and the third consisting of formats that have a more complex structure and are domain specific (e.g., Federal Geographic Data Committee (FGDC) Content Standard for Digital Geospatial Metadata, MAchine Readable Cataloging (MARC), Government Information Locator Service (GILS)), or that are part of a larger semantic framework (e.g., Text Encoding and Interchange (TEI) headers, Encoded Archival Description (EAD)). They compare each of the three bands on six characteristics: environment of use, function, creation, designation, associated search protocols, and status. Despite the rich structure of their typology, the authors acknowledge that it is a preliminary attempt because of the emerging nature of most of the metadata standards and the blurring of categories.

Gilliland-Swetland (1998) offers yet another classification of metadata. She provides a table of types of metadata (administrative, descriptive, preservation, technical, and use) and their functions. She also arranges a table of attributes of metadata (source of metadata, method of metadata creation, nature of metadata, status, structure, semantics, and level), along with characteristics of each attribute. The existence of multiple models for classifying and describing metadata reveals that the communities have not yet agreed on a common model, and that metadata is a fast-moving area of research and practice.

The Dublin Core
The Dublin Core is the most successful attempt to date at a metadata format that bridges these many different applications and communities. Its success is attributed to the consensus approach through which it is being developed. Representatives from scholarly and professional communities concerned with knowledge organization and management came together starting in 1995 to hold a series of Metadata Workshops. The purpose of these workshops is to define and develop metadata requirements for use on the Internet and in local applications, such that digital libraries and other electronic repositories can interoperate and exchange data (Baker 1998; Hakala, Husby, and Koch 1996; Weibel 1995; Weibel and Iannella 1997; Weibel and Miller 1997). These workshops have resulted in proposals for a core set of metadata elements that can be applied to "document-like objects," whether text, images, or other forms or genres, in almost any application. This set has come to be known as "the Dublin Core," because the first workshop was held at OCLC in Dublin, Ohio.

Initially, the Dublin Core was limited to intrinsic data, which is the description of the intellectual content and physical form of documents. Extrinsic data, in contrast, are external to the document, such as cost, access rights, and intellectual property ownership. Rights management, an extrinsic element, was added to the core in the spring 1997 iteration. The Dublin Core is extensible, providing mechanisms to allow the addition of other descriptive elements for application or site-specific purposes. It attempts to define a basic set of elements that all electronic resources should have to support interoperability and data exchange, recognizing that varying degrees of extensibility are required for different applications. The fifteen elements included in the Dublin Core at this writing are title, author or creator, subject and keywords, description, publisher, other contributors, date, resource type, format, resource identifier, source, language, relation, coverage, and rights management (Weibel and Miller 1997). Descriptions of these elements and continuous updates can be found at http://purl.org/metadata/dublin_core_elements.

The Dublin Core offers a potential solution for several pressing problems: the need for a generally acceptable simple resource description format that can be applied to a wide range of resources; a semantic base for metadata related to HTML (Hypertext Markup Language) on which the World Wide Web relies; and a base for semantic interoperability between richer metadata formats (Dempsey and Heery 1998). The Dublin Core conferences further concluded that a technical framework is needed for exchanging metadata packages of all formats. The response is a proposal for the Warwick Framework as an architectural component of computer networks (Dempsey and Heery 1998; Dempsey and Weibel 1996; Lagoze 1996). Dublin Core also is being extended to other languages, and the international community is wrestling with translation and transliteration problems and with variations in local practices (Baker 1998).

Organizing a Global Digital Library

As should be evident from the discussion of the wide variety of forms, genres, and metadata that form a foundation for a global digital library, and the many perspectives and communities involved, it is too soon to tell how such a system will be organized. One thing is certain: no single entity will be able to impose order on this universe from the top down. Rather, the solutions are more likely to be "bottom up," with individual communities of practice, communities of interest, communities defined by a common language, or communities defined by other means, establishing organizational mechanisms that work for them. At the higher levels, some bridging mechanisms such as Dublin Core will assist people in gaining access to information produced by multiple communities. At the lower levels, standards and practices for representing documents and subunits of documents will enable information resources to be discovered.

Representing and Encoding Digital Content

Standards and practices for representing and encoding electronic documents have been in place for many years already, and new ones are being established. SGML, the Standard Generalized Markup Language, was first accepted as a standard in 1986 (Marcoux and Sevigny 1997; Mason 1997). SGML supports many variations, each with its own DTD, or Document Type Description. HTML is perhaps the best known of these DTDs (Flynn 1997). XML, Extensible Markup Language, is another SGML DTD that is becoming popular for encoding electronic documents (Bray and Sperberg-McQueen 1997). SGML architectures work well for textual documents, with or without embedded graphics and other media. Other formats exist specifically for encoding still or moving images, sounds, etc.

Some metadata formats first were established for print materials and later extended to electronic formats. An important example is MARC (MAchine Readable Cataloging), which was created by the library community in the 1960s as a means to exchange cataloging records that are based on the Anglo-American Cataloging Rules (Avram 1975). MARC is widely implemented around the world, and by now hundreds of millions of cataloging records exist in variations of this format. Other important initiatives such as those for geographic content (GILS and FGDC), museum objects (CIMI), and archives (EAD), are described by Dempsey and Heery (1998).

From Encoding to Access

Rather than explore the many mechanisms for representing, encoding, describing, and managing digital content that arise from individual communities (such an exploration would be of little value, in view of the rapid evolution of practices, standards, and bridging mechanisms), this section focuses on common properties.

The problem of resource discovery, explained earlier, is analogous to the question of whether a tree falling in the forest makes a sound if no one is there to hear it. Is an electronic document informative if no one can discover its existence? Probably not, nor is it useful or usable. Nor would a global digital library be useful if it consisted merely of a flat space of electronic documents without any organizing principles. More accurately, it would not be a digital library at all, for organization is a defining feature.

Metadata serve many important functions in organizing individual digital libraries and groups of digital libraries, including a prospective global digital library. The ability to discover the existence of resources online is only a starting point. Users often need to know about a resource's history; its ownership; its accuracy; its integrity; its relationship to other sources; its intellectual property rights; its technical features regarding how to run, display, or otherwise use it; the terms and conditions under which the material is available; and many other such matters related to usefulness, usability, economics, etc. (Dempsey and Heery 1998). Metadata are far more than descriptive; they serve these functions and others. Nor are metadata necessarily static, for additional metadata can accrue over time as individual resources are used and as their status changes (Gilliland-Swetland 1998).

Drawing on models provided by several authors, I will identify some basic functions of metadata that can serve to organize a global digital library and individual digital libraries.

Description

Description of a document, a document-like object, or a resource is a function of metadata common to all models reviewed here (Dempsey and Heery 1998; Gilliland-Swetland 1998; Hayes and Becker 1970; Weibel and Miller 1997). Gilliland-Swetland (1998) simply refers to descriptive metadata as that which is used to describe or identify information resources. Her examples include cataloging records, finding aids, specialized indexes, hyperlinked relationships between resources, and annotations by users. Hayes and Becker (1970), in the context of library automation, view bibliographic description, or a complete and accurate description of the document, as a primary function of catalogs and indexes. Catalogs typically describe full bibliographic units (e.g., books, journals); indexing and abstracting tools typically describe smaller units (e.g., chapters in a book, articles in a journal). Descriptive metadata enable a user to identify a document uniquely and thus distinguish each individual document from similar ones. Each document in a digital library requires a complete, accurate, and unique description.

Administration

Metadata serve essential functions in administering and managing digital libraries, many of which assist users in determining the usefulness and usability of resources. Gilliland-Swetland's (1998) examples of administrative metadata include acquisition information (e.g., how and when the document or resource was acquired), rights and reproduction tracking (e.g., what rights the organization has to use the material; what reproductions exist and their current status), documentation of legal access requirements (e.g., who may use the material and for what purposes), version control (e.g., what versions exist and the status of the resource being described), and location information. Hayes and Becker (1970) treat location as a component of the physical-access function, rather than grouping it with administrative metadata. In their model, physical-access metadata may indicate which libraries hold copies and the precise location of an item (such as the shelf location of a book or the cabinet in which a map is stored). In digital libraries, the "physical location" of an item may be a computer address, such as the URL (uniform resource locator), or some other mechanism for locating and obtaining a specific digital entity.

Hayes and Becker (1970) also include management information such as the usage of materials for making decisions about acquisitions, discards, and remote storage, in administrative functions. Gilliland-Swetland (1998) incorporates similar management functions under the category of "use metadata." Her examples include use and user tracking, content re-use, and exhibition records.

In electronic environments, administrative metadata also support access functions. Metadata from multiple processes can be linked to create new ways to discover resources. For example, users can follow links between versions of a document. They can locate and retrieve content from multiple online and offline locations. Whereas card catalogs indicated only what was owned by an institution, online catalogs also indicate what is on order, in process, and in circulation. Administrative metadata also improve management by making it possible to identify not only what materials are used, but when, in what form, and by whom (by category or by individual, depending on the privacy considerations).

Intellectual Access

More often than not, people are searching digital libraries to learn "about" something, rather than trying to obtain a specific, known item. They wish to discover documents, document-like objects, or other resources on the topic of interest or that may contain some information that will answer a question or that includes a particular fact, etc. Metadata that describe what a document is "about" serve an intellectual access function. In manual or paper-based systems, intellectual access is the process of assigning terms or classification codes to reflect what a document is about. In view of how subjective "aboutness" can be, intellectual access usually involves some degree of human judgment. In computer-based systems such as digital libraries, varying degrees of automatic indexing are possible. Significant terms can be extracted from textual documents and relationships among terms can be identified, for example (Korfhage 1997). Describing nontextual material is more problematic and less subject to automatic indexing (Fidel 1995; Layne 1994; Svenonius 1994).

Some common techniques for creating intellectual access metadata include "document-centered indexing," which reflects the content of the document, and automated indexing, which is necessarily documented-centered, being based on the stored content. "Request-oriented indexing" attempts to anticipate queries that might seek the document, thus describing meaning (Fidel 1995). Intellectual access is a major concern in digital libraries, in view of the array of content and types of materials contained, the heterogeneity of the potential audiences, and the variety of uses to which the contents might be put. Hayes and Becker (1970) classify intellectual access as one of the major categories of metadata, as does Gilliland-Swetland (1998), who labels it "semantics." Dempsey and Heery (1998) include aspects of intellectual access in several categories, such as whether the metadata are created manually or automatically, their function, and their environment of use.

Intellectual Organization

Most metadata in catalogs, indexes, and digital libraries can support intellectual organization, such that documents or other resources can be grouped or organized based on commonalities and relationships (Hayes and Becker 1970). All the documents by a certain author or creator can be brought together, as can all the documents on a certain topic. Documents can be organized by date, version, rights, format, or any other metadata element present in the record. Thus, metadata can be employed to bring together ("collocate") documents by one or more elements of interest to the user.

Collocation is far easier said than done, however, hence the need for metadata that represent data elements in a consistent manner. For example, metadata standards impose a consistent format that enables common dates to be collocated and different dates to be distinguished. Computers do not recognize "12/10/98" and "December 10, 1998" as the same date without some translation. The fact that "12/10/98" is interpreted as October 12, 1998 (or 12 October 98, or 12th October 1998) in most parts of the world adds to the confusion. The inability of most computers to distinguish between "00" in a date field as the year 1900 or as the year 2000 is at the root of the "Y2K" problem. Newer metadata formats typically require four digits for the year field. Some applications, such as those in historical or archival applications, also need to code for century. A search for "eighteenth century" should retrieve all dates from 1701 to 1800, or from 1700 to 1799, depending on how the century is delineated, for example.

Collocating personal names is an essential form of intellectual organization in most digital libraries, and metadata can assist by standardizing name formats and by providing links between variant forms (Borgman and Siegfried 1992). In bibliographic databases, authors may be listed under a variety of spellings, pseudonyms, nicknames, and combinations of names and initials, for example. One form of name, known as an "authority record," is established in catalogs and then all variant forms are referenced to the preferred form, thus collocating them. Imposing intellectual organization on personal names where the documents come from many sources is more difficult, as is the case with police records, consumer credit databases, and genealogy records. Names often are misspelled. Nicknames and married names introduce variation. Fraudulent use of aliases complicates matters further.

Most difficult is imposing intellectual organization on documents "about" a topic, as documents can be "about" something that is not mentioned in the document. Further, "aboutness" is often in the mind of the user or searcher and may be different from that of the author, creator, or indexer of the document. For example, a search for background information on the current debates over "diversity" in California would involve related concepts such as immigration, preferences based on race or ethnicity, university admission policies, hiring practices, and the names of specific laws such as "Proposition 209." A search for materials more than a few years old also would include concepts such as "civil rights movement" and "affirmative action." An historical treatment would include the term "slavery," which was used as an index term for an array of civil liberties topics until recent years. All of these are politically potent terms and may be included in documents only as veiled phrases, complicating the search process further. Conversely, a search on "California and diversity" also would yield documents on population diversity among plant and animal species. Similarly, someone seeking medical documents or patient discussion groups on "breast cancer" may have her search query blocked by software that filters out pornographic web sites, and may also retrieve recipes for cooking chicken parts.

These are but a few of an endless array of examples that illustrate the need for intellectual organization in digital libraries. Many methods exist for organizing individual digital libraries. Scaling these techniques to the scope of a global digital library, and developing new techniques, are among the greatest research challenges. Digital libraries offer the potential for vast improvements in intellectual organization, as links and pointers can be created among documents (and subunits of documents) in multiple digital libraries scattered across the network, using metadata to establish links among related versions, among items of interest, and among people, places, and organizations.

Technical Specifications

Gilliland-Swetland (1998) includes technical metadata as a category for metadata related to how a system functions. Her examples of technical metadata include hardware and software documentation, digitization information such as formats, compression ratios and scaling routines, and authentication and security data such as encryption keys or password methods. Dempsey and Heery (1998) also include "associated search protocols" as a form of technical metadata; these indicate which, if any, standard network search mechanisms will operate on these metadata. Their examples include specific standards such as Z39.50, common indexing protocol, and

CGI form interface. All of these technical metadata serve to indicate how usable and useful the metadata and associated document or resource are to any particular user. Once a document is discovered, a prospective user can employ these metadata to determine whether the content is readable, playable, computable, displayable (etc.) on available hardware and software, and whether it meets other technical requirements. Such metadata also can be included in the search process to select only resources that meet a specified set of technical parameters. Some technical metadata can be generated automatically from "self describing" software, while other technical metadata must be manually supplied.

Preservation Management

Only Gilliland-Swetland's (1998) model has a specific category for preservation metadata, although aspects of preservation can be incorporated in other models. Here she includes metadata related to the preservation management of information resources. These metadata include documentation of physical condition of resources and documentation of actions taken to preserve physical and digital versions of resources, such as refreshing and migrating data. In view of the growing problem of digital preservation, preservation metadata are likely to take on increasing importance in the future.

All the metadata functions described here apply to hybrid digital libraries, but the distinctions between digital libraries containing documents and those containing document surrogates is more apparent in the case of preservation metadata. Digital libraries that consist of metadata describing physical artifacts can be rich resources in and of themselves. One document can generate a far greater volume of metadata than the volume of the document itself. Consider the array of intrinsic and extrinsic metadata that can be associated with a single work of art like the Mona Lisa or a one-page historical document like the Magna Carta, for example.

A digitized image of a physical artifact is itself a document, but at the same time it is a description or representation that augments other forms of metadata. Preservation metadata, which would be updated as the digitized images are refreshed and migrated to new technologies and as physical artifacts are conserved or repaired, are essential to tracking and maintaining all manner of business and government records and educational and scholarly materials. As Gilliland-Swetland (1998, p. 8) comments, "metadata provides us with the Rosetta Stone that will enable us to decode information objects and to transform them into knowledge in the cultural heritage and information systems of the twenty-first century."

Summary and Conclusions

Among the many promises of a global information infrastructure is to improve access to information, in its many forms, regardless of the location of either searchers or resources. The potential exists for enriching people's lives, increasing social equity, and accelerating commerce via improved information access. These are laudable goals, but accomplishing them depends on what is meant by "access to information," by how a GII is developed and deployed, and by the policies employed. This chapter has explored definitions of "access," "information," and associated concepts such as digital and digitized information, data and metadata, and methods of organizing information.

The concept of access to information has roots in library services, telecommunications policy, and other arenas. For the purposes of this book, "access to information" is defined as connectivity to a computer network and to available content, such that the technology is usable, the user has the requisite skills and knowledge, and the content itself is in a usable and useful form. Several related factors are relevant to access in various contexts, including affordability and the role of information providers. Users can be sources of information, and thus they can also be providers.

"Information" is a rich concept and one whose definition has been a source of philosophical discussion for centuries. Information can be viewed as signals, as elements of communication, as culture, as process, as knowledge, as containers, or as things. A pragmatic definition that is accepted in the information sciences suits the purposes of this book: Information consists of things that can be managed in information systems such as digital libraries. Similarly, "documents" and "document-like objects" are viewed as things that are collected and organized in digital libraries on the behalf of a community of users and that are informative to those users. Documents can represent information that may exist in many other forms. This set of definitions enables us to distinguish between a global digital library and a global information infrastructure.

Documents collected in digital libraries can be "born digital" or can be digitized versions of materials that originated in other forms. In either case, providing digital documents online can make their contents far more widely accessible than is the case with most other forms. As with any new technology, digital formats have tradeoffs compared with print, film, and other physical formats. Content is encoded in discrete bits, often losing subtle shadings in images and sounds. Preserving content in digital forms looms as one of the greatest challenges of the information age. Digital content is not "eye legible;" it can be read, used, run (etc.) only with the appropriate technology. Digital media must be refreshed and content must be migrated to new technologies as they are invented and as old ones become obsolete or unavailable. No single or simple solution yet exists.

Metadata, or "data about data," are essential components of computer network architecture. Metadata include both intrinsic data about what is in a document and extrinsic data about it, such as its history, ownership rights, preservation condition, and hardware and software requirements for its use. Some metadata can be generated automatically, while others must be created manually. Some are generated at the time the documents are created or digitized, and other metadata accrue over the life of the document's use. Taken as a whole, metadata provide mechanisms to describe and represent documents, document-like objects, and cumulative resources such as digital libraries. They are essential for organizing individual digital libraries, a global digital library, and aggregates of digital libraries at levels in between. Metadata serve a variety of organizational functions in improving access to information, including description, administration, intellectual access, intellectual organization, technical requirements, and preservation management.

In sum, access to information is a rich concept that incorporates a host of behavioral, philosophical, technical, and policy issues. It draws on knowledge in many disciplines concerned with computing, networks, telecommunications, information systems and services, documents and documentation, social and behavioral issues, and social institutions such as libraries, archives, and museums.

4

Books, Bytes, and Behavior

The title of this chapter is borrowed from those of several recent books and journal articles that address the evolution of publishing, libraries (both physical and digital), and new media. These include *Books, Bytes, and Bucks* (Lesk 1997a), a book about designing and implementing digital libraries; *Books, Bricks, and Bytes,* a collection of essays on the role of libraries as institutions for an electronic age; and "Silicon dreams and silicon bricks" (Odlyzko 1997), an article on electronic publishing and the evolution of libraries. Lesk's use of the word "bucks" (American slang for dollars) indicates the importance of economic issues in these discussions. Most important, I add "behavior," to reflect the centrality of human behavior in determining the adoption and adaptation of media and institutions.

One of the most contentious developments arising from digital media and computer networks is electronic publishing. Attitudes toward electronic publishing reflect the striking dichotomy between visions of a continuous future and visions of a discontinuous future, as was noted in chapter 1. To characterize these views in their simplistic and basic forms: The discontinuous future favors electronic publishing on the grounds that it is less expensive than print, that it offers faster and wider distribution, and that it will continue to become less expensive and more accessible as technology gets cheaper and better and as more people have access to computer networks. In this view, electronic publishing is inevitable and will replace print publishing for all but niche materials. A corollary effect will be that libraries and publishers, as we know them, will no longer be needed, as people will acquire their own content directly from computer networks.

In contrast, the view of a continuous future favors print publishing on the grounds that electronic materials are unpleasant and uncomfortable to read on screen and that electronic formats are most useful as a means of selecting content to be printed on paper for reading. In this view, print publishing continues unabated and is preferable for most materials. Print being a proven technology, its portability, combined with the ability to flip through pages, offers advantages unmatched by any electronic form. Electronic forms have an important niche but never will replace print. Libraries will continue to be necessary to select, collect, organize, conserve, preserve, and provide access to content in many media. Publishers will be needed to provide editorial, marketing, distribution, and other services.

Both positions overstate their cases in defense of their preferred forms of publication. Most such scenarios are ahistorical, not recognizing the continuity of debate over forms of media. Gutenberg's improvements in movable type were decried by those who feared the loss of handcrafted manuscripts (Nunberg 1996). As Odlyzko (1997) comments, even Plato decried the invention of writing, fearing the loss of oral tradition and of reliance on human memory. Yet we still have oral traditions, handwriting remains a basic skill of literacy, and handcrafted books are valued more than ever. Television did not replace radio, but each of these media evolved into their own niches. Now they co-exist with many other broadcast media, including cable and satellite television, and online news and entertainment services. Print newspapers co-exist with online versions, some of which are complementary products of the same publishers; others are competitive ventures. The emphasis on form in most of these discussions obscures the role of content, which is the substance of any medium.

The new media offer opportunities to improve the form and distribution of content. As people adopt new media, they also adapt them to their habits and practices. Thus, behavior, institutions, and media evolve together. Useful aspects of old technologies are carried over into new ones, and less useful aspects often disappear.

Electronic Publishing

Eisenberg's (1989, p. 11) assertion still rings true:

We are, with electronic publication, approximately where printing was in the year 1469. The foundations have been established; the technology is spreading from central to peripheral areas; only a minority of holdouts remain completely opposed. There is a sense that great changes are coming.

By now some of these "great changes" have indeed arrived for some forms of publications in some fields, yet much of the content distributed electronically is printed on paper before being read, print publication continues at a steady pace, bookstores are more popular than ever, public library usage is growing, and conferences on "the future of the book" and "the future of print" abound. The future of electronic publishing is not much clearer than it was a decade ago. If anything, the situation is more complex as a result of the proliferation of formats, media, and channels of distribution, changes in copyright laws and intellectual property practices, and changes in the economics of publishing.

Underlying this complexity is the difficulty of defining "electronic publishing." Simple characterizations, such as those noted above, tend to focus on electronic distribution of content, such as electronic journals, monographs, or newsletters. Yet electronic technologies pervade all aspects of the publishing process. Authors write their texts on word processors and send them to their publishers online or on disk. Images, tables, and graphics also are likely to be created on computers. Even if the authors do not create content initially in electronic forms, most publishers key, scan, or otherwise digitize content for production. Editing, page layout, and other production tasks take place online, regardless of whether the final product appears in print or electronic form. The hand setting of type is largely gone, except for specialized presses in the book arts and publishing in countries that lack adequate computing and technical infrastructure. Newspapers distribute national print editions for home delivery across the United States not by airplane, but by distributing the content electronically to regional printing sites and delivering the physical copies from those multiple sites.

In sum, most aspects of modern publishing are electronic. Manual production no longer is cost effective for most mainstream trade and scholarly publishing. In view of the fact that so much of the publication process is electronic, why are so many publications, including this one, transferred to paper form for distribution? If the issues surrounding form of publication were merely technological, most content would be distributed and read in electronic form by now. Technology is only one determinant of the most appropriate form to produce and distribute content, however, and multiple forms of print and electronic publication will exist indefinitely.

Debates about electronic publishing involve the interaction of technological, psychological, sociological, economic, political, and cultural factors that influence how people create, use, seek, and acquire information. Predictive models for the future of publishing interpret these factors differently and assign different weights to them. Wildly differing predictions of the form and the rate of change are the result. All manner of data exist to support each argument, making it difficult to compare them. Only time will tell whose assumptions and choices of supporting data are most accurate. More important for the purposes of this book is an analysis of the factors involved in creating, seeking, using, and acquiring information, which helps to make implicit assumptions explicit.

The Electronic Publishing Scenario

Rather than attempt a review of the large and growing literature of electronic publishing, I will analyze the discontinuous view of the future: that electronic distribution soon will replace most print publication. This approach is employed as a means to identify factors and assumptions that can be explored in more depth in subsequent sections. To represent the discontinuous view, the scenario and the arguments presented by Odlyzko in a series of influential papers (1995, 1996, 1997, 1998) are examined. Odlyzko's is among the most fully developed, documented, and articulate of the discontinuous views. Further, he incorporates or makes reference to most of the other widely circulated scenarios, including those of Ginsparg (1994, 1996), Harnad (1990, 1995a,b), Nelson (1987), and Rawlins (1991) and the counter-arguments of Brent (1995) and Fuller (1995a,b).

The authors noted above focus primarily on scholarly publishing, for several reasons. One reason is that scholarly publishing is more amenable than trade publishing to electronic forms, in view of the much smaller audience and the lack of economies of scale. A second reason is that expertise in electronic publishing exists in the university, research, and development communities, and most scholars have access to computer networks. A third is the great pressure to change the structure of scholarly publishing. Both the number and the price of scholarly journals (in print and electronic forms) are growing at far greater rates than the budgets of libraries. As a result, research libraries are able to acquire an ever-decreasing portion of the extant scholarly literature on behalf of their constituencies.

Odlyzko (1995, 1996, 1997, 1998) draws most of his examples from mathematics, the primary field in which he publishes, and physics, a field in which great successes in electronic publishing have been shown (Ginsparg

1994, 1996). He extrapolates to scholarly publishing in general, predicting that most scholarly journals will exist only in electronic form within 10–20 years. He views this result as desirable, envisioning a future system that will provide better and faster reviewing and will be less expensive. Let us look more closely at these arguments and at the assumptions underlying them.

The argument is most fully developed in a long early piece (Odlyzko 1995). Aspects are updated and extended in subsequent articles (Odlyzko 1996, 1997, 1998). At the outset, Odlyzko claims that the changes in scholarly publishing are due to the confluence of two trends: the growth of scholarly literature and the growth of information technology. His argument for the demise of traditional print forms of scholarly journals and their replacement by electronic journals is based on the following points:

• Costs of electronic publication are "negligible" when compared to print publication, according to his economic analysis. Electronic forms can provide most of the same services as print publications, but for less.

• Technology is getting cheaper and easier to use. The cost of disk storage is dropping quickly. Scholars can post their own works to an electronic repository, and can search for materials on topics of interest.

• Electronic journals can be operated by scholars without charging fees for access. Costs are minimal because they are using available resources provided by grants, universities, or corporate employers. Publishers are less necessary as intermediaries.

• Electronic journals offer various advantages over print, including dynamic formats, hyperlinks between articles and journals, and speed of dissemination.

• Libraries will be less necessary, as scholars can locate the materials they need for themselves and can do so without paying subscription fees. Only a few centralized depositories will be needed. Equity will increase because journals can be distributed cheaply around the world online and on tape.

A brief analysis of these arguments reveals that the relationship between technology and scholarly publishing is greatly oversimplified. Several of the underlying assumptions are questionable, especially when extrapolated beyond the fields of mathematics and physics.

The Growth of Literature and Technology
The exponential growth and increasing specialization of scholarly literature over several centuries is well documented (Meadows 1998), as is the rapidly improving price-performance ratio of computer speed and storage

capabilities. Scholars, publishers, provosts (the university administrators who usually are responsible for academic budgets), and librarians are bound together by scholarly publishing in a delicately balanced equilibrium; no single party has full control over the relationship. Each of these players recognizes that a "crisis" exists in scholarly publishing (Hawkins and Battin 1998; Kling and Covi 1995; Lamm 1996; Lyman 1996; Okerson 1996; Pew Foundation 1998), but they do not agree on its causes or solutions. Most arguments that electronic publishing will supersede print publishing focus on the mechanics of publishing rather than on the socio-technical system in which scholarly publishing is embedded (Kling and Covi 1995). Odlyzko (1998), Ginsparg (1994, 1996), and others suggest that scholars can manage much of scholarly publishing's universe, wresting control from the other parties. Other proposals, such as that by the Pew Foundation (1998), place more control in the hands of universities, changing the publishing system by altering the processes of tenure review and the criteria for evaluating library collections. Recent and proposed changes in copyright and intellectual property laws to favor publishers may further limit the control of scholars and libraries, undermining both of the prior approaches (*Bits of Power* 1997; Lyman 1998; Mann 1998).

The Economics of Scholarly Publishing

One way to reduce the costs of scholarly publishing is to perform fewer of the editorial services now provided by publishers. The resulting loss in publication quality is deemed acceptable by Odlyzko (1998), at least for the types of content he has in mind. Economic models for scholarly publishing vary owing to differences in assumptions about format, content (e.g., plain text, mathematical equations, diagrams, color plates), number of copies, form of distribution (e.g., payments to wholesalers and jobbers, direct mail services, postage and handling), sales rate (e.g., rapid cost recovery vs. warehousing costs), etc. (Bot, Burgmeester, and Roes 1998; McCune 1998). If publishers' editorial practices remain unchanged, the primary cost savings of electronic journals are in printing and distribution. Printing may constitute as little as 9 percent of revenues; distribution costs are more variable (McCune 1998). Thus, the actual cost savings will vary widely, depending on the circumstances of publication and what services and functions are included.

Odlyzko's (1995, 1998) economic model also assumes that journal editors are rarely paid and that reviewers almost never are paid for their services. Though most journal editors may not receive a salary supplement (although some do), they are no more altruistic than other professionals, and they expect some perquisites in return for spending their time on editing rather than on their own research and teaching. His model includes some publisher-paid costs, such as administrative assistance to editors, but omits many other real costs that are paid by publishers or universities. These include office space, computer equipment and services, travel monies, and teaching releases. The latter are particularly expensive to universities, as other teachers must be paid to cover the editors' courses. As universities' budgets tighten, academic departments are seeking ways to recover costs for activities such as journals, especially in fields without substantial amounts of grant funding. New economic models for journal publication will include costs that formerly were hidden.

Much of Odlyzko's (1995, 1998) cost savings in electronic journal publications are gained by removing publishers' profits from the equation. He envisions an altruistic model of scholarly publication in which payments for intellectual property play a minimal role. In his later writing (1998), however, he acknowledges "the perverse incentives in scholarly publishing" that enable for-profit publishers to maintain control over intellectual property. Scholars decide where to place their work, and their incentives are to place it in high-prestige journals. They have no direct incentive to place it in low-cost outlets, as the costs of journals are paid by others, principally by libraries. Key to the reforms favored by librarians and provosts are publishing models that provide incentives for scholars to publish in lower-cost outlets, whether by bearing some of the costs directly or by changes in tenure and evaluation criteria (Pew Foundation 1998).

Some publishers, both trade and scholarly presses, are seeking domestic and international legal reforms that give them more control over intellectual property (Lyman 1996, 1998; Mann 1998; Samuelson 1995, 1996). If they were to prevail, electronic publishing could become more expensive to scholars, libraries, and consumers than print publishing is today (*Bits of Power* 1997; Lyman 1998). In sum, the economics of publishing are complex and are becoming more so.

Technology Trends

Computing technology is getting cheaper, and computers are becoming somewhat easier to use. However, each of these is relative. Odlyzko's economic model includes the cost of acquiring hardware and software and overhead costs of scholars. It does not appear to include the costs of hardware and software maintenance, particularly expenses such as personnel for training, configuring systems, installing software upgrades, and maintaining local networks. A study by the Gartner Group estimated the actual cost *per year* of acquiring, operating, and maintaining a desktop computer to be about $10,200; hardware and software are about 15 percent of the total cost of ownership (*Bits of Power* 1998). Other studies attribute from 4 percent to 30 percent of the total cost of ownership to hardware and software (Barnes 1997; Hudson 1996; Slater 1997; Strassmann 1997). Thus, the actual costs of information technology to an organization are not necessarily dropping.

The availability of computer technology is far greater in the heavily grant-funded scientific disciplines than in the social sciences, the arts, and the humanities. While computers are now widely available in most disciplines, faculty and students in less-well-funded fields have basic personal computer workstations rather than high-end scientific machines that can support the typesetting software, disk farms, and screen displays to which he refers. Expertise in producing and managing electronic journals also varies widely across disciplines.

Ease of use is relative too. Producing electronic journals has become far simpler over the period of Odlyzko's writings, the earliest of which predate the proliferation of the World Wide Web. Searching for information has become only minimally easier, or has become harder, depending on one's perspective. Internet search engines allow broad sweeps at the expense of precise retrieval. The explosion in size and number of digital libraries is making comprehensive searching more difficult because information retrieval is sensitive to scale. Despite the extensive effort being devoted to this research challenge, neither search engines nor intelligent agents will provide the easy retrieval that Odlyzko (1995) suggests any time soon.

Scholar-Controlled Publishing

Odlyzko (1995, 1998) proposes a model for scholarly publishing that is controlled by scholars and distributed without fees. A great portion of the production costs of articles already are assumed by scholars and their employers and by funding agencies. These include the salaries of scholars and research assistants, grants to conduct research, and equipment on which to write articles. If scholars and their employers were to assume the remaining costs, publishers could be avoided and library costs could be minimized. The scholar-controlled model has several weaknesses noted earlier, including the variety of cost accounting methods, the "perverse" incentive system, and intellectual property rights. If such a model could be implemented, some editorial quality would be lost, and some improvements in the reviewing process would be gained, along with cost decreases.

Odlyzko and many others (see, e.g., Harnad 1990, 1995, 1997; Hibbitts 1996) point to the physics preprint server managed by Ginsparg (1994, 1996) as the most salient example of the success of electronic publishing. The server (http://xxx.lanl.gov) contains primarily preprints, although other types of "e-prints" can be submitted. Some areas of mathematics, nonlinear sciences, and computer science are covered in addition to physics. Anyone online can acquire copies, without charge, from the server. The high level of participation has led to rapid dissemination of research findings in physics. It also has led to international equity of access, since distribution is not limited to the circle of the authors' colleagues as was the case with print publications.

Although Ginsparg's success is to be lauded, the transferability of this model to other fields is questionable. As Odlyzko (1998) acknowledges, Ginsparg's physics server received a $1 million grant from the National Science Foundation for software development; other costs are borne by the host institution, which is federally funded. Scholars are submitting preprints to the server after the articles are accepted by journals, as Odlyzko also acknowledges. Whether such a system would be successful without external funding and without the imprimatur of reputable journals remains to be seen.

Many publishers (including scholarly societies) in other fields are looking less favorably on online posting of preprints than are those affiliated with physics. Some publishers consider any form of online posting to constitute prepublication, and will not consider posted works for journal publication. In other cases, copyright agreements explicitly forbid the posting of versions that are substantially the same as what will appear in the journal. These are but a few of the intellectual property problems that remain to be resolved in electronic publishing.

Advantages of Electronic Formats

The real power of technology in electronic publishing may be in new formats for publishing, as Odlyzko and others suggest. New genres can be created that provide better searching, sorting, and displays, hyperlinks between documents, and links from citations to the full source. Except for hyperlinking, we have yet to realize most of these gains. The first forms of any new technology look much like the old; familiarity helps to gain converts. Even hyperlinking is not universally seen as an advantage. Books and journals are not read serially, in most cases. People skim them and flip through for charts, graphs, images, indexes, and reference lists. Scholars typically browse through many journals per year, reading only a selected number of articles in full, whether in print or online.

A study of chemists revealed that the most important use of electronic journals is for printing, followed by the ability to browse graphics and text; portability also ranked highly (Stewart 1996; Meadows 1998). Another study found that offices that introduce electronic mail increase paper consumption by 40 percent (Mann 1998). Most people prefer to read journals while sitting in a comfortable chair or couch, rather than on screen at a desk. Paper is still easier to annotate, highlight, and skim than is an electronic display. Screen displays are improving, albeit at a slower rate than improvements in disk storage and processor speed. Portable electronic books with annotation and scrolling abilities are appearing on the market (Silberman 1998). As the technology improves, and as design improves to take advantage of new capabilities, electronic publications will become more attractive.

Scholarly publication in scientific fields probably is the kind most amenable to technological adaptation. In the social sciences and in the humanities, where speed of publication is less critical and technology penetration is lower, adoption is likely to be slower. In the trade presses, we are likely to see many different niches, with different technological devices, genres, formats, and audiences. Reading a novel on an electronic book while traveling by air seems probable. Putting *Alice's Adventures in Wonderland* on an electronic book seems more analogous to watching a video or playing a computer game than to bedtime reading for a child. However, these are merely extrapolations from present technology and habits, in view of the difficulty of predicting new uses of new media.

The Diminished Role of Libraries and Publishers

Odlyzko's model cuts the costs and increases the speed and breadth of distribution largely by reducing the roles of libraries and publishers. Libraries and publishers alike recognize that the present system has serious problems. Some go so far as to say that the traditional university library is unsustainable in its current form (Hawkins 1998). Neither set of players will relinquish their roles voluntarily, and both are in the throes of substantial change.

Publishers play a variety of roles, including improving content through editorial processes, advertising, and distribution. By retaining control over intellectual property rights, they can repackage content in various forms over long periods of time. Scholars, universities, and other institutions will assume some of these roles in some situations. The publishing industry is changing rapidly through acquisitions and mergers and through revisions of copyright law. These developments likely will affect the future of scholarly and trade publishing far more than technological advances will.

The models of Odlyzko and others focus almost exclusively on the distribution of current content as it is produced, not on access to the continuing record of scholarship. Libraries do play a "middleman" role, acquiring materials at the time they are available. What Odlyzko (1995) fails to note is that they play an essential role in preservation by maintaining access indefinitely. Preserving electronic formats is an expensive process owing to the degradation of electronic media, the rapid obsolescence of hardware, continual software upgrades, and the need to maintain dynamic links to other systems and software. Neither publishers nor journal editors are willing to accept long-term responsibility for the scholarly record; they prefer to leave this role to libraries.

Whether the majority of scholarly journals are free (an unlikely scenario) or not, some mechanism is needed to select, collect, and organize those materials that are needed for academic programs. Scholars may know precisely what journals they need for their own research, but students and lay people do not. Nor do scholars wish to take on the role of librarians in selection and acquisition. The quality of a collection that supports an academic program remains an essential part of the accreditation process for that program, and this is unlikely to change soon. Great library collections still attract great scholars to universities, despite attempts to find other means to evaluate library services (Pew Foundation 1998).

Odlyzko (1995) analyzes at great length the need for abstracting and review journals, concluding that they still would be required under his proposed model. Organizing collections is one of the essential roles of libraries. Scholars are a distinct group of information seekers because they know the journals and authors of their specialty areas so well that they rarely use indexes and catalogs. However, they need these organizational tools when they explore new topics, and their students need them for their own research and for the searching they do on behalf of the scholars for whom they work.

Most of the activities of scholars, publishers, and libraries are likely to be conducted differently with the proliferation of information technologies, the availability of a broader array of formats, and the shifting economics of scholarly publishing. Librarians see advantages to electronic journals, as do other players. They can provide electronic journals on demand to their user communities, 24 hours per day, without incurring the costs of physical storage space on library shelves. Electronic journals are searchable in more ways than print journals, and they can be packaged in a variety of ways to provide new services. Though publishers and libraries may operate much differently a decade or two hence, they will continue to exist and to be essential.

Creating and Using Documents

Articles in electronic journals are but one of many forms of documents that will be collected and organized into digital libraries and made accessible via a global information infrastructure. Electronic monographs will be available, as will objects such as reports, maps, memos, graphs, charts, moving images, and numeric data sets. Many documents large and small exist online already, such as electronic mail messages and web pages, which in turn may be subdivided into units of a paragraph, an image, or less. In principle, any information that can be captured in electronic form can be treated as a document or set of documents in a digital library. Further, metadata that describe documents, objects, or other entities can serve as documents in digital libraries. Whereas living beings such as humans, animals, or plants cannot be stored in digital libraries, descriptions or representations of living things can be. A biography, a personnel record, or a child's essay about a pet can all be electronic documents. Whether something is or is not a document is a function of the use to which it is put.

Are documents merely "things" that contain "information" to be manipulated in digital libraries? From a technological viewpoint, yes. These are objects that can be collected and organized in information systems, managed, searched, and made accessible to those who seek them or their contents. From the viewpoint of those who create and use them, however, they are far richer entities. As Brown and Duguid (1995) so eloquently state, documents have a "social life." People have reasons for creating documents and for using them. The meaning of a document may reside in a community and in the document itself. Religious documents, such as the Bible, the Torah, and the Koran, are focal points for their communities, for example. These are not static documents, despite having been written centuries ago. They continue to be discussed, analyzed, and interpreted. Marginal notes, annotations, and commentaries are associated with these documents, whether physically attached or not. Individual readers can make their own annotations and interpretations and have access to those of scholars past and present. Documents that form the basis of governmental systems also have meaning and social significance far beyond the words written on paper, be they the Constitution of the United States or the works of Marx or Mao. They, too, are associated with a plethora of interpretations, commentaries, laws, and rules.

Academic disciplines have documents that are landmarks for concepts, theories, findings, or ways of approaching their field. Some salient examples are Shakespeare's plays for modern language and literature, Einstein's theory of relativity for physics, the Turing test for computer science, Brandeis's formulation of personal privacy for law, and Vannevar Bush's article "As we may think" for information science. These works have different interpretations on their "home fields" than in other disciplines and contexts.

The documents we create every day have a "social life." Research reports from a scientific laboratory reflect a process of negotiation within a team for what story will be told, how it will be told, the choice and format of data to support the results, conclusions and interpretations to be drawn, and who will receive authorship credit. Readers of the report will not interpret it in isolation. Rather, they will compare it to other work on which it builds or with which it may conflict. Readers' interpretations will be influenced by intangibles external to the document, such as their opinions of the journal, authors, laboratory, and funding agency. Research funded by tobacco companies, for example, will be interpreted differently than research funded by the National Institutes of Health, regardless of the results.

The more we understand about the social context of documents, the better we can design electronic publications and digital libraries. We need to know more about how, why, when, and for whom people create documents if we are to build better tools for them to do so. Similarly, we need to know more about people's criteria for selecting and evaluating documents if we are to build better tools for seeking information. We need to know what people do with documents once they have them, so that we can build tools for reading, browsing, annotating, manipulating, and otherwise using documents. Hence, we need to study and test implicit assumptions about information-related behavior if we are to design better systems to support that behavior.

The preceding analysis of electronic publishing demonstrates the importance of looking beyond technological factors. Similar predictions based on technology trends indicated that the "paperless office" would be in place by now (Lancaster 1978). Yet not only does paper persist; its use in offices is increasing. Studies are confirming anecdotal reports that people prefer to read documents on paper rather than on screens, as was noted above. Taken together, the design challenge is to understand the reasons for the preference of paper. Is it due to the quality of screen displays? If so, would better displays suffice? Is it due to the ease of manipulating paper? If so, would better browsing and skimming capabilities make electronic forms more attractive? Is it due to the ability to annotate paper? If so, would annotation facilities help, if they were simple and useful enough? Is it due to the portability of paper? If so, electronic forms would need to be very light and malleable. Or is it a preference for comfortable seating and lighting, in which case a lightweight portable device with a high resolution screen may be suitable? If no substitute exists for paper, should the electronic formats support high-quality printing features? Printing may be the only option for those who prefer paper for its low cost and its ease of replacement with new copies. Compared to paper, electronic devices are expensive, heavier and bulkier to carry, subject to theft, and time consuming to replace (because the application environment must be reconstructed). Similarly, paper may be the only option for those who prefer its reliability, compared to electronic devices that require power sources and occasional repairs. All these design approaches, and more, are being tried (Brown and Duguid 1995; Dillon 1994; Meadows 1998; Silberman 1998; Stewart 1996).

Surely all these reasons and preferences apply, and thus we need to determine which solutions are appropriate for which situations. Empirical testing in multiple situations is the only feasible way to determine the appropriate devices and delivery models for electronic documents. Most people do not think much about why they like paper; they find it difficult to say which alternatives would suffice and when.

Process and Structure

Most literate people create documents every day, whether grocery lists, work orders, memoranda, email messages, notes to their children's teachers, or journal articles. Many of these documents are ephemeral and thus not likely to be collected into digital libraries. What processes do people use to create these documents? What are the structural characteristics of these documents? How can we utilize process and structure to design digital libraries?

One approach is to study how people manage information in their day-to-day lives, regardless of whether the documents created have any lasting value. Another approach is to study the processes by which documents intended for storage, retrieval, and access are created. Scholars are a rich source of material for the latter approach. The scholarly record, though incomplete, dates back as far as the written word. A considerable amount of knowledge exists about how scholars create, use, and seek information resources. We also know much about how to collect, organize, and provide access to the scholarly record—in print, electronic, and other media.

Although scholars represent a small portion of the users of a global information infrastructure, they have the longest history of usage. These examples also are likely to be familiar to a substantial portion of the readership. Thus, I draw many but not all of my examples from scholarly communication.

Writing and Creating Documents

Creating information is more of a community-driven process for scholars than for most other groups (Agre 1998). Though all authors or creators have an audience in mind for their work, scholars are actively engaged with their audience. They write for each other, while most other creative work represents a one-way flow from author to audience. Scholarly research activities vary by field and may include collecting original data through laboratory experiments, field studies, surveys, qualitative studies, analysis of archival resources, or other research methods. In all disciplines, with varying degrees of emphasis, scholars think and talk to people about a research topic, read extant studies in the area, study original sources and make notes, draft an original contribution to the literature, and revise the document for publication (Case 1986; Stone 1982). Reading and discussion may take place throughout the process, and intervening reviews, both formal and informal, will lead to revisions in the document.

The actual process of authoring is receiving renewed attention as more creative activities involve the use of information technologies such as email, word processors, and collaborative writing tools (Beck 1995; Bruce and Sharples 1995; Dillon 1994; Ruhleder 1995). Writing practices and styles are highly individualized, making collaborative authoring a challenge under the best of circumstances. Although the amount varies by academic discipline and local circumstances, the quantity of collaborative research and publication appears to have increased significantly with the growth of computer networks. The number of authors per paper, the proportion of international collaborations, and the size of work groups in the sciences have increased substantially since the early 1980s (Walsh and Bayma 1996). Thus, scholars are heavy users of computer networks for the purposes of writing and creating documents, as well as seeking them. They need collaborative writing tools that support shared document creation among groups of increasing size (more than just pairwise collaboration) and that are effective for asynchronous communication, in view of the number of time zones over which collaboration often takes place.

Most studies of authoring involve the creation of texts. With the advent of electronic publishing, documents can include images and sounds, and can be dynamic rather than static. For example, in place of a static table of results, a running simulation can be included. Full data sets, including audio and video, can be appended, along with software to run them. References to supporting literature may be dynamic hyperlinks, enabling readers to retrieve the cited material directly. Readers may be allowed to append commentary and links to related materials. To create such dynamic documents, authors need far more sophisticated tool kits than the word processing software of today. Readers also will need more sophisticated retrieval mechanisms to obtain and use these dynamic documents. We need to know more than we do about the processes of creating textual documents, and much more about the processes of creating multimedia documents. Studies of the early adopters of multimedia electronic journals should be fruitful in determining some of the capabilities required for tools to support creation, use, and searching of dynamic documents.

Information and Structure

The community basis of scholarship is evident in the structure of the documents they create. Authors in all fields cite their sources for evidence and use the arguments of others to buttress their own, and to provide links that indicate the relationship between one work and other works in the same field and in other disciplines. Citations also are made for other purposes, such as refuting prior work, acknowledging mentors or major figures in the field, and displaying the authors' knowledge of the literature (Kochen 1989; Moravcsik and Murugesan 1975; Small 1978, 1982). Scholars are well acquainted with the literature of their fields, and thus the references at the end of a document often tell them more about its contents than does the author's name, the title, or the abstract. Reference lists also are valuable in bringing together work on a topic of interest. The aggregate of citing to cited relationships among documents reveals a network of communication among scholars that can be utilized in electronic environments (Borgman 1989b, 1990a; Paisley 1989, 1990; White 1990).

The community nature of documents is especially evident in electronic environments, scholarly or not. References to sources, people, related documents, graphics, images, sounds, advertisements, and so on can be embedded in electronic documents that reside on computer networks. Relationships between documents that once were static now are dynamic. Rather than being fixed information in a document, references become actionable items. Readers can click on references and be transferred directly to the document being referenced. They can click on an author's name to obtain background information, and often they can send email to the author as a function of the same software package. This feature only applies for living authors, of course. The World Wide Web, which originated in the physics community, has brought dynamic, community-based documents into the mainstream. Readers now can follow paths to people and products, as well as to scholarly publications.

Evaluation

Not all documents are created equal—nor all authors, journals, universities, publishers, libraries, companies, web sites, and other players in the information life cycle. Creating, using, and seeking information involves a continuous process of evaluation. Authors decide to which journals, conferences, and publishers they will submit their work. Readers decide whose work they will read, which web sites they will visit, and which documents they will retrieve from long lists of options. Universities decide which scholars they will hire and promote. Libraries decide what materials they will select, collect, organize, and provide for access. Students decide which universities they will attend, and universities decide which students they will admit. All these decisions, and more, are based to some degree on judgments about the quality of documents and the information they contain. Many of these judgments are subjective, and they vary widely by individual and by circumstance. To the extent that such judgments can be characterized or quantified, they can be used in designing digital libraries. Process and structure characteristics, as identified above, also can help in adapting digital libraries to the information-related behavior of their users. Search, display, and retrieval capabilities can be adapted, at least partly, to the practices and preferences of digital libraries' users.

Process and structure characteristics long have been employed to study scholarly communication (Borgman 1990b). Now that so much communication—interpersonal communication, collaborative writing, searching, and publishing— is conducted online, we can use these indicators and methods to improve the usability of digital libraries.

Indicators and Measures

Despite the continual evaluation of information in daily life, much of it is subjective. Newspaper readers generally agree that *The New York Times* is the national newspaper of record in the United States, but few except journalists and mass media researchers can state explicit criteria for why they believe this to be the case. Similarly, people trust certain television stations, newscasters, and magazines more than others. Within their communities of friends, family, and colleagues, people place more trust in some individuals than in others. Those who emerge as "opinion leaders" in their communities have considerable influence in those areas where their opinions are valued. Opinion leaders play a key role in the diffusion and adoption of new technologies, from microwave ovens to electronic mail (Rogers 1983, 1995). In the academic community, much information flows through "invisible colleges" of scholars with common interests, whether across a country or around the world (Crane 1972; Lievrouw 1990). The social context of documents is embedded in these communities and relationships (Brown and Duguid 1995).

Relationships and influences involved in current judgments about information can yield insights into future judgments. Surveys of registered voters are used to predict the outcomes of elections, for example. The influences of media coverage, political advertisements, and opinions of friends and family on voting behavior are assessed again after the election. Comparisons of these data are used to design more effective political campaigns and to improve predictions of subsequent elections.

Scholarly communication is particularly amenable to tracking and assessment not only because so much of it is conducted online but also because a long historical record exists. The record is documented in a variety of ways. Indexes and abstracts of journal articles are organized by author, title, subject, laboratory, and features specific to individual fields, such as chemical structure or testing instrument. Journals are described in directories, with analyses that include the historical record of editorship, scope, publisher, name changes; price and availability; and which indexes and abstracting services cover it, how comprehensively, and for which periods. Books are recorded in catalogs and bibliographies. Field-specific dictionaries, encyclopedias, glossaries, and other resources establish core concepts, their histories, and the relationships between them.

Among the most influential documentation for evaluation purposes are the citation indexes published by the Institute for Scientific Information (the *Science Citation Index*, the *Social Sciences Citation Index*, and the *Arts and Humanities Citation Index*). The primary access provided by these computer-generated indexes to current scholarly journals is by author, title, and keywords. Additional indexes provide access by institutional affiliation and include author contact information. What is unique and most valuable in these indexes is access to the references in journal articles, and from the cited publications back to the documents that cite them. A reader can look up the entry for a current article and view the list of references made. Such reference lists can serve as topical bibliographies for retrieving the referenced documents. Conversely, a reader can look up a previously published article to see what newer articles have cited it in the time since it was published. Following the path of references is particularly effective when searching for information on new or emerging topics, as the citing papers may form a body of work that builds upon the earlier paper.

Citation indexing of scholarly literature follows principles established in the late nineteenth century by *Shepard's Citations. Shepard's* has been published continuously for 125 years, providing a rich network of legal literature. "Citators," as they are known in the legal field, are used to verify the current authority of a legal source. A legal citation search typically begins with a court decision or a legislative statute. The citator provides data on whether, when, and by whom the decision or statute was later reviewed. It may have been reversed, affirmed, criticized, questioned, overruled, or followed, for example. Citators are an essential component of legal research and are basic features of legal databases. The community basis of law is evident in its reliance on the relationships among legal documents. The value of a court decision or statute as the basis for legal argument depends entirely on its current authority. A precedent that might have been the basis for a winning case last week, once overruled, can become an argument for the opposing side in a lawsuit.

The source material for legal citators consists of court decisions, federal and state statutes, and related legal literature. The source material for the scholarly citation indexes is a set of current journals selected by an editorial board, but the materials cited in journals may come from many other sources, including books, reports, and journals not included in the original set. As a result, these citation indexes can be used to draw rich and complex maps of scholarly literatures. Several secondary analyses of these data are produced on an annual basis that rank authors and journals by their frequency of citation. These analyses are further aggregated to determine the relative impact of journals in a field, and to rank the productivity and impact of authors, academic departments, and institutions.

Indicators from citation indexes, other forms of indexes and abstracts, and other documentation of the scholarly record can be used to evaluate information for a variety of purposes. Use of such data for these purposes is not without controversy. The point here is to illustrate ways in which the social life of documents can be employed to assist people in creating, using, and seeking information.

Choosing Channels

The "perverse incentives" of scholarly publishing discussed in the context of electronic journals are particularly evident in scholars' choices of publication channels for their work. An article that appears in a prestigious journal is assumed to be more accurate and important, having passed through a rigorous review and selection process, than one that appears in a lesser journal or in a conference proceedings. The perceived credibility of journals, monographs, edited books, conference proceedings, reports (etc.) varies widely within and between fields, and varies over time. Individual scholars have their own opinions on which journals or conferences are the most prestigious or the most effective channels to reach their audience. Academic departments often have lists, some official and some unofficial, of appropriate journals in which to publish for getting tenure. One reason that channel choice can be so subjective is that it may vary between research topics of a particular scholar. The best journal in which to publish the results of one project may not be the best to publish the results of some other project, for example.

Complicating the choice further is the relationship between journals. Papers rejected by a first-tier journal often are submitted to second- or third-tier journals. This iterative process of manuscript submission is part of scholarly communication. Authors may benefit from critical reviews by first-tier journals. While editors complain about receiving poor quality manuscripts, they also pride themselves on their rejection rates.

Channel choices also are influenced by the stage of a project. Talks, conference papers, and technical reports may be the best means to get feedback on early findings or conceptualizations. In some fields, conference papers are considered an authoritative statement of research. More commonly, conference papers are viewed as preliminary presentations for purposes of discussion; the journal articles that follow are considered to be the authoritative statement. In most fields, book chapters are summaries of prior work, and carry minimal weight in tenure reviews. In other fields, they are treated more like journal articles.

The unit of publication and the basis for authorship also varies widely. In some fields, each experiment is the basis for a paper, while in others, one journal article reports on multiple studies, synthesizing months or years of work. Books are considered the highest form of scholarly contribution in some fields, particularly the humanities, but are rarely part of scholarship in others. Some disciplines regard sole authorship as the essence of scholarship, while others attribute authorship to everyone with a research relationship to the project, sometimes resulting in dozens of authors on experimental papers in fields such as physics.

The mechanisms that document and organize the scholarly record reflect many of these community relationships. Inclusion in indexing and abstracting publications reflects the perceived importance of a journal to a community. It also can become a self-fulfilling prophecy. Editors and publishers lobby indexing and abstracting services to cover their journals, since coverage increases the visibility of the journal, improves access to its contents, and may increase subscriptions. Established journals thus have an inherent advantage in attracting readers over newer journals, whether published in print or electronic form. Indexing coverage and age of journals are among the indicators that could be used to weight retrieval in digital libraries. In deciding where to publish, for example, prospective authors could set parameters for whether they wish to see only journals published for at least 10 years, or they might specifically request newer journals.

Scholars with sophisticated knowledge of publishing and documentation already can use these tools to select publication outlets (Borgman 1993). For example, with tools presently available in most libraries, an author can begin with a topic and see which journals or conferences are covering that topic, in what depth, and over what period of time. Alternatively, an author can begin with a candidate set of journals and see which ones are most highly cited, and by which other journals. An assessment of what audiences might be reached by a journal could be based on which indexing and abstracting services cover it. As more digital libraries come online, these analytic capabilities should become more widely available (Paisley 1990).

Case in point: A colleague and I wished to position a technical article that included data from humanities sources and business sources (Borgman and Siegfried 1992). The target audience was a technical one, but we also wanted to reach people conducting research on information retrieval specific to humanities and business topics. First we identified the ten most-cited information science journals, using the *Science Citation Index* and the *Social Science Citation Index*. These tools also enabled us to determine which other journals, and from which fields, were citing these journals, providing an indication of the target journals' visibility in those fields. As a next step, we used a directory of journals to identify where the target journals were indexed and abstracted. Somewhat surprisingly, our analysis of core information science journals revealed that despite similar content, similar authorship of articles, and similar citation rankings, some journals were indexed in computing and technology sources while others were indexed in arts and humanities sources. Of the journals highly ranked in computing and technology areas, we selected the one with the greatest visibility in arts and humanities. The article was accepted and published in that journal and indeed has been well cited in multiple disciplines in the time since it appeared.

Evaluating People and Institutions

Citation data can be used to rank the influence of individual scholars and can be aggregated to provide rankings of departments, laboratories, universities, and other institutions with which scholarly authors are affiliated. Citation indicators often are used in hiring, tenure, promotion, and accreditation decisions. Use of citation data for these purposes has been challenged on the grounds that these are indicators and not true measures of value (Borgman 1990a; Cronin 1996; Edge 1977, 1979; Rice et al. 1989). As with any indicators or measures, these data should be used with care and with an adequate understanding of the assumptions underlying them. People are unlikely to be hired or promoted solely on the basis of the number of their publications or the number of citations received. However, the data remain useful for comparing candidates and assessing the influence of an academic department on its field. For purposes of information retrieval, they can be useful for such purposes as distinguishing between authors central to a field and those on the periphery, and between those more and less influential on a topic.

More generally, these data are useful for drawing maps of academic disciplines, identifying key players and changes in a discipline over time (Borgman 1990a; Rogers and Cottrill 1990; Small and Greenlee 1990; White 1990; White and McCain 1997).

Evaluating Content

Digital libraries, web search engines, and other forms of information retrieval systems usually allow searching by names, titles, keywords, and subjects. Some database-specific features, such as dates, businesses, identification numbers, and chemical structures, may also be included. The results often are overwhelming. Information systems do not enable people to search by evaluative criteria such as the "best," "most significant," or "core" works on a topic.

Generally speaking, it is possible to construct search algorithms for anything that can be specified explicitly in a database. Names, document titles, and keywords are in databases and thus easily matched; labels for "the best" generally are not. Yet we can use community-based indicators to approximate these judgments, especially when data from multiple sources can be applied. For example, it is technically possible to retrieve the most-cited articles, the most-cited authors, work from the laboratories receiving the largest amounts of grant funding in an area, the oldest journals, the most widely indexed and abstracted journals, and the most frequently reviewed books. In combination with other search methods, such indicators can assist in the retrieval process. They should not be used exclusively, of course, as they are merely indicators and not true measures of value. Nor would it be desirable to disenfranchise newer or younger scholars, laboratories, journals, publishers, and other parties involved in the scholarly communication process.

A variety of mechanisms are being developed to extract implicit and explicit patterns of information in databases. The best known of these are "data mining" and "knowledge discovery" techniques (Trybula 1997). One such technique that relies on the community basis of documents is "collaborative filtering" (Filtering and Collaborative Filtering 1997; Green, Cunningham, and Somers 1998; Miller, Riedl, and Konstan 1997). The underlying principles are most easily explained by example. If two people like the same set of documents, such as the same three novels or movies, then each of them probably will like other novels or movies that the other party likes. To conduct collaborative filtering, the group of participants would be offered a list of novels or movies and asked to select their favorites. When all have made their selections, people with similar tastes are clustered. Each participant is then given a list of novels or movies he or she has not yet read or seen, but which are favorites of people with similar tastes to theirs.

Collaborative filtering and citation analysis operate on similar assumptions. Each counts indicators on the assumption that if the sample is large enough, the trends are reasonably reliable. Neither technique attempts to ascertain the meaning of individual relationships. People may like the novels or movies for different reasons, but if the sample is large enough then the recommendations are reasonably reliable. Similarly, authors cite other works for different reasons, but if the sample is large enough, the influence relationships are reasonably reliable. The trend data have a number of applications. Already, online bookstores are using collaborative filtering to recommend books, music, and movies to customers based on commonalities of taste. Collaborative filtering is being used with automated intelligent agents to improve information retrieval. Citation data can be utilized alone for retrieval and analysis, or in combination with other measures to assess trends and relationships (Lievrouw et al. 1987).

Information vs. Literature

A fundamental difficulty of determining what is "best," "most significant," "core," etc., is that evaluative criteria depend heavily on the viewpoint of the observer. Scholars have perspectives on the literature of their fields, learned through apprenticeships and experience, that influence their quality assessments. From a scholar's viewpoint, a literature has a structure and an ideology that includes a history of ideas, founding texts, and landmark documents. It also has a set of practices such as research methods, standards of evidence, and forms of argument; and a set of institutional relationships that reflects mainstream and dissident schools of thought, powerful and marginal research groups, accepted publication outlets, and funding sources (Agre 1995b).

Students learn the literature of their fields not by studying objective indicators, but by learning the informal map from their teachers and advisors. Scholars instruct their students in the most important sources and authors to read. Graduate students take qualifying examinations that assess their mastery of the core literature of their fields. Establishing the literature that students are required to study, and the contents of required courses in a field, is a highly contentious process in any academic department, owing to the variety of opinions on what constitutes the essential content of a field. Yet when people are searching vast bodies of published literature, they would often find it useful to know what works are considered essential and by whom.

Selecting, Collecting, Preserving

Far more materials are published, in print, electronic, and other forms, by trade and scholarly publishers and by individuals and organizations, than can be collected by libraries or otherwise preserved. Some judgment must be applied to determine what to select, collect, organize, preserve, conserve, and provide for access to present and future generations of readers. Libraries are the institutions charged with this responsibility. Their primary obligation is to their community of users, whether it is a university, city, town, country, corporation, or other entity. In consultation with members of the community, they establish a collection development policy that includes general guidelines for what they do and do not acquire. Such policies apply regardless of the form of material acquired (Buckland 1988).

Academic libraries rely on a number of indicators in determining what to select. The usual starting point is the academic curriculum. Subject depth is determined by the topics in a curriculum and by degrees offered. Collections are most extensive if they support Ph.D. programs, and less extensive if they support only undergraduate programs, for example. As curricula change, so do library collections. Beyond these general guidelines and consultations with faculty, librarians rely heavily on directories and on indicators such as citation rankings and journal impact factors. These indicators are influential not only in determining which materials to collect, but which subscriptions to cancel as prices rise. In turn, these decisions determine what is available to present and future generations of students and scholars. Thus, these indicators are influential throughout the information life cycle.

Some inherent conflicts exist between the objective, long term view of collections that librarians attempt and the rich subjective, contextual view of the current and past literature that scholars take. Reconciling these views in ways that assist in creating, using, and seeking information is one of the challenges of digital library design. Librarians are well aware of the ideological disputes involved in selecting and collecting information resources. They attempt to treat all perspectives with similar respect by representing multiple points of view in a collection. They also endeavor to organize materials in neutral ways that will stand the test of time and ideology.

Organizing collections based on scholars' views of their literature is problematic because of the variance of opinions. Yet students are left to rely on the guidance of their teachers to identify which of the vast array of extant materials and sources on a topic are most worthy of their attention. Others rely on the opinions of family, friends, colleagues, and the mass media. Librarians guide readers to authoritative sources, but their professional stance on ideological disputes usually remains neutral. Library catalogs and indexes, organized on premises of neutrality, are of minimal assistance for evaluative purposes.

Neutrality is more easily achieved when organizing by objective elements such as personal names, document titles, and descriptive data than when organizing by content or subject. No classification or indexing system is neutral, despite the best efforts of its creators. Choices of terminology for indexes, abstracts, and catalogs inherently carry ideological meaning (Bowker and Star 1999). Ideology and interpretation vary over time and circumstances. As a result, catalogs and indexes are full of terms that once were appropriate but may now be obsolete, obscure, irrelevant, or offensive. For example, some labels for racial and ethnic groups (e.g., Negro,

Black, Colored, Afro-American, African-American; Mexican, Hispanic, Latino) that were socially acceptable when first employed may be offensive in many contexts today. Terms such as "pro-choice," "anti-abortion," and "pro-life" are highly politicized descriptors; no neutral terms exist that would retrieve documents from all sides of the discussion. A search for "Vietnam war" in the *Library of Congress Subject Headings,* the most commonly used vocabulary for organizing catalogs, yields only a few peripheral topics, such as "Herbicides—Vietnam—war use." The primary subject heading is "Vietnamese conflict, 1961–1975," which reflects the political fact that Congress never officially declared war on Vietnam.

Other established terms, such as "cookery" and "aeroplane," simply appear quaint. Leaving older terminology intact provides a cultural context for the period in which the documents were written, yet it makes the material difficult for current searchers to locate. Updating terminology also is problematic, since new terms may not be direct equivalents for the old ones. Any pair of terms usually is synonymous only in a specific context. For example, "dog" and "canine" may be equivalent in biological contexts, but not in literary references such as "dog day afternoon." "Heat" and "thermal" are more equivalent in physics than in kitchen cooking methods.

Seeking Information

Digital libraries support the process of seeking information better than they support the creation or use of documents, and they support active searching better than other kinds of information seeking. Searching and acquisition of information can be grouped in four categories: passive attention, passive search, active search, and ongoing search (Wilson 1996, 1997). Passive attention includes activities such as listening to radio and watching television. Information might be acquired, even if not intentionally. Passive search is where someone acquires relevant information in the process of searching for something else or performing some other activity. Active search, the most widely studied of these activities, is the intentional pursuit of information. Ongoing search is the case where active searching has established a basic framework, and occasional searching updates the results or the framework.

Information seeking is a continuous process, involving active and passive behaviors and formal and informal communication. The cycle of creating, using, and seeking information can be viewed as a series of stages, but these stages often are iterative. People move back and forth between stages, and they may be actively creating, using, and seeking information concurrently. People tend to manage multiple information-related tasks, each of which may be at a different stage in the cycle at any particular time.

Information Needs

In most models of the information-seeking process, the cycle is initiated by a seeker's "information need" (see, e.g., Allen 1969; Bates 1977, 1979, 1984; Belkin, Oddy, and Brooks 1982a,b; Case 1986, 1991; Case, Borgman, and Meadow 1986; Crane 1971; Dervin 1977; Dervin and Dewdney 1986; Dervin and Nilan 1986; Ellis 1989; Kuhlthau 1988a,b, 1991; Marchionini 1995; Meadows 1974, 1998; Paisley 1984; Stone 1982; Taylor 1968; Wilson 1981). The "need" stage may begin when a person senses that it might be useful to know something not presently known by him or her. In some models, the stage begins when a person formulates a statement of an information need. Alternatively, an explicit search statement sometimes is viewed as the starting point for studying information needs.

An information need is inherently subjective and occurs only in the mind of the seeker, making all these approaches problematic. A "need" is a psychological construct, closely related to other constructs such as motivations, beliefs, and values. Needs cannot be observed by a researcher or librarian, much less by an automated "intelligent agent." Only indicators or manifestations of needs are observable. Various studies have found information needs to be influenced by personal characteristics; by emotional, educational, demographic, social or interpersonal, environmental, and economic intervening variables; and by the social context in which the need arises (Wilson 1996, 1997).

Theories of Information Seeking

Much of the research on information seeking focuses on how people conduct searches in library resources or on how they interact with information systems such as digital libraries. Although at least 50 years of these studies exist, most are descriptive of specific systems and situations; few resulted in generalizable theories (Wilson 1994). Part of the problem with theory development is the difficulty of separating how people "naturally" do things from the way that they use tools. These descriptive studies consistently reveal a tight coupling between information systems and behavior. People search using the tools available; as the tools change, their activities change accordingly. People found innovative ways to use manual tools such as card catalogs and printed indexes. Later, they learned to use the first crude mechanized systems. As systems improved, more people used them, and to better effect. Lessons learned from studying the use of each generation of technology provided knowledge to improve the next generation, even if little behavioral theory resulted. Thus, technology and behavior evolve together.

Theories did emerge from later research on information seeking as a form of communication behavior. Dervin's (1977; see also Dervin and Dewdney 1986) theory of "sense making" is among the most popular of these. The theory of sense making holds that information seeking arises from a situation, or context, that lacks sense to the individual. When a person realizes that a gap exists, he or she pursues ways to close the gap. The steps taken depend on the intended use of the information for making sense of the situation. Dervin's model also has practical application in training librarians to elicit people's information needs. Cognitive theories propose similar motivations for information-seeking behavior and sense making: that people have a cognitive need to fill gaps in their knowledge (see, e.g., Daniels 1986; Ingwersen 1984, 1996).

Psychological theories of stress and coping offer other building blocks for general theories (Wilson 1996, 1997). Stress occurs when people feel they are exceeding the capacity of their personal resources or feel endangered. Coping is the set of cognitive and behavioral responses toward controlling or reducing stress. Wilson identifies an array of psychological research containing evidence that the lack of information contributes to stress and that seeking information is a common coping behavior in resolving problem-related stress (Folkman 1984; Kleiber, Montgomery, and Craft-Rosenberg 1995; Krohne 1986, 1989, 1993; Miller and Mangan 1983; Slangen et al. 1993; van Zuuren and Wolfs 1991). In the context of health information, individual differences in stress and coping behavior are especially evident. Some people seek information as a method of coping with a threat, while others cope by avoiding information about the threat (Krohne 1986, 1989; Miller and Mangan 1983). Cognitive and sense-making theories are consonant with the first set of behaviors, but do little to explain the second. People in the latter category are more stressed when presented with a high amount of information about their illness, raising ethical issues about the design of information systems and services.

Much evidence exists that information seeking follows the principle of least effort. Depending on the information and the reasons for seeking it, people often talk to their family, friends, neighbors, and colleagues before pursuing documentary sources of information. They may talk face to face with people nearby before making phone calls or sending email. People often start with local sources in their own offices (desks, bookshelves, file cabinets, and in their computers), their colleagues' offices, and other nearby locations before consulting library resources, whether physical or digital (Bishop and Star 1996; Case 1986, 1991; Case, Borgman, and Meadow 1986; Kwasnik 1991; Meadows 1974, 1998; Ruhleder 1995; Taylor 1968). Similarly, people will search for information via desktop terminals before going down the hall to a computer lab, much less across campus or across town.

Information-Seeking Behaviors

People exhibit a variety of behaviors in the process of seeking information. Some of these are idiosyncratic to individuals and circumstances; others occur in consistent patterns. As patterns emerge, they can be employed to improve the design of digital libraries. Let us look briefly at known activities and patterns of information seeking that can be supported in the design of information technologies.

Information-Seeking Activities

People conduct a wide array of information-related activities throughout the day. Some of these, such as email, discussion lists, telephone calls, and face-to-face interaction, involve informal interpersonal communication. Others involve formal channels, such as reading and writing for publication. Early research tended to draw a firm dichotomy between informal and formal information seeking (Garvey and Griffith 1964; Menzel 1966; Paisley 1965). This dichotomy was questionable even in the days before electronic mail, computer networks, and the World Wide Web. Formal and informal information-related activities now are intertwined and inseparable. Users of computer networks easily shift between interpersonal communication and information retrieval, and from seeking information to using or creating it.

Scholars are particularly active information seekers, as they need to stay current with their fields. They seek information actively in support of specific research projects or teaching, maintain ongoing searches in support of continuing interests, and gather information through passive search and by paying attention to the world around them (Meadows 1974, 1998). They put the information gathered to a variety of purposes, including identifying new research topics, framing ideas with respect to the work of others, buttressing their arguments, putting their conclusions in context, and establishing priority for new contributions.

Despite the ease of online communication, scholars still travel great distances to spend time with other scholars, continuing to regard personal discussion as the "essence of scientific communication" (Meadows 1974, 1998). Although computer networks are contributing to an increase in international collaboration, these collaborations typically are initiated and maintained through periodic same-time, same-place discussions among members of a work group (Walsh and Bayma 1996). Airline travel for business purposes continues to increase, despite early predictions that electronic mail, audio and video conferencing, and other information technologies would diminish the need for physical travel (Rice et al. 1984; Rogers 1986). Conferences often bring together communities that are active online. Electronic communication complements, rather than replaces, many aspects of face-to-face communication (December 1996; Newhagen and Rafaeli 1996; Parks and Floyd 1996; Plowman 1995; Rice et al. 1984; Rogers 1986). Thus, we need tools that support relationships among tasks and activities, rather than assuming that new technologies will supplant old ways of doing things.

Patterns of Information Seeking

Patterns of scholarly communication reveal consistency within and differences between disciplines. Fields vary in their choice of publication channels, which is one reason that transferring electronic publishing models between fields is difficult. For example, social scientists use monograph and journal literature about equally, while natural scientists rely more heavily on journals (Skelton 1973). Humanists typically are heavy users of textual materials, as archival materials rather than experimental data often are the substance of their work (Bates et al. 1993; Case 1986, 1991; Crane 1971; Stam 1984; Stone 1982). The physical and biological sciences, medicine, and most technical fields rely almost entirely on recent publications. New scientific data lose value more quickly than data in the social sciences and humanities. Thus, digital libraries of preprints, reports, and current literature are essential tools in science, technology, and medicine. Not surprisingly, these fields were the first to develop online databases. In contrast, humanities scholars may rely on primary source materials that cover centuries and are scattered throughout the world. The proportion of a field's materials that exist in electronic form vary widely, with the physical and life sciences, technology, and medicine better served by digital libraries than the social sciences, the arts, and the humanities.

Patterns of information seeking also vary by seniority in a field (Meadows 1974, 1998). Over the course of their careers, scholars develop rich interpersonal networks of colleagues in their research areas, known as "invisible colleges" (Crane 1972; Lievrouw 1990). They rely heavily on their network membership to exchange ideas and to be alerted to significant developments. They receive new work prior to publication via preprints of articles exchanged among colleagues, making them minimally dependent on catalogs, indexes, and tables of contents.

The creation of preprint servers and the practice of posting preprints, reports, and other documents on web sites is changing the balance between junior and senior scholars, however. Even with the availability of more resources online, junior scholars, graduate students, and others new to a field lack the interpersonal network that supports information seeking and lack senior scholars' complex heuristic knowledge of the literature. This group is much more dependent on catalogs, indexes, abstracts, and search engines to locate information on a topic of interest. These formal methods of organizing and providing access to information are essential for those who are not intimately familiar with the literature of a field. Senior scholars may employ these tools only to refine search topics or to explore unfamiliar territory.

Librarians sometimes complain that senior scholars do not use the catalogs, indexes, and other organizational tools provided, instead sending their graduate students to retrieve specific items or to find information on their behalf. Scholars counter that they do not need these tools because they already know their literature, or that the tools are not organized in a form useful to them. Graduate students, in turn, rely heavily on these tools and on their academic advisors to guide them through the informal landscape of the literature that is lacking in the formal tools. These patterns suggest that the design of digital libraries should be based more on the needs of novices in a field than on the needs of experts.

Patterns of information seeking also vary by the availability of information resources and by the degree and means of informal communication. Scholars and students at prestigious and well-funded research institutions in developed countries have many advantages. Those at top institutions have access to a local group of colleagues, to more local computing and information resources, to a continuing flow of visitors who infuse new information into their environment, and to travel funds to attend conferences and collaborate with colleagues elsewhere. Those with fewer information resources compensate in a variety of ways. Computer networks are increasing the participation by scholars at peripheral institutions in invisible colleges and increasing their access to documented sources of information, but the results are mixed on whether networks are increasing the equity among institutions (Walsh and Bayma 1996).

As was discussed above in the context of the economics of scholarly publishing, it is unlikely that the majority of journals will be distributed free of charge, whether in electronic or print forms. Computer networks offer new ways to seek information, whether formally or informally, actively or passively. Scholars, students, and other interested information seekers still can acquire resources that their institutions or public libraries provide, resources that are available without charge (whether online or offline), and resources for which they are able to pay. Those with minimal financial resources have access to a larger volume of documents via computer networks than they did in manual systems, but they still have lesser access to the body of current literature. Similarly, those with fewer funds to attend conferences or to travel can maintain more interpersonal relationships via electronic mail than they could with postal mail alone. Even so, it is much easier to maintain relationships online that are established in face-to-face contact than it is to establish new collegial relationships online. Technology alone will not erase inequities in access to information.

Summary and Conclusions

In this chapter I have addressed a wide range of issues in the information life cycle and the evolution of publishing, technology, and institutions. The growth of computer networks, the increasing availability of computer workstations in homes and offices, and advances in information technologies such as digital libraries combine to offer new ways of creating, using, and seeking information. At the same time, the production of scholarly literature continues to increase, as do costs of printed publications, leading to a situation that appears to be economically unsustainable. Many people are proposing that information technology offers the most promising and cost-effective solution to the "crisis in scholarly publishing," and that it also offers attractive options for trade publishing. Most aspects of print publishing already are automated, from document creation to editorial processes and page layout. Yet printing on paper and physical distribution of copies persists. Predictions of the "paperless office" date back more than two decades, yet the use of paper is increasing with the advent of information technologies, not decreasing.

Arguments for the predicted conversion from print to electronic journals oversimplify the relationship between technology, behavior, and economics. Scholarly publishing, the primary example, operates on a delicate balance between authors, publishers, libraries, and readers or consumers of publications. Each of these players has different incentives for their behaviors, and each favors systemic reforms that would give their sector more control. Changes in the academic incentive system, in economics, and in regulations over intellectual property will have far more influence on the future of scholarly publishing than will technological developments.

From a technological perspective, documents are merely "things" to be manipulated in information systems. From a behavioral perspective, however, documents have a "social life." They are created for a purpose and for a community; their meaning lies in the community as well as in the documents themselves. The more that can be understood about how and why documents are created and used, the better that information technologies such as digital libraries can be designed to support those behaviors. I explored a variety of behaviors involved in creating and using documents. By making implicit behaviors explicit, it is possible to identify characteristics that can be employed in design. These include the process of creating documents, structural features, and judgments involved in choosing channels of publication, in evaluating people, institutions, and content, and in selecting, collecting, and organizing documents for communities of users.

Though many of the decisions and judgments that are made throughout the information life cycle are subjective, a number of objective indicators and measures exist that can be used to approximate and support human judgment. I reviewed some of the indicators that are widely used in scholarly publishing and in law, showing how they also can be used to improve information retrieval and other aspects of document creation and use. A variety of new data-mining and knowledge-discovery techniques are being developed that will take further advantage of process and structure characteristics of documents and of community relationships associated with them.

Knowledge of the processes and relationships associated with the creation and use of documents also yields insights into information-seeking behavior. Information seeking is a complex process that involves informal, interpersonal communication and formal activities in search of documentary sources. Some activities are passive and some are active. The process is generally assumed to start with an "information need," although needs are defined in a variety of ways, depending on the research approach taken. After many years of descriptive studies, some promising behavioral theories of information seeking are appearing. These include sense making, cognitive theories, and stress and coping as responses to situations of uncertainty. Descriptive studies have yielded knowledge about activities and patterns of information seeking that are used in improving information retrieval systems. Taken as a whole, these studies reveal the co-evolution of technology and behavior. People use the tools that are available and adapt them to their needs; the next generation of technology attempts to incorporate the adaptations.

5

Why Are Digital Libraries Hard to Use?

If national and global information infrastructures are to serve "every citizen" (Bangemann Report 1994; Computer Science and Telecommunications Board 1997a), then digital libraries should be reasonably easy to learn and to use. But how easy can we make them? Some suggest that information systems should be as easy to use as automatic teller machines, but the comparison is unfair. ATMs support only a few procedures for withdrawing or depositing funds. Other widely adopted information technologies, such as radios, televisions, and telephones, also support only a small set of actions, but even these technologies are becoming more complex and harder to use. Turning on a television, changing channels, and adjusting the volume are easy, yet programming a video recorder to schedule the recording of a television program is notoriously difficult. Similarly, most people are capable of making and receiving telephone calls, but advanced features such as call forwarding, call waiting, and three-way calling are prone to error.

One of the reasons that technologies become more complex as features are added is that the relationship between the task and the tool becomes less visible. An ATM has few enough features that each one can correspond to a single key or menu choice. Audiocassette-based telephone answering machines have a direct mapping between task and action: press "play" to hear messages, press "delete" to delete messages. Voice message systems have these functions and many more, with the result that the mapping becomes abstract: log onto the system with a user identification number and password, after which new messages may play automatically, but to delete a message press "76."

Desktop computers are especially abstract in regard to the relationship between form and function. One cannot inspect a computer and identify its functions in the same way that one can identify the functions of a telephone or a television. Keyboards, pointing devices, function keys, and screen displays can be programmed to support almost any imaginable application. Because of this generality, the same physical actions may produce different results in each software application. In the abstract world of computing, the "real-world" clues are gone, replaced by pull-down or pop-up menus, screen displays, searching tools, and lists to browse. Usability depends heavily on users' abilities to map their goals onto a system's capabilities. Also missing in automated systems is the safety net of human assistance. Instead of a store clerk, a librarian, or some other intermediary who listens carefully to an ambiguous question and responds with an interpretation such as "What you may be looking for is . . . ," the options for assistance may be an automated help system, an email query, or a telephone help line. These are not acceptable alternatives in most cases. Information systems will achieve wide acceptance only if they are easy to learn and use relative to perceived benefits.

Designing Information Systems for Usability

Information systems continue to be difficult to learn and to use, despite the technological advances of the last two decades. Many of the design challenges identified early in the 1980s have yet to be solved (Borgman 1984, pp. 33–34):

The change in the use of computing technology is a fundamental one. Once the computer began to be used by people who were not experts, the access requirements changed dramatically. The technology-oriented expert who uses a system daily can learn (eventually) to use almost any mechanism, no matter how poorly designed. The situation is different with the new community of users. Most of them lack both a technological orientation and the motivation to invest in extensive training. The new class of users sees a computer as a tool to accomplish some other task; for them, the computer is not an end in itself. This new generation of users is much less tolerant of "unfriendly" and poorly designed systems. They have come to expect better systems and rightly so.

The technology has moved much more rapidly than has our understanding of the nature of the tasks for which we use it or our understanding of the human ability to adapt. Indeed, an important issue is whether the user should adapt to the computer or the computer adapt to the user. Computers have turned out to be much harder to use than we had expected, and design and training problems have resulted. We have had many calls for more "user friendly" systems, but we don't understand human-computer compatibility well enough even to agree on what "user friendly" means. Thus we are left with several distinct challenges: 1) we need to determine what factors make computers difficult to learn and use; 2) we need to define a set of characteristics for "user friendly" systems; and 3) we need to apply the research to design.

Although these same three challenges remain, a larger array of design factors now are recognized. Research on human-computer interaction in the 1980s was just that: research on the relationship between an individual user and the computer in direct interaction. "User-friendly" design addressed screen displays and functional capabilities, but it did not delve deeply into task motivation, much less the relationship between a computer user and the work, educational, or leisure context from which the task arose. People were expected to adapt to systems, and considerable effort was devoted to user training. Today people have higher expectations of information systems. Digital libraries should be easy to learn, to use, and to relearn, and should be flexible in adapting to a more diverse user population.

Usability Evaluation

Perspectives on usability shifted substantially over the course of the twentieth century. The initial purpose of ergonomics was to place people into the technological order. Human skills were measured relentlessly, so that people could be matched with the machine task to which they were best suited and machines could be operated by those with the requisite capabilities (Edwards 1995; Gilbreth 1921). By the early 1980s, however, the focus of ergonomics (also known as "human factors") had shifted toward shaping technology to human capabilities and needs. This period also marked the transition from mainframe computing systems operated by skilled professionals to desktop computing for end users. Landmarks in this transition include the Association for Computing Machinery's first conference on Computer-Human Interaction (1982), the publication of Ben Shneiderman's textbook *Designing the User Interface* (1987) and of Donald Norman's popular book *The Psychology of Everyday Things* (1988), the Scandinavian movement toward the work-oriented design of computer artifacts (Ehn 1988), the first conference on participatory design in the United States (Namioka and Schuler 1990), and university courses in human-computer interaction and user interface design (first offered in departments of computer science and information studies, later spreading to the social sciences, humanities, and other fields). A large body of research on human-computer interaction now exists, and it has led to general principles and guidelines for the design of information technologies.

Despite these advances, establishing generalizable benchmarks for usability remains problematic owing to the variety of applications and the diversity of user communities served. Many criteria for usability have been derived from the findings of research in human-computer interaction. The criteria proposed for "every citizen interfaces to the nation's information infrastructure" (Computer Science and Telecommunications Board 1997a, p. 45) are particularly applicable to digital libraries: Systems should be easy to understand, easy to learn, tolerant of errors, flexible, adaptable, appropriate and effective for the task, powerful, efficient, inexpensive, portable, compatible, intelligent, supportive of social and group interactions, trustworthy (secure, private, safe, reliable), information centered, and pleasant to use. Other applicable criteria are the user interface design rules established by Shneiderman (1992, 1998), as adapted to information retrieval by Shneiderman, Byrd, and Croft (1997):

Strive for consistency.
Provide shortcuts for skilled users.
Offer informative feedback.
Design for closure.
Offer simple error handling.
Permit easy reversal of actions.
Support user control.
Reduce short term memory load.

Nielsen (1993) identifies five usability attributes for information systems (which also are suitable for other applications): learnability, efficiency, memorability, errors, and satisfaction. The above criteria offer general guidance for design, but they are far from a "cookbook" for constructing any individual information system. Principles such as "easy to learn" must be adapted to the application and to the user community. A system that supplies daily weather reports to the public must be much easier to learn than one that supplies geophysical data to researchers, for example. Setting appropriate criteria for any system involves evaluation with members of the target audience and comparisons to similar applications.

Though the value of making systems easier to use may be self-evident to users, it is not always self-evident to software vendors, to programmers, or even to the managers who acquire software on behalf of end users. The literature of human-computer interaction abounds with studies indicating that companies release software without basic human factors testing out of a belief that market timing, number of features, price, and other factors are more important to business success than is usability, or that usability testing itself is too expensive or is ineffective (Computer Science and Telecommunications Board 1997; Landauer 1995; Nielsen 1993; Sawyer, Flanders, and Wixon 1996; Shneiderman 1998). Studies to determine the veracity of such beliefs are revealing hard evidence that improving usability is cost effective, both for software producers and for the organizations that implement software (Computer Science and Telecommunications Board 1997a, Nielsen 1993). Almost half of the code in contemporary software is devoted to the user interface (Myers and Rosson 1992), and the greatest source of cost overruns in software development lies in correcting usability problems (Nielsen 1993). Even a small amount of usability evaluation in the development process can pay for itself several times over in cost savings from lost productivity (Computer Science and Telecommunications Board 1997a; Landauer 1995; Nielsen 1993; Sawyer, Flanders, and Wixon 1996).

Relevance

As was noted in chapter 4, seeking, using, and creating information involves a series of judgments. People also make judgments about the usability of information systems and about the value of the content they retrieve. Thus, information systems can be judged by their effectiveness in retrieving relevant results, and by the time, effort, and cost required to achieve those results.

Classical measures of the effectiveness of information retrieval systems depend on relevance judgments. "Precision" and "recall," the most widely applied of the classical performance measures, date back to the earliest days of automated information retrieval (Cleverdon 1964; Lancaster 1968; Perry, Kent, and Berry 1956). Precision is the ratio of relevant items retrieved to the total number of items retrieved; recall is the ratio of relevant items retrieved to the total number of relevant items in the database.

Measures that depend on relevance assessments are reliable only to the extent that relevance can be quantified, however. Relevance is inherently a subjective concept, because it involves human judgment (Harter and Hert 1997; Saracevic 1975; Schamber 1994). The question "relevant to what?" quickly arises. Are the results relevant to this search query, to other items in this set, to items ever seen before, to the underlying need, or to the problem to be solved? On whose judgments is relevance based? Are the results relevant to a motivated searcher, to a librarian searching on someone's behalf, or to an experimenter? These are but a small sample of relevance criteria. Schamber (1994b) lists 80 relevance factors reported in published research. Relevance-based measures of retrieval are complemented by a variety of other quantitative and qualitative measures that consider both the process and the products of a search. These include time to learn a system, time to search, amount of search reformulation required, number of errors, and subjective satisfaction (Borgman, Hirsh, and Hiller 1996; Harter and Hert 1997; Robertson and Hancock-Beaulieu 1992; Salton 1992; Tague-Sutcliffe 1996).

Although exact relevance measurements are problematic, recall and precision remain useful as a framework for conceptualizing the search process. In theory, they are inversely proportional—as recall increases, precision decreases, and vice versa. Expert searchers employ this inverse relationship in searching. Searching goals can be viewed on a continuum from finding everything that exists on a topic (high recall) to finding a few very good matches with as little noise as possible (high precision). A search designed to achieve high recall tends to retrieve many irrelevant matches too; one "casts the net widely," adding many synonyms, subject headings, classification codes, and other attributes that might possibly match something of interest. Conversely, a search designed to achieve high precision misses many relevant items by "casting the net narrowly"—that is, restricting the search query to attributes central to the desired topic. Tradeoffs between recall and precision can be incorporated into the design of user interfaces and retrieval algorithms in digital libraries, assisting searchers in framing their queries as narrowly or widely as desired.

Content and Community
Design guidelines and evaluation criteria can be employed to build more usable systems, but only to the extent that design goals are appropriate for the application. At the core of effective digital library design is the rela-

tionship between the content to be provided and the user community to be served. Design goals can originate from either perspective.

Design often originates with an existing collection and a goal of making the content available in a digital library. An organization may own (or hold the rights to) one or more collections, such as photographic images of animals, maps of a region, historic literary texts, or instructional materials. Any of these collections could be used in a variety of ways, to serve a variety of purposes. In deciding on the features of a digital library to support these materials, the next step should be to determine who would use the content, how, and why. For example, a set of animal images could be valuable in biology classrooms at the elementary, the secondary, or the college level. In a digital library to serve any of these applications, each image could be described by common and biological names, the search capabilities could be simple enough to be learned by students in a few minutes, and the display capabilities could support one or a few images at a time on basic desktop machines available in classrooms. If the same set of animal images were to serve an audience of biological researchers, a more elaborate taxonomic description would be required, in addition to more extensive searching and display capabilities. If the animal images were intended for advertising purposes, they could be described in terms of the emotional impact sought, such as "peaceful," "pastoral," "aggressive," "leadership," and "tension." Colors, image size, granularity, and the cost of using the image in different media would be essential descriptive elements. The search capabilities would have to be simple enough for nontechnical users, yet they would have to support browsing through various combinations of elements. High-quality displays on larger screens would also be necessary.

Alternatively, digital library design can begin with the audience to be served. Law firms, for example, serve the information needs of their attorneys with multiple digital libraries. Attorneys need resources on statute and case law that apply to their current cases. They often need related technical, social, or policy materials too. The actual searching of digital libraries may be done by librarians, paralegals, or attorneys, all of whom are familiar with legal terminology and resources. Many of the information needs can be satisfied with commercially available digital libraries of statute and case law. The content of these digital libraries is collected and organized for the information needs and work practices of the legal profession.

Accordingly, these systems provide sophisticated searching features that assume legal expertise. Some initial training and continuing education are required, which is acceptable because these systems are used frequently. Similarly, work product, litigation support, and other databases of materials internal to law firms are designed for the information needs and work practices of the firm.

These same digital libraries of legal resources contain materials that are of considerable value to members of the lay public who need legal information for purposes such as contracts, wills, marriage, divorce, death, purchasing property, or landlord-tenant disputes. However, the commercially available systems targeted at the legal community are rarely usable by a lay audience, whether because of the technical expertise required, the time investment necessary to learn the systems, or the cost. This does not mean the systems are poorly designed, however. Usability is relative and must be judged on the basis of intended goals. The lay audience is served by a complementary set of resources tailored to the information needs, technical skills, and financial resources of those who are not legal professionals. The best known of these are the Nolo Press materials on basic contracts, wills, and divorces.

The tradeoffs involved in designing digital libraries for single or multiple communities are exemplified by the seemingly simple question "Why is the sky blue?" This is a question that can be answered at many levels. Most children are curious about this topic by the age of 8 years, yet it is also of interest to astrophysicists. Even if the question is phrased in similar terms, the child and the adult astrophysicist intend different questions and expect different answers. The child is happy with a simple answer—a few sentences, a picture book, or a multimedia science game might do. In contrast, the scientist probably wants some recent journal articles, data from satellite observations, or maybe an experimental kit to explain concepts such as light, color, and atmosphere to an introductory class. Although this a reasonable question to pose to a global digital library, it contains few clues as to the results desired. In what form should the digital library produce an answer? In what medium (text, images, sounds)? In what language—only the one in which the question was asked, or in other languages if appropriate content exists? For what kind of computer and operating system should the results be formatted? What text, image, video, audio, and statistical software does the user have to manage the results?

More generally, how much diversity in user populations or in content can be supported by a system? When should the design of a digital library be based on providing one community with access to multiple collections? When should the design of a digital library be based on providing one collection to multiple communities? When should a community's needs be supported by a single collection and when by independent access to multiple collections? When should access to multiple collections be aggregated in a single system? To answer the "Why is the sky blue?" question, for example, scientists may need sophisticated data analysis facilities, while children may need rich but simple-to-learn browsing capabilities. The scientists' user interface may require "high-end" hardware and software, advanced computing skills, and extensive domain expertise, and thus it may be usable only by that small and specialized user community. Conversely, the children's user interface to those same data may run on "low-end" hardware platforms, require minimal computing skills and domain expertise, and be usable by a broad audience.

Knowing the Users

The degree of tailoring to user communities will depend on the goals of the application, on what is known about the community, on the extent to which users have participated in the design, and on characteristics of the application. If the scope of the user community is well defined (e.g., employees of a company or students in a university), a representative sample can be studied and design participation can be solicited or appointed by management. If the scope of the user community is less well defined (e.g., prospective users of a new product or service), designers still can sample from the target audience. Marketing studies may provide baseline data. Research on primary and perhaps secondary target audiences may identify common elements and requirements and the degree to which needs and interests vary. Such studies provide a starting point for design. Prototypes can be tested on samples of the target audience, and the design refined. However, digital libraries on a GII will serve larger, more diverse, and more geographically distributed audiences than most systems of today. Scaling methods of design and evaluation to this complex environment is another of the challenges in constructing a global information infrastructure.

Individual Differences

Another consideration in designing digital libraries is the range of skills, abilities, cognitive styles, and personality characteristics within a user community that may affect usability. Collectively, these factors are known as "individual differences." Studies of human-computer interaction with information retrieval systems, word processing software, and computer programming reveal a variety of individual differences that influence human performance (Egan 1988). Population characteristics known to influence usability of digital libraries include computer skills, domain knowledge, familiarity with the system, technical aptitudes such as reading and spatial abilities, age, and personality characteristics such as those measured by the Myers-Briggs tests (Borgman 1989; Egan 1988). Other social and cultural factors thought to influence usability are even harder to isolate and study (Computer Science and Telecommunications Board 1997a; Leventhal et al. 1994; Shneiderman 1998). Thus, even when content is being selected and collections are being organized for well-defined communities, considerable differences within groups often must be accommodated.

Two brief case studies illustrate the process of designing digital library applications for specific user communities.

Case Study: Energy Researchers and Professionals

We had two goals in this set of studies for the US Department of Energy: to identify behavioral characteristics of energy researchers and professionals that influenced usability of an operational system and to apply the results of the behavioral study to make the system easier to use. The system had a terse Boolean interface typical of its day and a large database of bibliographic records. Neither the content nor the organization of the database could be changed, but usability could be improved by constructing a "front end" client to the system and by developing a simple instructional module. The extant body of research on the information-related behavior of scientists, discussed in chapter 4, provided a baseline for designing the study.

The first phase of the study was to interview a sample of the scientists currently using the existing system, so that we could identify their information needs and uses (Case, Borgman, and Meadow 1986). The interviews revealed considerable individual differences in information-related behavior within the community on factors such as frequency of use, skills, habits, and purposes.

The second phase of the project was to design the client. Most of the scientists and professionals interviewed used only basic features of the system, so we focused on simplifying those features rather than on specialized techniques. Most respondents were intermittent users, so design also focused on reducing the time to learn and relearn the system.

The third phase of the study was to evaluate the client and the instructional module in an experimental setting, with subjects drawn from the user community. Results indicated that the client user interface provided significant usability gains over the native system (Borgman, Case, and Meadow 1989; Meadow et al. 1989).

Case Study: Elementary School Students Studying Science

The Science Library Catalog Project was an outgrowth of a project, based at the California Institute of Technology, whose goal was to improve instruction in elementary school science, specifically biology and physics (Borgman et al. 1995). Among the weaknesses of science instruction identified was that students were not learning how to search for new information beyond what they learned in the classroom. Our goal was to supplement "hands-on science" with "hands-on information searching." The audience was school children between the ages of 8 and 12. The project constructed online catalogs of science and technology materials, with longer-term goals of extending the system to include full text, images, students' reports, and other materials. The Science Library Catalog was developed and tested iteratively with multicultural populations in Southern California over a five-year period. Research was conducted in public and private schools and in a major public library. In most of the experiments, the catalog data were those of the schools or public libraries studied.

At the time of the initial study, little prior research existed on children's information-related behavior. Few had studied how children search for information in either paper-based or electronic environments. Lacking a baseline specific to information-related behavior, we started by identifying what was known about cognitive development and about the technical skills of children in the target age group. Research in education and in psychology revealed that children in this age range typically lacked basic skills requisite for the online catalogs of the day, such as typing, spelling, alphabetizing, and science vocabulary. However, children have other skills that could enable them to use alternative designs. These skills include the ability to use a pointing device, to browse, and to recognize terms and concepts that they may not be able to recall from memory.

The design was radically different from online catalogs, information retrieval systems, or other digital libraries available at the time. Science and technology topics were displayed on cascading bookshelves, and only a mouse was needed to navigate. Topics were presented in a subject relationship (based on the Dewey Decimal Classification system, although the numbers were not displayed), providing context that is not evident in most online or card catalogs even today. Catalog records were reformatted to display as pages of the book. Basic catalog data were displayed as a title page, in the familiar form they would appear in a children's book. Page corners were dog-eared so they could be turned to reveal more information, where available. A map of the library was tucked in a book pocket, which resembled the glued-in pockets commonly used to hold lending cards and date-due slips. When the map was clicked, footprints traced a path from the location of the computer to the location of the shelf where the item was held. Children found the metaphor familiar and appealing. Most could find books of interest in a 1500-record database in a minute or so. We refined the user interface in a series of experiments, improving screen displays and navigation features. Ultimately we developed a system that was easy to learn and highly effective for this user community, and results were consistent across the schools and the public library studied.

We studied the system in enough different situations to believe that the results could be generalized to other elementary-school-age children. In the hope of achieving generalizable results, we relied on widely available hardware, software, and content. The Science Library Catalog was developed in HyperCard on Macintosh computers, a common platform in elementary schools at the time. Input consisted of catalog records in the MAchine Readable Cataloging (MARC) format, following international standards. However, we encountered problems of scaling and of migration to subsequent generations of technology. The largest database studied was about 8000 records, and that size strained the usability of the hierarchical browsing structure. Schools did not yet have internal networks, so the catalog could be used only from computers in the library. The metaphor was tied to a physical location, so that a path could be traced from the computer to the physical location of the items described in the catalog. Considerable redesign, based on additional studies of user behavior, would be required to maintain the same level of tailoring while adapting the system to larger databases, to networked environments, or to be interoperable with other systems in real time.

In sum, whether digital library design begins with the content, collections, or the user community to be served, understanding the behavior, context, practices, expertise, and requirements of the prospective users is essential for improving usability.

Search Knowledge and Skills

The use of digital libraries can be approached from a number of theoretical and practical perspectives. Information-seeking behavior includes an array of formal and informal communication processes, some of which may involve digital libraries. Information needs, variously defined, are the usual starting point for information seeking. Other approaches consider problem situations, anomalous states of knowledge, or user goals (Belkin, Oddy, and Brooks 1982a,b; Dervin and Nilan 1986; Hert 1996; Ingwersen 1984, 1996), or focus on the interaction between users and systems in searching for information (Belkin and Vickery 1985). Yet another approach is to view the search for information as a form of problem-solving behavior.

Problem Solving in Digital Libraries
Problem solving has been studied much more comprehensively than has information-seeking behavior. Problem solving offers a model for examining the nature of information-related problems, for studying methods of finding solutions, and for studying expert and novice behavior. An information need is a type of problem, and the solution is the information that fills the need. This subsection examines problems and solutions from this perspective.

Problems

From a cognitive perspective, all problems have three basic components (Glass, Holyoak, and Santa 1979, p. 392):

1. A set of *given information,* a description of the problem.
2. A set of *operations,* or actions that the problem solver can use to achieve a solution.
3. A *goal,* or description of what would constitute a solution to the problem.

Multiple types of problems exist, as do multiple types of knowledge that may contribute to solving them. Problems can be classified by the degree to which they are "well defined" or "ill defined" (Reitman 1964; Simon 1973). Well-defined problems are those in which the given information, operations, and goal are clearly specified. An example is an elementary algebra problem. Ill-defined problems tend to be open-ended—the given information is not clearly specified, much less the operations or goal. Information problems usually fall in the latter category.

The lack of definition of some problems—such as "How can this device be improved?"—is immediately apparent. Others—such as "How many Japanese cars were manufactured in 1999?"—may appear at first to be well defined, but upon further exploration turn out to be ambiguous. In the global economy, design and assembly can be distributed over multiple countries; this makes it difficult to determine national responsibility (Reich 1992). If the second query were to be interpreted as "How many cars were manufactured in Japan in 1999?" then cars manufactured by Japanese companies in plants outside Japan would be excluded. Also ambiguous are the terms "cars" and "manufactured." Import and export regulations distinguish passenger vehicles, utility vehicles, trucks, and vans; thus, "cars" could be counted in different ways for different purposes. Similarly, "manufactured" could mean design, production of individual parts, or assembly.

Regardless of how the question is interpreted, the answers could lie in a number of different digital libraries, each with different representations and search capabilities. Documents containing automobile industry statistics are likely to vary in structure and content depending on their origin (e.g., US government trade statistics, Japanese government trade statistics, statistics of other governments, the automobile industry, the manufacturing companies, and industry analyses in the popular and trade presses). Statistics might be found in television news broadcasts, company promotional films, web sites, and many other places. To obtain precise results with the intended meaning would require considerable expertise in the organization of content in individual databases, in the mechanisms for controlling terminology, and in the functional capabilities of each digital library searched. The final answer is of little value unless qualified by an explanation of how the concepts were interpreted and represented.

The "Japanese cars" problem is ostensibly one with a factual answer. Even more difficult to articulate clearly are questions "about" something. Most concepts can be expressed in multiple ways, and individual terms often represent multiple concepts that vary by context. People typically generate queries from what they know about their problem, rather than from what they know about information resources, much less about the representation of concepts in those resources. As a consequence, their initial queries may contain clues that lead them toward their goal or away from it.

The effect of initial queries on the path of a search can be illustrated by the question "Do you have any books about Brazil?" Upon further elaboration by a human (or automated) intermediary, this might become "Do you have any books on Brazilian fish, written in English, and published after 1980?" Taking the question literally, the system would answer with records on books containing the words "fish" and "Brazil" or "Brazilian," written in English, with a publication date of 1981 or later. Whether the result is relevant to the underlying information need is another matter. Further discussion with a skilled information professional may reveal that "Brazilian fish" is only the entry point for a much different problem, such as the following:

I'm gathering some background information for my neighborhood campaign to prevent a new development project that might pollute our river. I've heard that the Amazon River fish population was severely damaged by development in the 1980s. Maybe some of the data the environmentalists gathered there would be useful for our testimony, but I can't read Portuguese. What I really need is environmental data on local species and local river conditions, and Brazil seemed like a good place to start.

The most useful information in response to this query may have little to do with Brazil. A better result would be environmental studies performed in conditions similar to those of the local river, experiences of community groups in challenging development projects, and guidance in presenting testimony to government agencies. Furthermore, the most relevant content may exist in papers, records, reports, articles, videos, films, or tapes, rather than in books. It is possible (though not evident in the refined query) that Brazil could be relevant for other reasons. Perhaps one of the people hearing testimony has experience there and would find Brazilian examples particularly salient.

Another applicable finding from the literature of problem solving is that the degree to which a problem is well defined or ill defined is partly a function of the knowledge and skills of the problem solver (Glass, Holyoak, and Santa 1979). For example, in the queries above, an expert such as an automotive-industry analyst or an environmentalist could articulate the queries more specifically and completely than could a novice to the domain. Similarly, an expert in the use of a particular information system could specify a problem in terms appropriate to that system better than someone not familiar with that system. Human search intermediaries combine their knowledge of a subject domain and of information-seeking behavior with their skills in searching information systems to assist people in articulating their problems. They often ask people about the purposes for which they want information (e.g., obtaining a job, finding child care, researching a term paper, establishing a business), and elicit additional details concerning the problem.

Solutions

Much of the work on problem solving follows from Polya's classic model, which has been applied in contexts ranging from mathematical problems to creative thinking (Glass, Holyoak, and Santa 1979; Koberg and Bagnall 1972). It is particularly useful as a model for solving information problems.

As Glass, Holyoak, and Santa (1979, p. 393) explain, Polya (1957) divides the problem-solving process into four steps: understanding the problem, planning a solution, carrying out the plan, and checking the results. These steps are iterative; the results are checked at multiple points in the process. For example, a plan for a solution may include some preliminary searching to explore the problem, then more detailed searching along the most promising paths identified. Interim results are assessed to determine subsequent actions.

The amount and the type of planning that goes into solving an information-related problem are affected by several things. One is the degree to which the problem is defined. Well-defined problems (e.g., finding an email address) require less planning than ill-defined problems (e.g., finding a birthday gift for a friend). Information problems that appear well defined often can turn out to be ambiguous, as was illustrated above. In many cases, some initial searching is required to determine the scope of the problem before developing a plan. Another factor is the amount of expertise the searcher has in the problem domain. Expertise is relative to the problem at hand. Everyone is an expert with regard to some things and a novice with regard to others. Even in an area of expertise, the amount of knowledge about a problem may vary by stage of search. People gain more knowledge of a problem through exploring it, which influences subsequent steps in the search process. A third factor that influences planning is knowledge about the resources and operations available to solve the problem. In the case of information problems, searchers need some knowledge of relevant information sources and how to search them. As people become familiar with the range of sources and search capabilities, their planning and their searching improve. For example, students in medicine and law gradually become more proficient searchers as they become more knowledgeable about technical terminology, information resources in their fields, metadata available to represent those resources, and the search capabilities for each system and each collection.

Search Process

Despite the number of years people spend in formal education, few receive formal instruction in general problem solving or in searching for information. Information searching is a process that most people learn through experience. Knowledge may be gathered through experiences in libraries, archives, museums, and laboratories and by using information systems. Some people are able to extract general principles that can be applied to multiple systems and situations and become expert searchers. A few become proficient intermittent users, but most remain "permanent novices" with respect to searching digital libraries.

Research on the use of information retrieval systems reveals great disparities in the use of system features. Novices tend to rely on the most basic features, often in short search sessions, rarely taking advantage of sophisticated search refinement capabilities. Intermittent users may use a few more features, but rely on a small set of familiar capabilities. Experts are those who use a combination of features, often taking an iterative approach that tests multiple strategies for finding the information sought. Experts are able to combine features in sophisticated ways appropriate to a problem. Although experts may draw on a common set of known strategies, they tend to develop individualized approaches to searching. Given the same statement of a problem, expert searchers often produce diverse sets of results from the same system as a result of differences in interpretation of the problem, in choice of terminology, and in choice of features (Borgman 1989a).

Studies of expert searchers reveal knowledge and skills that contribute to effective and efficient searching. These are techniques that can be taught to novices. Some techniques can be incorporated into system features, such as offering users prescribed tactics for broadening or narrowing searches. The requisite knowledge and skills for searching can be categorized in a variety of ways. General knowledge of computing has been divided into categories such as syntactic and semantic (Shneiderman 1980), objects and actions (Shneiderman 1998), and conceptual, semantic, syntactic, and lexical (Foley et al. 1990). Combining models for computing, problem solving, and information seeking, I proposed a model of the knowledge and skills required to search for information in digital libraries: conceptual knowledge of the information retrieval process, semantic and syntactic knowledge of how to implement a query in a particular system, and technical skills in executing the query (Borgman 1986b, 1996b). Below I explore these three categories, drawing examples from online catalogs, bibliographic and full-text databases, geographic information systems, and web-based information systems.

Conceptual Knowledge

Conceptual knowledge is the user's model or understanding of a type of system, whether it is digital libraries, spreadsheets, or word processing. Users employ their conceptual knowledge of the search process to translate an information need into a plan for executing a search. Experts analyze the problem, determine goals, break the problem into component parts, survey the available sources that may contain relevant information, and make a plan for conducting the search in one or more digital libraries. They carry out their plan, continually checking progress toward their goals, and revise their strategy accordingly.

Studies of skilled searchers on bibliographic retrieval systems in the 1970s and the 1980s were distilled into strategies and tactics for information retrieval that could be taught to novices and codified in textbooks for online searching (Bates 1979, 1981, 1984; Borgman 1989a; Borgman, Moghdam, and Corbett 1984; Lancaster and Fayen 1973). More recent studies of the World Wide Web and geographic information systems are yielding similar results about the role of conceptual knowledge in searching. The ability to construct a mental model of "an information space" continues to be a key predictor of searching success in multiple types of digital libraries (Dillon, in press; Dillon and Gabbard 1998; Priss and Old 1998).

Expert searchers know how to manage searching processes that typically confound or discourage novices. Searchers commonly encounter one or more unsatisfactory situations: search failures (no matches), excess information (too many matches) (Larson 1991b), and irrelevant matches. Studies of searching the World Wide Web reveal similar patterns, with about 30 percent of searches resulting in no matches on some search engines, despite the massive amount of content online (Shneiderman, Byrd, and Croft 1997).

When experts encounter no matches, they typically expand the search by framing the topic differently. They refer to term lists, thesauri, or other tools to identify synonyms or more general terms that will improve recall, for example. They may release constraints on the topic, such as date, language, or format. Experts are aware that "known" facts such as personal names, places, titles, manufacturers, and dates often are incorrect, and searching for them should be generalized. Similarly, when experts encounter too many matches, they may frame the topic in narrower terms, add constraints, or search for a subset of the problem, all of which may improve precision. When experts encounter too many irrelevant matches, they recognize that their choice of terms or parameters may not match those in the digital library adequately. They may reframe the search with other terms and tools in that digital library or look for other collections that may be more suitable.

Vocabulary continues to be the most difficult aspect of searching for any type of information, whether for text, images, numeric data, audio, or any combination of these. Documents, places, ideas, and objects are described differently by those who create them and those who seek them. Metadata play an essential role in access by describing and representing content in consistent ways. Even so, mapping from a searcher's "entry vocabulary" or starting point to unfamiliar metadata vocabularies remains difficult (Batty 1998; Buckland et al. 1999). People searching for train schedules from Rome to Naples must map their vocabulary to terms such as "rail," "railway," or "Eurorail" rather than "train," and to "Roma" and "Napoli" rather than "Rome" and "Naples," for example. These simple mappings are relatively unambiguous and often can be done automatically. Less obvious, and less familiar to those not speaking the local language, are the equivalence of Vienna (English), Wien (German), and Becs (Hungarian) for the capital of Austria, or Prague (English) and Praha (Czech) for the capital of the Czech Republic.

More complex mappings require more conceptual knowledge of how vocabularies are structured. Buckland et al. (1999) offer the example of searching for "rockets" in the Census Bureau's "US Imports and Exports" database, which employs a specialized categorization scheme. The plural "rockets," for example, yields only one category: "bearings, transmission, gaskets, misc." The singular "rocket" yields three other categories: "photographic or cinematographic goods," "engines, parts, etc.," and "arms and ammunition, parts and accessories thereof." "Rocket" appears only in a subcategory of the latter term: "missile and rocket launchers and similar projectors." Missing altogether from searches on "rocket" and "rockets" are general categories probably of interest: "guided missiles" and "bombs, grenades, etc." Specialized vocabulary structures such as these enable experts in the subject domain to specify precise categories, yet also require that they explore the structure sufficiently to identify all possibilities. Automatic mapping between terms is difficult because relationships depend on context. Categories that are synonymous for one problem are not for another, unlike the simple mapping between "Vienna" and "Wien" on rail schedules. Even "rail" and "train" are synonymous only in certain contexts.

These are but a few of many examples of strategies and tactics that experts use in planning and executing online searches. General patterns exist, such as "berry picking" relevant results from multiple digital libraries over multiple searches (Bates 1989). Some patterns are indirect, such as "pearl growing," which starts with a core of one or a few known relevant documents and spirals outward for other materials that are related to the starting set (Borgman, Moghdam, and Corbett 1984).

In comparison, studies of novices and intermittent users of online catalogs and other digital libraries reveal little evidence of search-planning or search-refinement strategies. Nonexpert searchers are more likely to search intuitively than to use advanced features intended to make searches more efficient and effective. For example, novices will use familiar terms as keywords without verifying that their chosen terms are used in the database. They have particular difficulty recovering from problems involving subject terminology. In contrast, experts will employ tools such as subject thesauri, classification structures, and name authority files to identify the most promising terms and appropriate synonyms. When experts retrieve unsatisfactory results, their reflex is to reframe the search. Novices, however, often are unaware of what they are missing, failing to distinguish between poor results because of the contents of the digital library and poor results because the strategy was inadequate. Vocabulary problems arise in all types of digital library searching (Bates 1986, 1989; Berger 1994; Bilal 1998; Blair and Maron 1985; Borgman et al. 1995; Crawford, Thom, and Powles 1993; Efthimiadis 1992, 1993; Hildreth 1993; Hirsh 1998; Lancaster et al. 1991; Larson 1991a–c; Leazer 1994; Markey 1983; 1986; Markey and Demeyer 1986; Matthews, Lawrence, and Ferguson 1983; McGarry and Svenonius 1991; Micco 1991; O'Brien 1994; Rosenberg and Borgman 1992; Taylor 1984; Tillett 1991; Walker 1988; Walker and Hancock-Beaulieu 1991). Even in online shopping, inconsistent description of products is emerging as one of the greatest sources of searching difficulties (Lohse and Spiller 1998).

Semantic and Syntactic Knowledge

Conceptual knowledge of the information retrieval process is used to plan and refine searches. Semantic knowledge is understanding the operations available to execute a plan, such as choosing among types of capabilities that exist for searching. Syntactic knowledge is understanding the commands or actions in a specific system (Shneiderman 1992).

Expert searchers' semantic knowledge includes familiarity with capabilities common to most information systems, such as keyword searching, Boolean combinations, browsing thesauri, typical sorting and display options, and hypertext features. Expert searchers also are knowledgeable about capabilities that may be specific to types of systems (e.g., text, numeric, image, geographic) and about multiple implementations of each.

Before searching an unfamiliar digital library, experts usually analyze the documentation and other explanatory materials to determine its features, capabilities, and data representations, then plan their search accordingly. Because search capabilities operate somewhat differently on each system, experts know to examine general retrieval functions and database-specific features and may experiment to determine the interactions between them (Borgman 1996b).

In the earlier example of the search for "rockets" (Buckland et al. 1999), novices might do only a keyword search on the term "rockets," retrieving an incomplete and unrepresentative set of results. Experts, by comparison, usually would employ their semantic knowledge of vocabulary structure to explore the hierarchy of categories. Experts want to know how results were achieved, and judge the completeness and accuracy of results accordingly. For example, they need to know whether "rocket" is matching singular and plural forms and whether it is a preferred form that is picking up synonyms. Novices, lacking critical skills to assess how the results were achieved, are more likely to accept the results provided.

Because Boolean operators are implemented in a variety of ways, experts pay considerable attention to Boolean execution algorithms in judging the results from a system. For example, whereas some systems would treat a search for the book title "Usability Engineering" (Nielsen 1993), if entered in that form, as an implicit AND, other systems would treat it either as an implicit OR as a "bound phrase" in which both terms, in the specified order, must appear. If it were treated as AND, only documents containing both terms would be retrieved. This could be a large set if each term could appear anywhere in a full text document; it could be a much smaller set if the search were restricted to titles, for example. If it were treated as OR, a massive set could be retrieved, containing all the documents that contain either term. In view of the frequency of the term "engineering" in technical databases, this would be an unwelcome outcome. If the title were treated as a bound phrase, then only phrases with these two terms in this sequence would be retrieved—a desirable result for this particular search. Alternative treatments include retrieving documents with these words in this sequence but allowing a small number of terms to intervene, truncating each term such that matches on words beginning with "usab" or "engineer" are retrieved, or ignoring the second term and matching only on "usability."

The market for information systems has changed profoundly since the early days of information retrieval. When searching was conducted primarily by expert intermediaries, extensive documentation was provided on search features. Searchers learned how to manipulate systems precisely, employing semantic and syntactic knowledge of specific functions and knowledge of the comparative features of different systems. When the same database was available on multiple search services, searchers would select which to use on the basis of the search engine's capabilities and on the basis of price and other features, such as the availability and quality of documentation (Borgman, Moghdam, and Corbett 1984). Most digital libraries now are intended for end users, and only minimal documentation or training is provided. The exceptions are commercially provided scientific, technical, medical, and legal databases that are marketed to experts and professionals and priced accordingly. Specific information on how search functions are executed—once well documented—now may be considered proprietary, especially by Internet search engines. Even expert searchers cannot ascertain how the terms they enter are being treated, and thus they cannot tell how to assess the completeness or reliability of results. In the present situation, it is often difficult to obtain enough semantic or syntactic knowledge about a system to evaluate or compare results.

Technical Skills

Developing syntactic, semantic, and conceptual knowledge about the search process requires basic computing skills. Among the technical skills needed to search any digital library are being able to use computer keyboards and pointing devices, being familiar with the arrangement of screen displays, and knowing to press "return" or "enter" after typing a command. Sometimes users must recognize that an on-screen button such as "enter," "start," or "search" is the equivalent of pressing "return" or "enter." User interfaces have become more consistent in recent years with the adoption of interface design guidelines specific to hardware platforms and operating systems. At a minimum, users can expect consistency in such basic operations as opening and closing windows, pulling down menus, and cutting, copying, and pasting text or objects. Beyond core features, however, each system remains unique, and users still must learn where to point and click and what to type, in what place on the screen, and when. These technical skills are obvious to proficient computer users, but must be noted lest they be taken for granted in the general population. Upon first encounter with a computer, the uninitiated often start by pointing a mouse directly at the screen like a remote control device, for example. The need to move a mouse on a flat surface perpendicular to the plane in which its reflection occurs is counterintuitive and has few "real-world" analogues. Telephone help lines are plagued with new users who ask where the "any" key is located, in their attempts to follow instructions such as "press any key to begin." These are not isolated examples, as anyone who ever has staffed a computer help desk can confirm.

The global information infrastructure is intended for wide adoption in homes, schools, libraries, museums, offices, and other institutions that support diverse communities. The level of technical skills required for searching digital libraries varies widely by application, from most basic novice to highly advanced. As digital libraries are designed for more general audiences, a broader range of skill levels will have to be accommodated in many applications. In addition to people who lack general literacy skills, people with physical, sensory, or cognitive disabilities account for 15–20 percent of the US population (Computer Science and Telecommunications Board 1997a, p. 38). Many of these disabilities involve reading, vision, manual dexterity, or other factors that limit use of computers. Systems that can accommodate people with disabilities tend to be easier for most people to use (Computer Science and Telecommunications Board 1997).

Summary and Conclusions

As tasks become more complex, and as the relationship between task and action becomes more abstract, technologies become more difficult to use. "Real-world" analogies disappear, replaced by commands, menus, displays, keyboards, and pointing devices.

Minimum criteria for usability, as derived from research on human-computer interaction, are that systems should be easy to learn, tolerant of errors, flexible, adaptable, and appropriate and effective for the task. Though evidence is mounting for the economic value of usability evaluation and iterative design, applying these criteria to design is neither simple nor straightforward. Systems vary widely in audience and application, and the criteria must vary accordingly. The design of digital libraries can begin with available collections or with a user community to be served. In either case, design must be driven by questions of who will use the content, how, and why.

People make judgments about all aspects of seeking, using, and creating information. They judge the usability of systems, the value of the content retrieved, and its relevance to their problem. Although relevance is subjective, it remains a useful construct for framing searches. Search goals can stress precision (casting the net narrowly to find a few good matches), or they can stress recall (casting the net widely to find the greatest number of relevant matches).

Searching for information in digital libraries is a form of problem solving. The problem-solving process can be divided into four steps: understanding the problem, planning a solution, carrying out the plan, and checking the results. Several kinds of knowledge are involved in solving information problems. Conceptual knowledge is applied to framing problems and formulating plans for solving them. Semantic knowledge enables searchers to choose among operations for solving problems. Syntactic knowledge is used to execute the plan. Technical skills in the use of computers are needed to employ all the other knowledge. Experts plan their searches, and they reformulate them when too many, too few, or the wrong matches are retrieved. Novices, in contrast, often are stymied by unsuccessful searches. They abandon searches rather than reformulate them, and they show little evidence of planning or strategic actions.

Experts use a variety of strategies and tactics to overcome poor design in digital libraries. Novices do not. Nor will novices tolerate poor design if they have other alternatives. The audience for digital libraries has changed radically since the early days of information retrieval, from expert search intermediaries to "every citizen" who has access to the network. The next generation of digital libraries must serve a large and diverse community and provide a large and diverse collection of information resources. Though we do not yet know how to build such a system, a starting point is to employ what is known about information-related behavior in the systems of today.

6

Making Digital Libraries Easier to Use

Of all that is known about information-related behavior and about the difficulties of using today's digital libraries, what findings should be applied in designing tomorrow's digital libraries ? What findings are relevant to digital libraries that are larger in size, collect an expanding array of digital content, employ increasingly sophisticated technical capabilities, and serve an increasingly diverse international population?

Rather than begin afresh with each new generation of technology, designers of digital libraries should build upon experience with earlier technologies and upon past research. Revolutionary new designs rarely work in operational settings, because people need opportunities to shape the technology to their own needs and practices. "Radical incrementalism" is a more reliable design method, because adaptation requires "extensive fine tuning in the real world" (Brown 1996, p. 30). Systems can be refined in the laboratory to improve many aspects of usability, but the true test of usability is effectiveness in field situations. Knowledge gained from experimental and operational settings can be combined with theory-building research to make incremental improvements in the next generation of digital libraries and other information technologies.

This chapter identifies four trends in digital library design that build upon research findings in information-related behavior and knowledge organization. These trends are predicated on several assumptions. One assumption is that the number and variety of digital libraries available on a global information infrastructure will continue to grow. Another is that the number of people with access to computer networks, both domestically and internationally, will continue to rise rapidly. Similarly, network capacity will increase quickly, as will the price-performance ratio of computing technology. However, the actual trajectory of these developments is subject to many factors that cannot be predicted. And although the price of computer workstations is decreasing, hardware and software represent only 4–30 percent of the total cost of ownership, depending on how these figures are computed (Barnes 1997; Bits 1998; Hudson 1996; Slater 1997; Strassmann 1997), and thus the true costs of information technology are not necessarily dropping. Patterns of access will change as people utilize simple "network access only" computers and mobile or otherwise "untethered" devices, in addition to desktop and laptop workstations. Network congestion is leading to differential pricing models for access, which will influence who uses what network resources, at what cost, and at what time (Lynch 1998). All these factors will affect the design of digital libraries.

These are the four trends discussed in this chapter:

from metadata to data   Early information retrieval systems consisted primarily of metadata that described offline, physical resources. The trend is toward digital libraries of full content, with associated metadata.

from independent to linked systems   Early systems were designed to stand alone and to be searched independently. New systems are being designed for distributed environments. Now links can be built between digital libraries, between documents in multiple digital libraries, and between digital libraries and other applications.

from searching to navigation   Query-based searching is complemented by navigational approaches that take advantage of features specific to the medium (text, images, colors, sounds, etc.) and to networked environments.

from individual to group processes   Most research on information-related behavior has focused on actions of the individual, independent of the group processes from which information needs often arise. The new challenge is to design digital libraries that are an integral part of group practice and that support work that is distributed across computer networks.

I will address these trends individually, identifying research questions to guide the design, development, and deployment of the next generation of digital libraries. The discussion draws on several other recent research agendas related to the social aspects of digital libraries (Bishop and Star 1996; Borgman et al. 1996; Computer Science and Telecommunications Board 1997a). The chapter does not provide a comprehensive review of this body of literature. Rather, the goal is to explicate the issues and illustrate them with selected research results. In addition to the sources specifically cited in this and other chapters, a wide range of other notable research exists on these topics (Adler 1940; Allen 1969; Allen 1991; Anderson, Galvin, and Giguere 1994; Baker and Lysiak 1985; Chen and Dhar 1990; Coyle 1984; Dolby, Forsyth, and Resnikoff 1969; Dumais and Landauer 1982; Furnas et al. 1987; Janes and Rosenfeld 1996; Lancaster 1992; Larson 1994; Levy and Marshall 1995; Lynch and Preston 1990; Pejtersen and Austin 1984; Richardson 1995; Shute and Smith 1993; Sloan 1991; Tagliacozzo, Kochen, and Rosenberg 1970; Turtle and Croft 1991, 1992; Wanting 1984; Wilson 1988).

From Metadata to Data

Research Issues

Earlier generations of digital libraries consisted largely of textual metadata describing offline, hard-copy materials such as journal articles, books, court cases, legislation, memoranda, and personal papers. The primary thrust of current digital library design is to maintain full content online. New materials are being created in digital forms, older materials are being digitized, storage costs are declining, and processing power is improving. As a result, full-content digital libraries have become technically and economically feasible. New forms of organization, user interfaces, and functional capabilities are being developed to address the changing environment for information systems.

Digital libraries containing only metadata continue to be valuable for identifying and locating offline sources. Many resources will continue to exist only offline, such as the holdings of libraries and archives that may have been collected over a period of centuries. No matter how inexpensive the technology becomes, scanning and digitizing will continue to be expensive owing to the manual labor involved in retrieving physical objects and in turning fragile pages. Even for the materials whose representations are available online, the metadata are essential for locating the originals.

Metadata provide information about resources that is necessary for understanding the content of those resources (such as who created them, and when), and for making use of them (such as the format in which they are stored, and the ownership of the intellectual property). Metadata can serve as the "Rosetta Stone" to decode information objects and to transform them into knowledge (Gilliland-Swetland 1998). Metadata also are needed to describe entire digital libraries, and to identify and locate collections of resources on a topic or relationships between resources. The availability of full content online, the shift from static documents to dynamic documents, and the distributed knowledge networks made possible by access in a global information infrastructure are forcing us to rethink the relationship between data and metadata.

Research Agenda

These are a sampling of the research questions to be addressed in the transition from metadata to data. Many other questions arise within the bounds of individual disciplines, and yet others will arise from application areas, such as business and industry sectors, government, medicine, law, arts, and humanities.

Text-Retrieval Mechanisms

Until recently, information retrieval consisted almost entirely of textual searching on metadata. Even when digital libraries contain objects in other forms, such as images and numeric data, the primary access may be via textual metadata that describe and represent those objects. When one is searching full-text content, rather than metadata, the characteristics of the data and the search process change. A comparison of the assumptions and characteristics between these two situations offers a means to identify the requirements for new forms of digital libraries.

In digital libraries that contain only metadata, the metadata usually consist of terms carefully chosen to describe and represent some document or object. Metadata on published materials, for example, usually consist of bibliographic descriptions (e.g., author, title, date, place of publication, physical characteristics) plus subject or index terms, and may include an abstract summarizing the content. As a result, each term in the record (with the exception of "stop words" such as articles and conjunctions) carries significant meaning about the document or object. When the full content of documents is searched, rather than just metadata, this assumption becomes problematic. One term among five in a title or among 200 in an abstract is more likely to be relevant than the same term found among 10,000 words in a journal article, much less among 100,000 words in a book. For the same reasons, Boolean operators are less useful in searching full content. If two or more terms appear in the same metadata record, the record is more likely to be relevant than if the same two or more terms appear somewhere in an article, a book, or a report.

In the 25 years or so that full-text databases have been available on commercial systems, many approaches have been tried. Most involve action on the searcher's part to constrain the matching of terms to specific fields in a record, to constrain the distance between term occurrences (e.g., within five words, within the same sentence, or within the same paragraph), or otherwise weight the match; or automatic techniques that weight terms by location in the record, frequency of occurrence in the record or in the file, or some other features. Manual approaches give more control to the searcher but require more semantic and syntactic knowledge about searching and about each digital library being searched. Automatic approaches require less operational knowledge but can produce unpredictable results.

Full-text search techniques continue to improve, but the tradeoffs in power and ease of use remain (Korfhage 1997; Lesk 1997a). More research is needed on these tradeoffs, with the goal of simple interfaces that are easily learned and relearned by novice and intermittent users while providing sophisticated capabilities for expert searchers.

Multimedia Information Retrieval

A growing amount of content in all media is being "born digital," and content that originated in other forms is being digitized. The costs of storage and processing are decreasing, bandwidth to transmit digital content is increasing, and representation standards are becoming more widely adopted. As a result, digital library technology is becoming technically and economically feasible for capturing, storing, distributing, and maintaining multimedia content. However, the technology for storing and displaying multimedia content is improving faster than the ability to search for that content.

Despite the problems with vocabulary control, text is at least partially self-describing. It is possible to search for words in textual documents, even with minimal indexing. The same cannot be said for sounds or images. A digital library containing any form of electronic records can be treated as a textual system if it contains only textual metadata describing other media, but this approach fails to take full advantage of the richness of the content.

Owing to the variety of possible interpretations, describing sounds and images with words is yet more difficult than describing textual documents. Photos, for example, are sometimes of interest because of who is represented and sometimes of interest because of who took the picture—neither of which can be generated automatically in most cases. Images can be described by features such as the subjects they contain (e.g., people, trees, buildings), colors, genre (e.g., nature scene, theater, crowds), size, date created, or creator. Some progress is being made in automatic recognition of such features as presence of human faces, presence of specific animals, and presence of certain shapes (Lesk 1997a; Pentland 1996). Similarly, recordings of music, spoken words, sound effects and other audio usually must be augmented with textual descriptions. Progress is being made in speech recognition to identify words and phrases, which then can be converted to text for searching. This is an imperfect process, as is exemplified by the aural confusion between "How to recognize speech" and "How to wreck a nice beach." Other content, when available, can be used to improve voice recognition. A notable example is the research at Carnegie Mellon University that combines voice recognition of newscasters' speech with text from closed captioning of the broadcasts (Wactlar et al. 1999). The same project is experimenting with voice input, converting the searcher's spoken words into text that can be searched against the text in the video collections.

Present retrieval mechanisms tend to be specific to certain media and certain applications. Methods that work for sound retrieval in one application are difficult to transfer to other applications, much less to video or graphics, for example. Designing true multimedia searching capabilities is among the great design challenges for digital libraries (Croft 1995).

Dynamic Documents

Most efforts in designing and maintaining digital libraries have addressed static documents (e.g., published materials or final forms of documents, whether text, audio, video, or other media). The next challenge is to describe, represent, and organize dynamic documents (e.g., continuously changing online versions). The metadata that describe dynamic documents must somehow distinguish between versions while identifying and maintaining relationships among versions of materials that are substantially the same. For example, when locating a document it is helpful to know that prior and subsequent versions also may exist, and that the content may exist in substantially similar forms that may be equivalent for some purposes (e.g., a transcript and an audio version of a speech; theater, broadcast, and airplane versions of a film; a conference paper and subsequent versions of a journal article). Determining whether versions of a document are substantially the same is often a matter of interpretation and may require information that is external to the documents themselves, all of which complicates the creation of standards and practices for document representation (Lynch 1993a,b).

Knowledge Organization for Diverse Communities

"Knowledge organization" is a general term that encompasses the many theories and practices involved in describing, representing, and organizing information. Multiple disciplines and professions approach these issues from different perspectives, such as the characteristics of the materials themselves, human behavior in categorizing and classifying objects and concepts, linguistic relationships among descriptive terms (e.g., broader, narrower, related term structures, faceted structures), and characteristics of the role or actions of the materials being described and organized. Each of these approaches, and many others, can be effective, depending on the collection, the content, and the community served by the digital library.

When the design of digital libraries was left primarily to information specialists, and when digital libraries contained primarily metadata, standard structures were more easily imposed on user communities. Now communities are creating and managing their own full-content digital libraries, and they may not defer to experts on knowledge organization. Organizing mechanisms are needed that can be employed by people who are specialists in the content of the collections, even if they are not specialists in information management. The resulting digital libraries must be useful to the user community and yet be sufficiently standardized that their contents can be migrated to new generations of technology as they appear. The Dublin Core is intended for use by diverse communities and for all manner of content. Among the primary goals for data and metadata are that they be transportable among applications and sustainable across technology generations.

Human vs. Automated Indexing

The challenge for knowledge organization in the transition from metadata to data is to identify when automated indexing is adequate and when human indexing is necessary. This can be done by studying how humans describe and organize materials, by identifying techniques that can be modeled in automated indexing, by analyzing how the productivity of human indexers can be improved through automated assistance, and by extending the known techniques of automated indexing.

Theory and practice for human indexing of materials has evolved over centuries by multiple information professions. Indexing methods now exist for describing, representing, and organizing materials in all media. Not only can skilled catalogers, indexers, abstracters, archivists, knowledge engineers, and other information professionals extract the meaningful terms or characteristics present in a document; they can augment the document with descriptors that supply context or interpretation. Often they assign descriptive terms from controlled vocabularies (general thesauri such as the Library of Congress Subject Headings, or specialized thesauri in fields such as medicine, engineering, biology, and business) or codes from classification systems, both of which serve to position the document in the larger information space. Professionals can add valuable metadata that may not be present in the document itself, such as who created or originated the document, who owns the intellectual property rights, how the document was created, and in what format it is stored. However, human indexing is labor intensive, time consuming, and expensive.

Computers can index most data that are contained in a document, including words and phrases, numeric data, size, color, and format, and can do so quickly and inexpensively. Human indexers are needed to interpret meaning and context. Without some human intervention, searching by text contained in artifacts is difficult due to the variation in uses of terms in different contexts (Paris, the city; Paris, the god; plaster of Paris), variation in terms for the same concept by different communities (e.g., botanists vs. gardeners; scientists vs. schoolchildren; physicians or lawyers vs. laypersons), and the variety of terms by which any concept is labeled. However, human indexing is too time consuming and expensive to be a complete solution. Machine indexing of identifiable features can be augmented by human indexing of aspects that require interpretation and judgment.

From Independent to Linked Systems

The transition from independent to linked systems raises a variety of challenges in organizing content, in supporting user communities, and in maintaining relationships between applications.

Research Issues

The set of digital libraries on distributed networks can be viewed collectively as a global digital library. In turn, a global digital library needs organizing mechanisms and searching capabilities that enable people to search this vast information space. Capabilities are needed to search multiple databases concurrently, to discover and locate individual digital libraries worthy of deeper exploration, to follow links between systems, and to trace paths between documents within individual systems. Similarly, by taking an "information life cycle" approach, content becomes transferable between digital libraries and other applications. The challenges are to design new representations, organizational mechanisms, and user interfaces in support of these links and to manage information throughout its life cycle.

An important goal for network architecture is to support linking, portable data structures, data exchange, and interoperability among systems and services (Libicki 1995a,b). Developments such as layered client-server models that can exchange data across different hardware and software platforms, and standards for encoding text and images, are making it possible to exchange data and to search remote systems with greater reliability and greater functionality. Despite the progress in standards for networked data exchange, however, full interoperability remains a distant goal (Lynch and Garcia-Molina 1995; Paepcke et al. 1998). Some of the problems are due to the wide variety of hardware platforms and software applications (which often span several generations of technology), some are due to the lack of appropriate software to translate between formats, some are due to usability problems in user interfaces, and others are due to lack of adequate skills on the part of users. Yet others are due to social, cultural, and policy differences that may be beyond the scope of technical solutions.

Research Agenda
Tailoring vs. Interoperability
Determining the appropriate balance between tailoring systems to communities and maintaining interoperability among systems is perhaps the most fundamental challenge in moving from independent to linked systems. On the one hand, the description, representation, and organization of digital libraries should be tailored to the community served. On the other hand, digital libraries should be interoperable, such that what exists on a topic can be identified regardless of location, format, language, or other characteristics. At the extreme of tailoring, the result would be idiosyncratic systems of little value outside their local context. At the extreme of interoperability, the result would be highly standardized systems that might serve no application well. Most of the research questions identified in this section reflect some aspect of this tradeoff.

Organizing within Digital Libraries
Challenges in organizing the content in digital libraries have arisen throughout this book, in the context of intellectual access (chapter 3), in the context of conceptual and semantic knowledge (chapter 5), and in the transition from metadata to data (in this chapter). The goal of most organizational schemes is to impose internal consistency on individual digital libraries. Concepts are mapped to a common term or category ("collocated"); broader, narrower, and related term relationships may be identified; and facets or other relationships may be specified. In the "rockets" example in chapter 5, relationships among many aspects of rocket products and rocket science were mapped.

Most organizational schemes were designed to link content relationships between documents, or between the metadata that describe documents, within a digital library. These schemes are being extended and others created to represent relationships among digital items such as whole/part, same origin of content in different medium (e.g., book, script, film, play), multiple instances of an artifact, original and translation, and similar content in multiple formats (text, numeric, images, audio, video), and to support hybrid digital libraries that combine metadata and data (Borgman et al. 1996; Leazer 1994; Tillett 1992).

Organizing between Digital Libraries

Organizing information between digital libraries takes place at two levels: Mechanisms that enable searching multiple digital libraries at once, bridging the organizing structures of each; and mechanisms that enable links between documents to cross system boundaries.

Many models exist for organizing materials in a single collection, but no similar model for organizing resources across multiple collections (Lynch 1993a). New methods are needed to bridge the organizing schemes that provide consistency within digital libraries but that may produce inconsistencies between them. Many factors introduce inconsistencies, one of which is perspectives inherent in schemes applied by different information professions, such as librarians, archivists, and curators. Digital libraries organized from each of these perspectives may contain related information, yet the information is structured and organized so differently that it can be hard to identify related documents.

For example, consider the variety of digital libraries that might contain information about the artist August Renoir. Library catalogs contain metadata on documents discussing Renoir's life and work, and on documents such as art books that include images of his paintings and drawings. Registrarial systems of museums that own works by Renoir contain records describing those works. Information systems of archives that hold letters written by Renoir include metadata describing them in a form known as "finding aids." A records management system of a gallery or auction house selling works by Renoir would include metadata describing those works. The catalog of a publisher selling Renoir reproductions licensed for sale would include images of those reproductions and metadata describing them. Any or all of these data, and more, may be of interest to a student, a scholar, a tourist, or a marketer, and creating links between the digital libraries and between the related documents would be of considerable value. One approach to the problem of varying data structures is to employ a common set of data elements, such as the Dublin Core, with additional elements suited to each application.

Another factor involved in bridging multiple digital libraries is the variety of terminology used. Each community has its own ways of expressing concepts. Multiple communities use different words to describe the same concept; conversely, the same word may mean different things to different communities. Any two terms are synonyms only in certain contexts. "Author" and "creator" may be synonymous when referring to the originator of a document, but the terms would not be equivalent in religious contexts. One might attend a "film" or a "movie," but in technical contexts film would be distinguished from video and digital formats. A search on "film" also may retrieve chemical compositions of different film media, depending on the collection.

A promising approach to the synonym problem makes use of "vocabulary switching" databases that consist of clusters of related terms from multiple disciplines and contexts (Atkins and Ostrow 1989; Horsnell 1988; Schatz 1997). Early research on vocabulary switching relied on manually constructed clusters; more recent research is experimenting with automatic generation of clusters. Results indicate that automatic switching of terms is risky, as subtle differences in meaning can produce such unpredictable matches that users' faith in the system is undermined. The technique is more effective when employed to guide the search process, providing users with a choice of alternate terms from which to choose.

Another element that complicates bridging between digital libraries is the level of representation. For example, text can be stored as characters or as images, and it can be searched by individual word or by metadata describing the image. Geophysical data might be organized at a level of detail that represents individual plants and buildings, or at the level of towns and cities (Hill, Frew, and Zheng 1999). Photographic images might each be described by multiple terms, or thousands of images might be described collectively by a single finding aid. Subject vocabularies may include hierarchical relationships, but documents may be described at the lowest possible level of detail and searchable only by the low-level terms. Few current systems are designed to retrieve narrower terms in response to a search for a broader term further up the hierarchy, for example.

Linking Digital Libraries and Other Applications

These are the early stages of transferring content from one step in the information life cycle to another. Technologies exist for creating and authoring text, images, and music, but few are available for organizing, indexing, storing, or retrieving the products of those technologies directly. Word processing files, for example, usually require manual markup for typesetting and further manual markup for indexing and retrieval in digital libraries. Even more intervention may be necessary for images, audio, and video files.

Linking digital libraries with other applications to support the information life cycle introduces several compatibility problems. One is compatibility between related application software (e.g., word processing, spreadsheets, databases) on the same hardware-and-operating-system platform (e.g., Macintosh, Windows, NT, Unix, Linux). Users with the same versions of software (e.g., Word 7.0) on the same platform may exchange files easily, but those with different versions (e.g., Word 6.0 and Word 7.0) may not. Conflicts between proprietary software packages on the same hardware-and-software platform are also problematic. Users with the most recent versions of competing products (e.g., Word and WordPerfect) often can exchange files by exporting to the competing format, but the more distance between versions (e.g., a new version of one package and a two-year old version of another) the less likely it is that exchanges will be successful. A third compatibility problem involves users with the same software package for different platforms (e.g., WordPerfect for Windows and WordPerfect for Macintosh). If the versions are current, they should be able to share files; however, compatibilities decrease with the age of software versions. Some of these compatibility problems can be overcome by converting files to an intermediate format, such as "rich text format" (rtf), or "page description format" (pdf). Intermediate formats do not always produce reliable exchanges, and some of them are proprietary. These are just a few examples of the compatibility issues involved in data exchange. As people rely more heavily on exchanging files as part of daily commerce and communication, and with capturing content in electronic form and maintaining it throughout its life cycle, standards and practices for interoperability will be increasingly important.

Legacy Data and Migration

It is rare for all the information an institution manages to be "born digital." Even when such is the case, it is unlikely that all the information will be in a consistent format. Constructing a digital library from multiple sources often requires that some of the content be restructured, reorganized, or otherwise converted to a common form. Often the content is in another physical form, such as paper, film, microfilm, or vinyl, in which case the content must be transferred to the desired form. The means depends on the originating and target formats. Clean text can be scanned and then converted by optical character recognition; degraded or handwritten text may need to be rekeyed. Sounds recorded on vinyl can be played and re-recorded digitally.

Any data not in a desirable form for a current application are considered "legacy data." Paper records are legacy data when computer-readable records are required for a digital library. Automated records are legacy data when they are in a structure or a format that is incompatible with the requirements of a new system on which they must operate. Legacy data are a major concern for digital library applications. Converting and restructuring data can be expensive, depending on the amount of manual labor required. Once in digital form, the data may be "migrated" (i.e., transferred) to other hardware and software multiple times, because data often outlive the technology by decades, or even centuries. Decisions about metadata, content representation, intellectual access, and organization should be made with a long view in mind.

Maintaining digital libraries over multiple generations of technology is a challenge when systems are independent. When they are linked over distributed networks, the links must be maintained too. Similar challenges arise when data are merged from multiple applications, platforms, or earlier systems. Minor variations such as punctuation and forms of names and dates determine whether records can be linked or merged automatically. Personal names are an obvious example (Borgman and Siegfried 1992). Some systems use one field; others use two (given name and family name); others assign middle names and initials to a separate field, with a fourth field for titles and prefixes such as Mr., Ms., Mrs., Miss, Dr., and Prof. If the full name is in one field, automatically determining which is the family name is risky because of variations in name order. In some parts of the world (e.g., Asia and Central Europe), family names are listed first; in other regions (e.g., the United States, Western Europe), given names are stated first. Parsing multipart names into separate fields also is problematic, owing to variations in practice and inconsistencies in recording names (e.g., Pedro Felix Hernandez-Ramos, Pedro Hernandez-R., Pete Hernandez; Mary Ann Smith-Jones, Mary Smith Jones, Mary S. Jones, Maryann Jones, Mary A. Smith).

Rarely are one-to-one mappings between fields possible, for one application makes finer distinctions than another, each of which has implications for some related system with which it must interoperate. Interpretations of content for each field and local practices vary accordingly. If data have been created over a long period of time, they usually reflect many generations of rules and practices for representation. Even when standards for data representation are faithfully employed, differences in interpretation and application of rules and differences in system implementation make exchanging or merging records a nontrivial task. Standards and practices for content representation and data migration are a continuing challenge. Research on methods to construct and maintain links through generations of technology will be another area of growing interest.

From Searching to Navigation

Research Issues
In the transition from digital libraries of metadata to digital libraries of full content, classical retrieval methods are becoming less effective. Similarly, in the transition from independent to linked systems, query-based searching is becoming less useful. Although structured queries are effective for some types of searches, browsing is a more flexible and adaptable means of searching than is submitting queries, and is well suited to distributed environments. The word "browsing" has many definitions (Marchionini 1995). Dimensions of browsing include scanning, intention, goals, and knowledge (Chang and Rice 1993). "Navigation" is used here as a collective term for browsing, for other forms of scanning through information, and for following paths within and between systems.

People often arrive at digital libraries with "anomalous states of knowledge" (Belkin, Oddy, and Brooks 1982a,b), rather than with well-formed statements of information needs. Information-related problems often are poorly defined, which makes query formulation difficult. In contrast, browsing enables people to recognize relevant information when they see it. Browsing and navigation features can enable users to follow paths from one related resource to another, whether from metadata to data, from one version of a document to another, or from one document related to another by subject, creator, owner, price, rights availability, features, or any other attribute that can be described and represented. Intelligent agents could follow these paths on a user's behalf, explore a collection of digital libraries scattered over a global information infrastructure, and return with a set of resources for the user to consider.

Despite the advantages of browsing over query formulation, the paradox of information retrieval remains: One must describe information that one does not have. The searcher still must establish a starting point for the navigation process, which requires selecting terms and features that describe the information resources sought. The searcher also must specify a starting point in one or more digital libraries, or the characteristics of target collections. Thus, the accuracy of the starting point for browsing is a major determinant of a search's effectiveness and efficiency.

Research Agenda
Navigation as Natural Behavior
Navigation and browsing appear to be natural behaviors based on two complementary principles of cognition: that people learn by making associations with prior knowledge and that people usually find it easier to recognize information presented to them than to recall it from memory (Anderson 1990). Systems that require the user to enter keywords rely on recall knowledge, since they require the user to generate terms. Systems that present an organized framework of terms from which the user may select rely on recognition knowledge. Recognition-based systems are particularly effective in subject areas that are beyond the user's everyday knowledge, as Borgman et al. (1995) found with a digital library of science materials for children.

Browsing and navigation also make a system's features more visible. Rather than having to examine documentation to identify a system's search capabilities, users can select from an array of choices: functions, terms, related documents, or related digital libraries. However, browsing and navigation are not direct substitutes for query-based searching. These approaches appear to be more effective in small, focused collections than in large, diverse systems, in which the choices may be overwhelming. Browsing also is better suited for ill-defined questions (for which exploration is often helpful) than for well-defined problems (for which a query statement may be more efficient). More research is needed to determine when browsing and navigation are most effective, to identify methods to assist in natural exploratory behavior, and to develop methods for assisting users in planning searches and in reframing unsuccessful searches.

Lost in Information Space

Among the greatest difficulties in searching for information is reframing the search when too many, too few, or irrelevant results are retrieved. Browsing overcomes the reframing problem partially by enabling users to follow paths rather than to submit queries that return sets of results. Even so, searchers still may have to browse through large sets of documents or long lists of options they have found by following links. Hypertext—which enables users to follow nonlinear paths, such as the links embedded in the World Wide Web—introduced new difficulties, however. Early research on hypertext revealed that users got "lost" in the system (Conklin 1987; Dillon 1994; McKnight, Dillon, and Richardson 1991). Various approaches to improving navigation in hypertext have been tried, including geospatial metaphors such as maps and signposts (McKnight, Dillon, and Richardson 1991). More recent research suggests that hypertext's effectiveness for learning and comprehension is limited, and that its value depends on individual abilities and learning styles (Dillon and Gabbard 1998).

Thus, the difficulties of search planning and reformulation exist in both navigational and query-based digital libraries. More research is needed on navigation, way-finding, and browsing through large and rich information spaces.

User Interface Design

Query-based interfaces often are simple and terse, whereas browsing-oriented interfaces are more richly structured, typically with multiple windows, menus, and other options. Color and position on the computer screen are used to distinguish among features. How information is presented or delivered will influence how it is received and interpreted (Borgman et al. 1996). Browsing-oriented interfaces work best when they are tailored to the content of a digital library and to the purposes of those who search it.

The design of a user interface for a browsing-oriented system must balance the tailoring-versus-interoperability tradeoffs discussed above. Tools for navigating through text should take advantage of textual characteristics; tools for navigating through music or videos should take advantage of their format and content characteristics. However, the more interfaces are tailored to content, the more likely it will be that searchers will encounter a new, different, and often foreign interface for each digital library. Similarly, people vary widely in their information-seeking habits, preferences, skills, and abilities. For example, those with strong spatial skills are likely to be adept at navigating spatially organized interfaces; people with weak spatial skills may be confused by them (Egan 1988). A single, simple user interface that will support effective navigation through text, images, audio, video, and numeric data is not yet feasible. A larger challenge is to design user interfaces that will help members of diverse communities with wide ranges of interests, purposes, and skills to navigate through mixed content.

Intelligent Assistance

Since the advent of graphical user interfaces, the dominant interface paradigm has been "direct manipulation" in which the user is always in control (Shneiderman 1987). Users manipulate objects on a screen, and the results of their actions are obvious and immediate. As applications become richer and more complex, the array of objects to manipulate grows and interfaces often become more complex. An alternative to direct manipulation for large and complex environments is "indirect management" in which "autonomous agents" collaborate with and assist the user (Maes 1994).

The indirect management approach is promising (although not without its detractors), but it is limited by the ability to diagnose a user's needs, interpret them well enough to act on them, and present a clear and helpful response (Computer Science and Telecommunications Board 1997a). Work on intelligent agents and related work on user models dates back to the 1970s or earlier. Not surprisingly, agents have proved most effective in narrow subject areas and with well-defined problems. General-purpose agents that can interpret ill-defined problems to be searched in complex environments such as a global information infrastructure are not yet viable. The challenge is to determine what tasks, under what circumstances, can be assisted by agents, and how to design user interfaces accordingly.

Balancing Human and Machine Control

Whether a user is submitting search queries or navigating through an information space, and whether by direct manipulation or indirect management, the fundamental challenge is to determine the appropriate balance of control between human and machine. These tradeoffs are part of a larger debate about the relationship of humans to technology. An underlying issue is the degree to which they should be trained to use "good," "effective," "efficient," or "productivity-enhancing" technology vs. the degree to which people should employ technology to assist them to be more effective, efficient, productive, or knowledgeable, or to make their work, education, or leisure more enjoyable. The debate can be informed by empirical data about performance and evaluation measures, but much of the discussion remains a matter of philosophy and opinion.

Navigating within and between digital libraries distributed across a global information infrastructure brings these debates into sharper focus. The world of digital libraries and information seeking is too complex and too messy to be delegated primarily to automated intelligent assistants. Too much human interpretation is required. In any case, better use of human interpretation can be made by relieving information overload where that is practicable, and by delegating those decisions that can be delegated. The challenge in seeking a balance for any community or collection is to distinguish between technical tradeoffs and larger philosophical issues.

From Individual to Group Processes

Research Issues

Whether conducted in print or electronic environments, most studies of information-related behavior focus on the activities of individuals in creating, using, or seeking information. When studied in library contexts, research tends to be bounded from the time one enters a building or an electronic system to the time one departs the premises or signs off the system. A few studies have addressed how people organize information in their offices and how they handle information resources throughout the work day, using the individual as the unit of analysis. Some researchers study how scholars collaborate in producing joint publications; others look at how scholars seek information in support of present and future projects (Case 1986, 1991; Case, Borgman, and Meadow 1986; Kwasnik 1991).

Despite the focus on the individual, most information-related activities involve group processes. People work in teams, negotiate with customers and clients, correspond with friends and colleagues, learn in classrooms, interact with their families, and spend time in leisure activities with other people. Few information-related activities are truly conducted alone. Questions asked by an individual often arise from interaction within a group. People read to one another and give oral presentations; they also read in private. Information resources sought and retrieved by one person may be annotated or otherwise adapted and passed on to others; any document may be handled or acted on by many people through the stages of creation, use, and disposition. As documents increasingly become mutable, malleable, and mobile, their use must be placed in social context (Bishop and Star 1996).

Collaboration is an essential part of work, education, and leisure, as studies conducted in communication, education, sociology, and other fields confirm. Yet why are group processes not considered in most studies of behavior related to the use of digital libraries? One reason is that individuals are easier to study. The activities of one person at one computer are easily bounded. However, the line between the individual and the group is becoming less distinct as more activities are conducted via computer networks. Groups share information resources online and hold discussions online, whether synchronously or asynchronously. Individual and group activities alternate between digital libraries and other applications on personal computers, intranets, and the Internet. The trend is away from using information technology to support isolated individual access to computer networks, and toward knowledge networking, in which fuller advantage is taken of the collective information resources and talent available on a global information infrastructure. Although more study of individual behavior is desirable, research also should incorporate social context and group processes involved in information-related behavior.

Research Agenda
Accounting for Social Context

What is studied about the information-related behavior of groups and how it is studied depends on many factors, such as whether the goal is the design of one or more digital libraries, incorporating digital libraries into work, education, and leisure practices, or building links between digital libraries and other applications. The results of analyzing human activities can influence design in at least three ways: by discovering which functionalities user communities regard as priorities, by developing basic analytical categories that influence the design of system architecture, and by generating integrated design processes that include empirical research and user community participation throughout the design cycle (Borgman et al. 1996). Bishop and Star (1996, pp. 369–372) propose a number of research questions related to issues of the social context of digital libraries, such as, "How do creators, librarians, and users collaborate in creating, finding, and using digital library documents?" "How does work change with the introduction of digital library access in the work place and the home and in the traditional library?" "How do digital documents structure social interactions (e.g., make, maintain and differentiate social groups)?" and "How do organizations make digital libraries usable or unusable for their members?"

Collaboration between People and Computers

As people increasingly use computers to communicate and collaborate with others, human-computer interaction becomes more than a relationship between one person and one computer. Rather, it becomes a set of relationships between many people and many computers. The Computer Science and Telecommunications Board (1997a) of the (US) National Research Council identified research on multiperson, multimachine groups as a top priority, recommending work on systems design and on theories of communication and collaboration in computer-mediated environments. More research is required that focuses on computer networks as a medium over which individuals and groups communicate. This work, in turn, should lead to better models of interaction between individuals and computers. Any research that results in improving people's ability to articulate their information needs should lead to better interfaces for digital libraries and to more effective autonomous agents that can assist in activities throughout the information life cycle.

Tailoring to Communities

Digital library design involves tradeoffs between tailoring systems to the community served and interoperating with other digital libraries and other applications. Whether design begins with content or community, relationships between users and capabilities must be considered. If communities are small and homogeneous, it is easier to identify who, how, and why information resources will be used than if the communities to be served are large and heterogeneous. Individual communities may be multicultural and multilingual, may include a range of skills from untrained novices to specialists, from one-time users to regular users with extensive searching expertise.

The underlying challenge in designing for a community lies in defining its membership. "Community" is a contested term, having many definitions in the social sciences; it usually implies some sense of interpersonal networks, common interests, or common activities, and it may or may not imply residence in a common physical locality (Wellman 1998). A community is generally larger than a family unit or working group but smaller than a city. In the context of a user community for a digital library, community members are united by their interest in the content and collections, but they may not have a social network (they do not necessarily know each other), nor are they necessarily in the same physical location.

In view of the wide range of digital library applications and user communities to be served, one set of challenges lies in determining what social, demographic, or other community variables should be considered in the design of a digital library. At a high level, the focus is on functionality and on analytical categories. Functionality may include retrieval mechanisms, navigation tools, display capabilities, import and export of content to other applications, and various user-interface features. Analytical categories include aspects of organizing knowledge, intellectual content, access points, and hierarchies. Different communities may need information resources stored at different levels of detail. Some individuals will prefer searching by image, others by textual descriptions.

Increasingly, digital libraries will be designed by and for communities of users without the assistance of information professionals. Those designers may be experts in the content and in the information-related behavior of the community but may lack skills in applying that knowledge to selecting, collecting, and organizing information resources, to designing user interfaces, or to other aspects of computer systems design. Thus, it is necessary to identify design principles that can be employed not only by information-systems professionals but also by user communities designing digital libraries on their own behalf.

Spanning Community Boundaries

The converse of designing for independent communities is making digital libraries useful to multiple communities. The same content may be pertinent to multiple audiences, each of which uses different terminology, has different levels of knowledge about the content, and has different requirements for organizing and navigating that content. For example, current legal information systems are predicated on technical knowledge of the law, yet nonlawyers also need legal materials. The same is true of most digital libraries containing medical and health information. Similarly, scientific data collected by and for scientists is of considerable value for business, government, and educational purposes. Scientists require a finely detailed organizational structure for these data and employ highly specialized terminology in describing content. Making the same digital libraries useful to businesspeople, teachers, and students requires simpler analytical structures, more common vocabulary, and user interfaces that demand minimal domain knowledge.

Digital libraries should span community boundaries both for economic reasons and for reasons of resource discovery. Digital libraries are expensive to construct and maintain; thus, it may be more economical to make one system available to multiple communities than to create multiple systems. Conversely, when people are seeking information on a topic, they may need to discover information resources located in digital libraries designed for a different community, and those digital libraries may be organized and represented in unfamiliar ways. Issues of linking digital libraries and of navigating across the boundaries of systems arise in spanning communities. Research is needed on bridging vocabularies, a common core of metadata, multivalent documents, multiple user interfaces, and other methods of achieving data exchange, portability, and interoperability (Bishop and Star 1996; Libicki 1995a,b).

Spanning Task Boundaries

As digital and analog technologies converge on the desktop, the laptop, the palmtop, and elsewhere in buildings and on bodies, the flow of information among tasks and activities becomes more seamless. Information resources captured from a digital library become input to other tasks and tools, and information generated from other tasks and tools becomes input for searching and navigating digital libraries. The fluidity of actions and the convergence of technologies create design challenges in determining what functions and capabilities to include in digital libraries and what functions to defer to other systems.

In chapter 2, a middle ground was established. There it was claimed that digital libraries available on computer networks could be considered together as a global digital library, and in turn that a global digital library is more than a set of organized collections and less than a global information infrastructure. A GII will provide access to information in a broader sense than will a global digital library, because a GII will support a wide range of information processes that do not involve information products directly. Thus, a distinction is made between obtaining information products in a useful form—a requirement for information access—and the capabilities for using those products. The continuing challenge in digital library design is to provide a coherent view of a collection, with content tailored to a community, while providing links to other digital libraries and to applications that support other tasks.

Summary and Conclusions

Correcting the known deficiencies in today's digital libraries is only a partial solution to making digital libraries easier to use. The next generation of digital libraries will have richer content, be linked to other digital libraries and other applications, be navigable in more flexible and adaptable ways than query searching, and be set in a larger social context. They will operate on a faster, higher capacity, and more widely distributed global information infrastructure than is available today. As the scope and the context of digital libraries evolve, new research questions must be addressed. This chapter outlined a research agenda for making the next generation of digital libraries better suited to people's information-related behavior in work, education, and leisure contexts and thus easier to use. The agenda is based on issues raised throughout this book, complemented by research agendas for digital libraries and information access recently proposed by others.

The research agenda is organized around four trends, the first of which is the transition from digital libraries that consist primarily of metadata to digital libraries that consist of full content. New forms of retrieval algorithms are needed to search the full content of materials. Digital libraries will contain new forms of documents, which will exist in multiple media. A diverse set of user communities will have a variety of requirements for knowledge organization and user interfaces. Human indexing for all these vast new resources will not be economically feasible, hence it is necessary to determine the appropriate tradeoffs between human and machine indexing, and to identify new methods of automatic indexing.

The second trend identified was the transition from independent systems to linked systems in which users can follow links from one document to another (within or between digital libraries) and links from digital libraries to related applications. Linking systems requires a balance between tailoring digital libraries to user communities and making them interoperable by means of a global information infrastructure. If a reasonable balance between tailoring and interoperability can be achieved, individual digital libraries can be discovered by network search engines and can exchange data with one another. The tradeoff between tailoring and interoperability raises questions about how to organize knowledge within and among digital libraries, how to port data between digital libraries and other applications, and how to transfer data from one system to another or from one generation of technology to another.

The transition from searching digital libraries by submitting queries to navigating through digital libraries as an information space is the third trend identified. Though navigation is more flexible and adaptable than query searching, people easily become lost in information space. Search planning and reformulation remain difficult. New forms of user interfaces that can assist in navigating, filtering, and displaying information are needed, as is automated assistance. Determining the appropriate balance of control between human and machine in this new environment is a matter of philosophy and opinion as well as a matter of technology.

The fourth trend identified is the transition from a focus on the individual user of digital libraries to the group processes involved in information-related behavior. Research must account for the social context of digital library use, must consider ways in which people use computers as a medium for collaboration, and must consider ways in which computers can assist the collaboration process. To the extent possible, digital libraries should be tailored to communities of users while also being capable of spanning the boundaries between communities. The goal is to make better use of resources and to improve knowledge discovery. Focusing on groups involves spanning the boundaries between applications; thus, it presents new challenges in drawing the boundaries between individual digital libraries, a global digital library, and a global information infrastructure.

Several lessons for the future of digital library design have been offered. One, reiterated throughout the chapter, is the fundamental challenge of balancing the need for tailoring digital libraries to a community of users with the need to construct a vast, interoperable, global digital library. Another is the reflexive relationship between human behavior and technology. It is difficult, and probably impossible, to separate the influence of one on the other. People use the technologies that are available and adapt them to suit their purposes. Subsequent iterations of technology reflect those adaptations in combination with new capabilities made possible by technological advances. In sum, technology and behavior evolve together.

The final conclusion is that usability is a moving target in the design of digital libraries. As the technology improves sufficiently to overcome earlier problems, it presents new opportunities that bring new design challenges. People have higher expectations with each technical advance and with each improvement in knowledge organization, in user interface design, or in system capabilities. As the research community addresses the challenges posed here, new challenges and new research questions will arise. Thus, access to information is an evolving concept.

7
Whither, or Wither, Libraries?

When libraries first began automating their internal processes, in the 1960s and the 1970s, librarians often were asked "Why does a library need a computer?" Most people were quickly persuaded of the need when given an explanation of libraries' activities in managing information. By now, the majority of libraries in developed countries provide information resources in electronic as well as physical forms and rely on computing technology and networks for their administrative operations.

Now the reverse question is being asked: "We have the Internet, the World Wide Web, and digital libraries, so why do we still need libraries?" Sometimes the question is explicit, as when organizations plan new campuses, buildings, or agencies, or when international development agencies allocate funds for telecommunications, computing, and library services. At other times it is implicit, as when government officials, parents, or volunteers invest in computers and network access for schools that may have no libraries (Borgman 1997c).

The question "Why do we need libraries?" suggests a dichotomous choice between libraries and computer networks. The challenge for the information age is not choosing between libraries and computer networks, however. Rather, the challenge is determining how best to provide access to information, and how best to support the marketplace for ideas. Libraries in democratic societies are part of social strategy "to promote the Progress of Sciences and useful Arts," to quote the US Constitution (article I, section 8). Public access to knowledge is necessary for an informed electorate, and to promote learning and invention (Buckland 1988; Lyman 1996). These cultural values are more permanent than the media of communication, whether print or electronic (Foskett 1984). Yet the distinctive features of the American public library system in particular are under threat from the technology and policy transitions currently underway. James Billington, the present Librarian of Congress, identifies four features currently under threat (Billington 1996, p. 36–37):

First, for democracy to be sustainable on a continental scale in a multicultural society, it must be based on the dynamic use of knowledge. . . . Second, this knowledge must be *openly accessible* to all people. . . . Third, public libraries expressed the *growing pluralism* of American society. . . . Fourth, public libraries were, nevertheless, a *unifying force* in the communities where they existed.

The social goals for libraries vary among democratic societies and between democratic and other social systems. They also vary among types of libraries, such as public, academic, special, and school, although libraries of all types cooperate with each other in the context of broader social goals. The means for implementing these goals were developed for a print culture, which has been the dominant form of communication during the period of modern democratic political systems. The present challenge is to support the social goals of democratic societies in a new technological environment for communication. Digital libraries have tremendous potential to enhance access to knowledge, to support learning and education, to promote progress in the "sciences and useful arts," and to inform the citizenry. At the same time, many scholars (e.g., Billington 1996; Dervin 1994; Lievrouw 1994a,b; Lyman 1996) are concerned whether the goals of free public access to information can be sustained while encouraging a robust market for information in economies where knowledge is a form of capital. The marketplace for ideas in a democratic society is characterized by a balance between the rights of the citizenry for the broadest possible access to information and the rights of creators of information to be compensated for their work.

Organization and Access in a Networked World

Organization of content is a defining characteristic of libraries, digital or otherwise. Information must be described, represented, and organized in ways that allow people to discover its existence, locate it, and obtain it in a useful and usable form. Documents or document-like objects should be described uniquely, so that their identity and authenticity can be verified. The component of network architecture that supports organization and access is metadata. Metadata serve a variety of functions in networked environments, including description, administration, intellectual access, intellectual organization, technical specifications, and preservation management.

Libraries have refined the theories, principles, and practices for creating metadata and for accomplishing these functions throughout the twentieth century. American libraries began sharing metadata for cataloging records around 1900. These practices spread around the world, and by the late 1960s international standards for sharing metadata in computer-readable form had been established and implemented. By now, libraries have more experience with creating, maintaining, and distributing metadata than any of the other links in the chain of producing and delivering information. They also have addressed a wide array of portability, interoperability, and scaling problems that others are just now encountering.

Library Principles and Practices
Among the core responsibilities of libraries are to select, preserve, and provide access to published materials on behalf of their user communities. This is usually a shared responsibility, as few individual libraries can acquire all materials of potential interest to their users. At a national level, one organization usually is responsible for preserving the published record of the country. Legislation supports the preservation of cultural heritage, typically requiring each publisher to provide a specified number of copies of every publication to a designated organization, which is usually the national library. In the United States, legal deposit laws ensure that the Library of Congress receives copies of US publications. In the United Kingdom, comparable laws require that British publications are deposited in the British Library. French publications go to the Bibliotheque Nationale de France, German publications go to the Deutsche Bibliothek, Hungarian publications to the National Szechenyi Library, and so on. Deposit libraries normally are responsible for cataloging these materials and creating the authoritative metadata for each document received. Collectively, the metadata they produce become the national bibliography of the country. Those metadata, in turn, become source material for other libraries that acquire the materials.

Throughout the world, legal deposit laws have been fairly effective in ensuring that printed books from major publishers are preserved in national collections. Acquiring books from new publishers, small publishers, or self-publishers who are not aware of their legal responsibilities always has been more problematic. Acquiring serial publications, pamphlets, and ephemeral materials that may be important parts of the national cultural heritage is yet more difficult. Electronic publications raise a host of new problems, not the least of which is determining what is a publication. Identifying what exists, who is responsible for it, and whether and how it should be acquired and preserved are among the other challenges to maintaining national collections and national resources of metadata.

Within each country, academic libraries and public and other government-supported libraries typically function as a collective entity to provide access to the materials held within their countries. In principle, the residents of a country should be able to use most materials held by any participating library in their country. Special libraries within private organizations also rely on these resources and may contribute as well. National cooperation, in turn, relies on international cooperation for sharing resources.

Managing Metadata

Metadata are essential to managing library collections and operations. Libraries use many types of metadata in their operations and services. Of these, cataloging data are the primary form of metadata used to manage local collections and to discover, locate, and obtain materials held elsewhere. Principles and practices for creating and managing cataloging metadata have evolved throughout the history of print publications and continue to evolve to support new media.

Cataloging is one of the most expensive operations in libraries: each item must be described physically, so that it can be identified uniquely, and intellectually, establishing responsibility for the work. Subject terms or classification are assigned so that works can be identified by topic. Early in the twentieth century, the Library of Congress (LC) began distributing cataloging records as a means to subsidize the cost of cataloging for the nation's libraries (Billington 1996). In the United States, the LC record is considered the most authoritative metadata for a work. Libraries can use the LC record, or a record from another authoritative source, rather than creating a new record for its own copy of that work. Further, if all libraries use the same catalog record, then the work will be described consistently across libraries, making it easier for readers to identify and locate. Substantial efficiencies and control of internal costs have been gained by sharing cataloging data (Cummings 1986; Becker, Dodson, and Yoakam 1984; Maciuszko 1984).

With the advent of online systems, it became possible to exchange records directly and immediately among many libraries, rather than the one-way flow from a central distribution point to individual libraries. Metadata from national bibliographies and other authoritative sources form the core of online shared cataloging systems. Participating libraries search the database to determine if a catalog record exists for a new document they have acquired. If so, the record is captured for local use; if not, the library catalogs the document and contributes the record to the database, where it is available for other participating libraries. Records in the shared database are extensible. Libraries can add data for their local catalog about their copy (or copies), such as the physical location of the item or extra access points (names, subjects, etc.) considered important for local uses.

The first major online shared cataloging system was OCLC (then Ohio College Library Center, now the OCLC Online Computer Library Center), established in 1967 (Becker, Dodson, and Yoakam 1984; Maciuszko 1984). Others quickly followed, such as RLIN (Research Libraries Information Network) and WLN (Western Library Network) in the United States, BLCMP (Birmingham Libraries Cooperative Mechanisation Project) and CURL (Consortium of University Research Libraries) in the United Kingdom, and PICA (Project on Integrated Catalogue Automation) in the Netherlands (Tedd 1993). In Europe, at least 30 cooperative networks existed in 14 countries by the early 1990s, offering a variety of services including online shared cataloging (Dempsey 1990; Hein 1991; Holley 1993). The European Union promotes multinational library cooperation, including the development of shared databases of major European collections (Day, Heery, and Powell 1999; Dempsey 1990; Rau 1990).

Shared cataloging systems, also known as bibliographic utilities, have become very large operations. OCLC alone serves more than 27,000 libraries in 64 countries, and its database contains about 40 million bibliographic records (OCLC 1998a) in more than 400 languages (OCLC 1998b). Analyses of library cataloging practices indicate that the vast majority of catalog records in the United States and the United Kingdom are obtained from these online shared cataloging systems. Records for materials in English are still more widely available than those for other languages, but the breadth of these databases is expanding rapidly as more countries contribute records (Chapman 1999; Leazer and Rohdy 1994). Thus, metadata exist in standardized, computer-readable form for a growing proportion of extant published materials.

Rules and Standards

Rules and standards are essential for managing metadata in networked environments. The establishment of standards for exchanging bibliographic data in computer-readable form in the 1960s led directly to the development of the shared cataloging utilities (Avram 1972, 1975, 1976; Buchinski et al. 1978; Library of Congress Network Advisory Group 1977a, 1977b; RECON Working Task Force, 1969, 1973). American and British libraries now have nearly 40 years of experience exchanging metadata in computer-readable form, based on international standards and rules. The Library of Congress began work toward the MARC (MAchine-Readable Cataloging) format in 1961, conducted a pilot project from 1966 to 1968, and began the MARC II distribution service in 1968. The British National Bibliography and the Library of Congress began work toward a UKMARC pilot project during the LC MARC pilot study, leading to the international exchange of records between the United States and the United Kingdom beginning in 1969 (Avram 1975). Also in 1969, the International Federation of Library Associations and Institutions (IFLA) convened an international meeting of cataloging experts that led to the establishment of the International Standard Bibliographic Description (ISBD) (Avram 1975; Gorman 1969). As other countries began to establish their own MARC formats, IFLA developed UNIMARC (UNIversal MARC) in the late 1970s to assist in international cooperation and data exchange between MARC formats (McCallum 1989).

Underlying these metadata standards are rules for how to describe and represent published materials. The Anglo-American Cataloging Rules (AACR), USMARC, and UKMARC were developed in concert in the late 1960s and are revised continually to accommodate changes in technology and in practices. AACR now supports the description and representation of various media, from videotapes to CD-ROMs, that did not exist in the

1960s. Despite common rules, national practices do vary, which is why AACR is mapped to multiple MARC formats (e.g., USMARC, UKMARC, CANMARC). AACR has been translated into multiple languages, with some adaptation to local practices. UNIMARC is used widely in Europe and elsewhere, especially with cataloging rules other than AACR. Various international efforts are underway to achieve convergence, or at least bridging mechanisms, among the multiple MARC formats. IFLA and the European Union are leading many of these efforts, in coordination with national libraries. The existence of multiple rules and formats is an example of the tradeoffs between tailoring to local practices and the interoperability of systems and services.

Catalogs and Content

A by-product of the sharing of cataloging records is the creation of union catalogs that reflect the collective holdings of participating libraries. OCLC alone has records on the existence and location of more than 660 million copies of 40 million distinct works that have been cataloged through the system (OCLC 1998a). Albeit the largest, OCLC is only one of many shared cataloging systems. Thus, these systems represent a significant step toward creating a global digital library of metadata indicating what information resources exist and where they are located.

Digital libraries of metadata facilitate discovery and location processes. They also can assist people in gaining access to the full content. Toward this end, shared cataloging systems provide services that execute resource-sharing agreements among participating libraries. Public and academic libraries in most countries lend materials to other libraries, and in return, they borrow materials from other participating libraries on behalf of their user communities. Interlibrary lending agreements often are supported by laws and by supplemental funds to redress imbalances between lending and borrowing libraries.[1] In this way, all the participating libraries in a country may function as a "virtual library collection" available to its citizenry.

The virtual library collection is accomplished by a variety of means. In some cases, library staff search databases such as OCLC or the British

---

1. In the context of librarianship, the words "loan" and "lend" are often used interchangeably. American libraries typically use the term "interlibrary loan"; British libraries and IFLA use "interlibrary lending."

National Lending Library at Boston Spa to determine the existence and availability of materials. These systems process the requests and submit them to the lending libraries, which deliver the materials to the requesting library. Materials such as books are usually sent by post, whereas journal articles may be sent by fax. The requesting library, in turn, lends the material to the requesting user. Materials delivered by fax or email can be provided directly to the requesting user. As more components of this process are automated, the number of steps decreases, the amount of handling decreases, costs drop, and delivery time shortens.

Commercial document supply services, for example, employ automation effectively to build upon existing resource sharing practices. They broker agreements with libraries to supply copies of articles from journals to which those libraries subscribe. The document suppliers' database of available journal articles is drawn from the online catalogs of participating libraries. Users request documents from the service, provide a fax number, email address, or other delivery address, and pay a fee. The service forwards the order to an owning library, which supplies the material directly to the requester. Fees paid are divided between the library for its subscription and staff costs, the publisher for copyright permission, and the document supply service for brokering the transaction. Libraries increasing rely on these sources as a form of outsourcing of interlibrary lending requests.

At present, electronic exchanges of materials are feasible only for short documents such as journal articles that are easily digitized, and only in parts of the world where telecommunications and computer networks are sufficiently reliable and available. Physical materials such as books and videos continue to be exchanged via postal mail owing to the expense of digitizing, limitations of bandwidth, and copyright policies.

Generalized Principles and Practices

The library principles and practices outlined above are predicated on the above-mentioned social goals for access to information in democratic societies. National bibliographies, shared metadata, resource sharing agreements, and copyright laws, taken as a whole, are the underpinnings of a "global virtual library collection." The form in which virtual collections are realized varies considerably within and between countries; this discussion has focused on common features. Many of these principles and practices also can be found in nations with other forms of government. These practices are by now well tested, are supported by available technology such as automated library systems and computer networks, and by resources such as shared cataloging systems that are accessible without political prejudice. "Automated library systems" is shorthand for enterprise management systems that support and integrate library operations such as acquisition of materials, serials management, cataloging, online catalogs, circulation of materials, and associated accounting processes (Barry, Bilal, and Penniman 1998; Borgman 1997a; Tedd 1993).

These practices were initially designed for print publications. Many of the assumptions on which they were predicated, such as one work existing in multiple copies, or the ability to specify precisely whether a document is subject to deposit laws, do not apply to digital documents that exist in networked environments. The world of electronic publishing and distributed access to information is far less ordered than is the world of print publication. Yet virtual collections are needed now more than ever. The necessity for mechanisms to identify, locate, and obtain information resources is increasing with the proliferation of digital content in many forms, in many languages, and in many places. Ways are needed to balance the rights of readers with the rights of authors, regardless of the format of information resources or the means by which they are delivered.

Deposit laws ensure that documents are acquired when they are available so that they can be preserved for future generations. In short, these laws ensure the persistence of content (Day, Heery, and Powell 1999). The lack of persistence is among the greatest challenges of managing digital documents; they may exist only as long as someone maintains access to them, and even if so, they often lack a persistent identifier or location.

Managing Metadata

Electronic documents rarely follow the "one work, many copies" rule. A work may exist in only one form and in only one place. The same work may exist in multiple versions, whether in one or many locations. Documents may exist in duplicate copies in multiple databases, such as digital libraries that are mirrored on multiple continents. If documents are unique, then only one copy of a metadata record is required, in which case shared cataloging is not an effective model. However, other services of shared cataloging systems continue to be necessary, such as registering what exists, where, in what form, and the means to obtain access. The question then arises of the appropriate methods to accomplish these functions, whether through centralized systems and services or through searching mechanisms that create dynamic virtual collections on demand.

One option is to shift responsibility for creating metadata to different stages in the publication process. Responsibility for cataloging monographs has been moving "upstream" in the process for some years already. "Cataloging in publication" (CIP) programs, for example, enable publishers to submit prepublication copies to national centers to generate partial cataloging records that can be included in the print publication. New programs in "Electronic CIP" (ECIP) enable publishers to submit prepublication copies electronically and have the records returned electronically, which shortens the turnaround time (Davis-Brown and Williamson 1996; Day, Heery, and Powell 1999).

Authors, creators, publishers, and other producers of electronic content can generate their own metadata, using standards such as the Dublin Core. Various international projects are underway to experiment with new ways of assigning metadata so that information resources can be discovered, located, and obtained in networked environments (Day, Heery, and Powell 1999). Other approaches involve the search engines that sweep the World Wide Web. These engines catalog, to varying degrees, what exists online at any point in time (Kelly 1999).

Though the principles and practices associated with legal deposit and shared cataloging are far from perfect in capturing, maintaining, and preserving a nation's cultural heritage, they go a long way toward providing a virtual collection for its citizenry. Most of the approaches proposed or tested to date for organizing electronic materials on computer networks are piecemeal. They also are more effective at providing access to what exists today than to creating a permanent and comprehensive set of resources.

Rules and Standards

Rules, standards, and practices continue to evolve with changes in technology, economics, and policy. The online digital world presents significant new challenges. One of these is the transition from cataloging physical objects to cataloging digital objects. The rules were intended for "book in hand" cataloging: the assumption that the cataloger can handle the item and inspect it for certain attributes. The Anglo-American Cataloging Rules, for example, originally presumed that the cataloger could determine the physical dimensions of the object and the number of pages, and could identify author, title, publisher, place, and other data on the title page and verso. In a digital world, catalogers are creating metadata for objects they cannot handle, and are reliant on other means to identify attributes of those objects. Creating metadata for electronic documents is easier and faster than for print documents only if the documents are structured in a way that data can be extracted automatically. Often, creating metadata for digital documents is more labor intensive than for printed documents. Rather than spending a few moments handling the object to identify metadata elements, the cataloger may need to visit a web site. Or, software may need to be installed and run to determine descriptive elements such as author, title, publisher and date, much less additional elements such as technical specifications.

The forms and genres of electronic publication are not stable, and may never be. This is the blessing and the curse of digital documents. Rules, standards, and practices for managing metadata are becoming more generic to accommodate the variance. Digital documents are often unique, and no equivalent yet exists for unique and persistent identifiers such as the International Standard Book Number (ISBN) or International Standard Serial Number (ISSN). Uniform Resource Locators (URLs), the current addressing mechanism, are notoriously unstable. Other proposals such as Persistent URLs (PURLs), Uniform Resource Names (URNs), and Digital Object Identifiers (DOIs) have yet to be adopted widely (Kelly 1999).

A related challenge is to adapt techniques developed for static documents such as books to dynamic or mutable documents that are updated continuously (Bishop and Star 1996) and to documents that may include links or pointers to other documents. Cataloging rules do account for relationships between documents that may be manifested in multiple ways (e.g., variations in copies, different editions) and in multiple forms (e.g., text, video, film). Research on the relationships that exist between documents in a world of static materials, such as equivalence, derivative, descriptive, whole-part, and shared authorship, are providing insights into the types of linking relationships needed in an online world (Leazer 1994; Smiraglia and Leazer 1999; Tillett 1991, 1992).

Catalogs and Content

In practical terms, the shift from print to digital forms only eliminates the last step in the information access process: obtaining a physical copy. Metadata continue to be essential for discovering and locating information resources, regardless of form. With print materials, the last step is to remove the item from a library bookshelf or request it via interlibrary lending or a document-delivery service. With digital documents, the last step may be simply to click on the name of the item, initiating the transfer of a copy to one's local computer.

As can be seen from the above examples, however, the shift from sharing cataloging data to sharing content is more than a technical matter. In the print world, legal deposit laws, shared cataloging systems, and interlibrary lending agreements combine to provide public access to information. The primary means for maintaining a balance between the rights of the citizenry for access and the rights of creators to be compensated adequately is through copyright and other intellectual property laws. US copyright laws include the "doctrine of first sale," which enables libraries to lend the print materials they have purchased, for example. They also include tests of "fair use" that permit a small number of copies to be made for educational purposes without additional payment to the authors or publishers. Copyright laws in other countries draw the balance somewhat differently, and international agreements govern sale and use between nations.

Copyright features such as the doctrine of first sale and fair use are being challenged for digital materials. Many publishers prefer to lease rather than to sell electronic content, for example. Others are providing electronic content only under contracts in which libraries forfeit certain copyright privileges. These are among the threats to library services to which Billington and others refer (Battin and Hawkins 1998; Billington 1996; Hawkins 1998; Lyman 1996, 1998). Finding the appropriate balance between the rights of citizens and the rights of producers may be the greatest challenge we face in providing access to information in democratic societies.

Form and Function, Space and Place

Libraries are more than collections and buildings. They exist in many forms, have many functions, and serve a variety of purposes, not the least of which is fulfilling social goals of their countries.

An Institution or a Function?

The simple definition of a library—an agency that selects, collects, organizes, preserves, conserves, and provides access to information on behalf of a user community—says little about how these activities are performed, the relative emphasis on each, or the relationship between them. Indeed, libraries come in so many types and sizes, encompass such a wide variety of activities, and vary so much by social context, that no single agreed-upon definition of "library" appears to exist. Libraries differ along such lines as type of institution ("academic," "school," "public," and "special" are the usual categories), and by politics, such as the contrast between public library services in democratic and totalitarian systems. Why they differ is little studied, however (Buckland 1988).

Libraries are social institutions that have evolved over a period of many centuries. They serve the information needs of their user communities, adapting collections and services as those needs change. Libraries tend not to be autonomous institutions. Rather, most are funded by governments to serve a defined community; by schools or universities to serve students, teachers, and staff; or by businesses, hospitals, museums, or other organizations to serve their employees and other constituents. Most libraries have a mission statement and collection development plan that identifies who they serve and what they collect, thereby drawing boundaries around their responsibilities.

Although libraries usually are the primary social institution that selects, collects, organizes, preserves, conserves, and provides access to information, few, if any, of these functions are unique. Archives and museums, for example, serve many of the same functions, for the same or similar user communities. The line between libraries and classrooms is blurring as courses are conducted via computer networks. Distance-independent learning environments rely on a steady flow of information resources between libraries, teachers, and students, and between libraries, homes, workplaces, and virtual classrooms.

Thus, libraries are both institutions and functions. Much of what distinguishes libraries from other information organizations is their professional principles and practices, rather than their functions.

Physical Place or Virtual Space?

Libraries serve as gathering points for communities, bringing together people, information resources in physical forms, access to information in electronic forms, and professionals to assist people in their information-related activities (Kent 1996; Lyman 1996; Mason 1996). In the 1990s grand new buildings or additions were constructed for public libraries in Los Angeles, San Francisco, Cleveland, and other major American cities. Britain, France, Germany, and Croatia recently have opened new showcase buildings for their national libraries. The Library of Congress has renovated its original Jefferson Building. These large investments of public monies signify a resurgence of interest in libraries as physical places (Dowlin and Shapiro 1996; Lehmann 1996). The new library buildings are designed to support the latest technologies while preserving existing materials in multiple formats. The new model for library services is not a print library or a digital library; it is a hybrid with complementary print and digital collections. The presence of complementary resources and services is having a crossover effect. People visiting a library building to borrow a book learn to use the Internet while they are there. Conversely, they come to the building to use computer networks, then browse printed materials and leave with a book (Mason 1996).

Many of the functions that libraries serve can be supported online, in a virtual space. People can search catalogs and databases from home or office, can consult with librarians or other advisors by email, and can convene meetings online. Libraries provide services to discover, locate, and obtain materials online, thus many are using libraries without even visiting their buildings.

Print or Electronic Resources?

People need information resources that exist in a wide variety of formats. Some wish their libraries would collect a greater proportion of print materials than they do; others would prefer a greater proportion of digital materials. These debates often degenerate into discussions of the portion of library collections that should be in electronic form—20 percent, 50 percent, 75 percent? Approaching collection development in terms of format begs questions of content and community, however. Traditional approaches to collection development begin with questions of who we are collecting for (community) and what they need (content). The choice of format (electronic, print, or other) usually follows from answers to the questions about community and content. However, these factors interact in complex ways. The materials selected must be in formats that are usable (readable, playable, etc.) on equipment available in the library or in the community, for example.

Even if the same content exists in multiple formats, consideration should be given to the ways in which print and electronic materials are used. Buckland (1992) draws a contrast between the uses of paper documents[2] and electronic documents. Paper is a solo technology, typically best used by one person at a time, and it is localized: the paper and the reader must be in the same place at the same time. Electronic documents can be used by many people at the same time, and they can be located at a different place from the reader (provided that the reader has a telecommunications connection to the site).

Other characteristics of form are relevant in collection choices. Paper documents often are more effective than electronic forms for discussions by a small number of people, for example. Paper is well suited for purposes such as explaining diagrams, where people need to point and make hand motions over a document. Paper generally is more suitable for making annotations and for browsing by flipping through pages than are most forms of hypertext (Dillon and Gabbard 1998; Silberman 1998). New technologies such as "electronic white boards" and "electronic books" try to replicate these features of paper. Paper is a very flexible medium, with many features that are difficult to support in digital environments.

The economic tradeoffs between print and electronic materials are complex and evolving. One factor is the difference in business models for print and electronic publication. Print materials normally are sold as individual copies or annual subscriptions, whereas electronic materials are subject to

2. Buckland (1992) regards other hard-copy materials, such as microform and clay tablets, as inconvenient variations on paper.

a variety of elaborate pricing schemes that may include annual fees, fees per use, fees based on size of user population, and combination fees based on acquiring sets of print and electronic resources from one publisher. Other economic considerations for libraries include the continuing costs of maintaining the materials, whether stored on a bookshelf, mounted on local computers, or access provided to remote computers, and the conservation and preservation of the materials as technology evolves.

The Public's View of Libraries

Libraries are a near-sacred social institution, and yet many question the need for their continued existence. The availability of information technology to create content in digital form, to digitize existing printed materials, and to distribute these resources over computer networks is provoking a broad public debate over the role of libraries. The debate involves other public and private institutions as well, and it is part of a more general discussion about the marketplace of ideas in a democratic society (Lyman 1996). Mason (1996) reframes the debate from whether we *can* do without libraries to whether we *should* do without them.

Many people have strong personal feelings about libraries, whether or not they use them. Every library has an intended community of users, such as those residing within the jurisdiction of a public library, or the students, faculty, and staff of a university served by an academic library, or the employees of a business or other organization served by a special library.

Public Libraries

Public libraries are the most familiar and visible type of library to most people. Their collections typically include popular reading materials for children and adults, basic reference sources, classics, and resources specific to the local economy and culture. Local history and genealogy are especially popular. They often lend materials such as software, videos, sewing patterns, and art work in addition to the usual books and journals, depending on the circumstances of their local communities. Public libraries provide services such as literacy programs, homework assistance, and public meeting rooms. Particularly in the United States, they serve as the "on ramp to the information superhighway," providing free public access to Internet resources.

People often turn to their public libraries when academic, school, and corporate libraries lack resources, and when they lack Internet access. When child care services are lacking, parents may send their children to the public library after school. Because these institutions provide such a diverse array of services to their local communities, they rarely attempt to build comprehensive research collections, leaving that responsibility to academic libraries and national deposit collections. Instead, they rely on interlibrary lending to provide materials beyond the scope of their collections.

The use of public libraries is growing, and budgets rarely keep pace with increasing demands. In the United States, and to some degree in Europe, libraries are supplementing their budgets with funds from a variety of sources, including private gifts, corporate partnerships, and fees for services. They also rely on volunteers from the community to supplement their paid staffs. Declining materials budgets increase the reliance on interlibrary lending and other cooperative agreements.

Public libraries serve diverse constituencies in their communities, provide a wide array of services, and make difficult choices among competing goals. They balance print collections with online services, physical places with virtual spaces, space for people with space for books, and buying with borrowing. Many of the choices they make occur behind the scenes and thus are not readily apparent to their user communities. Other decisions, such as the choice of certain books, put them in the spotlight. In their attempt to serve diverse communities and to provide open access to information from a variety of perspectives, public libraries sometimes offend the political, religious, moral, or cultural sensibilities of some of their constituents. These concerns are being transferred from print to digital materials with the advent of computer networks.

Most of the people, most of the time, are happy with the resources and services provided by their public libraries (Benton Foundation 1996). Some people, at some times, are not. An obvious example is the controversy over filtering or limiting access to Internet sites, a problem for which no easy answer exists. Filtering is ineffective, due both to the rapid appearance and disappearance of individual sites and to problems with information retrieval. Filtering on "bad words" restricts access to good sites. For example, simply blocking access to sites containing the word "breast" denies access to legitimate sites on breast cancer. Conversely, objectionable sites will slip through filters if they do not contain any of the specified "bad words." Purveyors of pornography are likely to be as technically sophisticated as those who wish to filter it. Some libraries are controlling access via policies such as requiring identification to use terminals. Others use screen filters that make the display visible only to the person seated in front of it. Yet other libraries refuse to filter or control beyond requiring parental permission for minors, applying the same policies as for print materials. A greater concern for many public libraries is people tying up library terminals for email and games, which diminishes the availability of the terminals for information access.

A less predictable controversy over public library policies is one that erupted at the San Francisco Public Library over the replacement of the card catalog with an online catalog and the "weeding" of the collection. That particular storm was preceded by an article in the *New Yorker* (Baker 1994) directed at these practices in public and academic libraries. Objections to online catalogs were based on the assertion that much information is lost in the conversion of catalogs to electronic form, such as notes on the back of cards. In fact, the reverse is true, as card catalog records usually are upgraded to modern cataloging standards as part of the conversion process (Schottlaender 1992). More subtle are objections to the loss of card catalogs as icons of a print culture and as familiar tools whose well-worn oak drawers and paper cards offer tactile pleasures unmatched by keyboards and computer screens. The card catalog controversy can be attributed partially to communication problems between librarians and their user communities. Librarians do not always include their user communities in decision-making processes for such momentous changes as catalog conversion, nor do they often communicate the reasons for their choices until a controversy arises.

Communication issues regarding the "weeding" of collections cut more deeply into principles and practices of library management. Baker's first *New Yorker* article stated that "the function of a great library is to store obscure books," and that "this is above all the task we want libraries to perform: to hold on to books that we don't want enough to own, books of very limited appeal" (Baker 1994, pp. 78–79). His later article focused directly on weeding policies of the San Francisco Public Library, expressing the view that it is that library's responsibility to preserve these materials for posterity (Baker 1996). Few American public libraries attempt to maintain research collections, leaving that responsibility to academic libraries and to deposit collections such as the Library of Congress. Storage space for books is expensive, especially in the centers of major cities. Today, public spaces for people to gather, to browse current publications, to read, and to use resources on site are usually viewed as higher priorities. Older materials that are in minimal demand often are stored off site or are "weeded" or "de-acquisitioned"—library euphemisms for "discarded." At such later time as a user requests an item not on site, it is retrieved from storage or requested through interlibrary lending. Libraries usually cooperate to ensure that at least one copy of each discarded item remains in the region and is available for lending. Much as digital documents are moved electronically to the point of demand, libraries are replacing "just in case" storage of physical documents with "just in time" delivery to the point of demand. By sharing this responsibility for low-demand items, they save money that can be diverted to other services.

These principles and practices are not widely known outside the library community. People understandably view the local public library as "their library." The fact that their library functions as part of a tightly coupled infrastructure of systems and services is not apparent unless explained. And even if explained, members of the community may not necessarily agree with the choices made. Such was the case with the San Francisco Public Library, one of the large American public libraries that had, in the past, attempted to maintain a research collection. Baker, members of the staff, and prominent members of the public disagreed (loudly and publicly) with the director's choices in placing other priorities over maintaining the research collection. These decisions were made in consultation with the city council and the library board some years earlier, in the process of designing a new building, but were not evident to the public until the building was opened.

There are no simple ways to resolve these debates, which are about how to achieve the social goals of public libraries in supporting learning, informing the citizenry, and making progress in the "sciences and useful arts." Managers in private companies regularly make tough choices such as "just in case" vs. "just in time" inventory management. Library managers make similar tough choices, but the subject is not spare auto parts; it is information resources that have cultural significance for their local communities. These debates will continue, and well they should. The public has the right to participate in determining the future of its social institutions.

Academic Libraries

The mission of academic libraries is more focused than that of public libraries: They serve the curricular and research needs of students, faculty, and staff of their parent institutions. They collect materials in direct relation to academic programs, with increasing depth for undergraduate, masters, and doctoral courses. As new curricula and programs are established, and as existing programs expand into new areas, library collections are expected to expand proportionately. Among the fundamental criteria for accrediting academic programs is the adequacy of library collections to support the curricula. Major research universities with extensive graduate programs and research facilities necessarily have more substantial library collections and services than do small colleges that focus on undergraduate education.

Even the most extensive academic library collection cannot serve all the needs of a university community, so academic libraries rely on cooperative arrangements for interlibrary lending and document delivery. They also rely on each other for specialized collections. If one library in a region has an extensive collection in one subject area, such as musicology, Latin America, or the history of medicine, other regional academic libraries may maintain only basic collections for those topics and build depth in other areas instead. Libraries borrow from each other and offer access and borrowing privileges to members of affiliated institutions. In Southern California, for example, the University of California at Los Angeles and the University of Southern California may be opponents on the football field, but they are partners in sharing library access. Their library users can observe the advantages of cooperative ventures in borrowing resources and in using the services of neighboring libraries. Less apparent to users is that they gain access to a larger body of resources when partner libraries share costs of expensive materials and decide jointly on which institutions will acquire, preserve, and conserve unique materials.

Major research libraries also serve as national and international resources. They catalog their materials in shared bibliographic utilities, making their holdings widely known. They collect materials in many, if not most, of the 400+ languages found in shared cataloging systems. Because they are building research collections, they do far less weeding than do public libraries. Storage costs remain an issue, however. Academic libraries often rely on off-site repositories, retrieving materials on demand. The nine campuses of the University of California, for example, share two large regional library facilities, one in Northern California and one in Southern California.

By now, the operations and services of most academic libraries in developed countries are highly automated. Integrated systems track materials from the time of ordering through receipt, payment, cataloging, physical processing (bar codes, spine labels, etc.), shelving, circulation, off-site storage, conservation, and any other handling or disposition. Metadata are exchanged online between library catalog systems and bibliographic utilities. Orders and payments may be exchanged between libraries and vendors through electronic data interchange (EDI), based on international standards. Integrated library systems are linked to other electronic resources, such as databases of abstracting and indexing services and digital libraries of text, images, and other content.

Academic libraries provide integrated access to hybrid collections of print and electronic resources. A common electronic gateway may enable access to a wide array of systems and services (Hyslop 1996; Olsen 1997). From computers in the library, in offices, in dormitories, in homes, in hotels, or elsewhere, members of the university community can identify what resources are owned by their institution, what is on order, and which physical materials currently are on loan to other borrowers. Some systems enable users to request items for delivery to their offices, place holds, extend the due dates for borrowed items, and request materials from elsewhere. Services often include digital libraries maintained on campus networks and on digital libraries located elsewhere. University libraries may pay for subscriptions to external services and provide access through a library or university gateway. Access privileges often are authenticated by domain name or other means. In this way, users are saved the trouble of maintaining passwords for individual systems and services. Users may be searching a rich array of digital collections without realizing that these are not publicly available resources or that their library is paying for their access rights. Many academic libraries are expanding their services to include electronic publishing, tele-learning, distance-independent courses, and other information technology applications for higher education.

Users of academic libraries are profoundly affected by the shifts in scholarly publishing discussed in chapter 4. The prices of scholarly journals have increased at far higher rates than either library budgets or inflation, resulting in substantial decreases in libraries' purchasing power, canceling of journal subscriptions, and reductions in purchases of monographs. Academic disciplines are affected to varying degrees, leading to tensions between departments. Science and technology disciplines rely more heavily on scholarly journals than on monographs, and a growing proportion of their information resources are available in electronic form. In contrast, the humanities and the social sciences rely on a mix of serial and monographic resources and fewer of their resources are available in electronic form. Heavy use is made of the digital resources available, but these supplement rather than substitute for collections of materials in print, microform, audio, and video formats, collections of photographs and other images, and archives and other collections of unique materials.

Users of academic libraries are acutely aware of the tradeoffs between access to physical items held locally and access to those held elsewhere. In the best of all possible worlds, all would have local and immediate access to all the resources they want, when they want them. Given that this option is neither technically nor economically feasible, librarians try to minimize the turnaround time to acquire materials on demand. The improvements in interlibrary lending and document delivery discussed above are reducing delivery times from weeks to days for postal shipments, and from weeks to hours for online or fax delivery. Such delays, though not desirable, may be acceptable for long-term scholarly research projects, and are an improvement over the situation prior to automation. Scholars frequently had to travel to the location where resources of interest were held. Humanities scholars continue to travel in search of rare or unique materials, although some of their research needs can be satisfied by online access to digitized resources.

The reaction of the academic community to the changes in their library services is mixed. Many items previously available only in print form, such as catalogs, journals, and indexing and abstracting services, are now available online and are more convenient to use. They appreciate the wide array of new resources available in electronic form, from data sets to digitized manuscripts. However, the majority of the academic community laments the decreasing availability of current journals and scholarly monographs, whether in print or in electronic form, because of escalating costs. Most proposals for new models of scholarly communication endeavor to redress the loss of access to materials of all types, in addition to extending access to new forms of publication.

Special Libraries

Special libraries in businesses, law firms, hospitals, museums, and other institutions are often the most innovative, responding quickly to the changing needs of their parent organizations. Special libraries operate under names such as "technical information center" or "resource collection" as well as "library." In networked organizations, special libraries offer online access to their resources and services and deliver information products in digital form to their users, in addition to the usual print-based services.

Special libraries are finding a new niche as information-related activities that once were discrete become integrated. For example, product designs and plans that are created online flow directly into the production process. Data about patients or clients can be maintained and used throughout the organization's relationship with those individuals. Similarly, electronic products such as publications, videos, films, games, or broadcast programs can be maintained online, and portions of them can be re-used in other products. The challenge in creating and maintaining information throughout its life cycle lies in describing and organizing content so it can be identified and located later by people other than those who created it, who may be seeking that content for purposes other than that which it was originally intended to serve.

The changing economics of information is influencing the role of special libraries in many organizations. Corporate libraries were the first to be funded as cost centers, such that services are charged directly to organizational units or to clients. The alternative, which is employed in many special and most academic libraries, is to fund libraries as part of overhead and to provide basic services to the user community without direct cost. Cost accounting for information services is problematic, however. The inputs are hard to measure, as collections are built and maintained over many years, making it difficult to apportion costs to individual transactions. Similarly, the outputs are hard to measure, since the value of the information provided may not become apparent for months or years after the transaction. Yet the costs are real, and libraries must demonstrate their value and justify their costs to their parent organizations no matter what financial models are applied. Internal costing is but one more challenge in developing an adequate economics of information.

The response of user communities to special libraries can be assessed only in general terms, since the services of special libraries are tailored to their unique communities and since studies of those services are usually proprietary. The job market for information professionals in private industry is expanding rapidly, and new job titles are appearing, such as "metadata specialist," "information analyst," "digital resources coordinator," and "digital archivist." At the same time, some special libraries are being closed as part of cost reductions in research and development, information services are being outsourced, and librarians' jobs are being eliminated, indicating that these units are not necessarily seen as essential to the future of their parent organizations.

Rethinking Libraries in a Digital Age

The question for the new millennium is not what to do about libraries but, more generally, what to do about access to information. What resources and services are needed, and by whom? Which are essential and which are desirable? What infrastructure is needed to support information resources and services? Who should provide them? These questions encompass a range of political, economic, and social issues. Historical democratic premises for providing open access to information through libraries are being challenged as information resources become a form of capital and as more aspects of information infrastructure are privatized.

Libraries are only one of many institutions in the midst of substantial structural changes. In North America, Europe, and elsewhere, fewer government funds are being devoted to public services such as libraries than in past decades. Professionals in the public and the private sector alike are expected to increase their productivity, which usually means more supervision of paraprofessional and clerical staff and a lower proportion of professional staff. Libraries are being asked to do more, often with fewer resources. Few of their traditional responsibilities can be abandoned, although many can be fulfilled more efficiently through automation and resource sharing, some can be deferred, and some can be relinquished to other agencies.

The present discussion of this vast range of issues will be limited to the evolution of libraries and to their present and future roles in providing access to information in a digital world. Four challenges faced by libraries are the invisibility of infrastructure, the changing nature of collections, the preservation of materials and content, and the boundaries between information institutions.

Invisible Infrastructure

Infrastructure tends to be visible only when it breaks down. The invisibility of information work in particular was identified many years ago (Paisley 1980). Infrastructure is embedded in other structures, is transparent, and is linked with conventions of practice of day-to-day work (Star and Ruhleder 1996). Much of what libraries and librarians do is not apparent to their users. Considerable professional time and vast amounts of paraprofessional and clerical time are devoted to the processes of selecting, collecting, organizing, preserving, and conserving materials so they are available for access. The selection process requires a continuing dialog with the user community to determine current needs, continuous scanning of available resources, and judicious application of financial resources. Once selected, the items are collected, whether in physical form or by acquiring access rights. This process, which requires negotiation with publishers and others who hold the rights to desired items, sometimes takes months or years, depending on the materials and the rights. As new items are acquired, metadata are created to describe their form, content, and relationship to other items in the collection. Once in the collection, resources must be preserved and conserved to ensure continuous availability over time.

Invisible Successes

If all these processes are done well, then people can find what they need, when they need it, in the form in which they want it. Users may encounter a catalog that is easily searched, a web site with a clear organization of relevant materials, a library building with good signage that leads them to desired resources, and professional staff who know the collection and can guide them in their information-seeking activities. Conversely, when these processes are not done well, users are aware of inadequate resources, poor organization, complex user interfaces, and a lack of staff to assist them.

Libraries risk being victims of their own success. The more ubiquitous their presence in their organizations and communities, the less apparent their role may be. The more services that are provided electronically, and the less need to visit a physical place, the less their users may be aware of who provides those services.

Invisible Content and Costs

The claim that the Internet will replace libraries often is based on questionable assumptions. Three common misconceptions are that all useful information exists somewhere on the Internet, that information is available without cost, and that it can be found by anyone willing to spend enough time searching for it (Borgman 1997c; Miller 1997).

online and offline resources   Only a small portion of the world's information exists in electronic form, much less on the Internet. Few journals or other print publications were created in electronic form until the late 1960s, and most of those early tapes and disks were discarded after the print products were published. Indexing and abstracting services began producing online databases in the 1970s, rarely converting print indexes that were created earlier than the 1960s. Vast portions of the world's knowledge resides in libraries, archives, museums, government agencies, and in private hands, in print or other hard-copy form, having been collected over decades or centuries. To use these materials, their existence first must be discovered, then access acquired. Catalogs, indexes, finding aids, and other forms of metadata, online and offline, serve the discovery function. Though some older materials such as rare and valuable manuscripts would gain a broader audience through digitization, relatively few older documents are in sufficient demand to justify digitization "just in case" someone wants them. Delivering physical copies or digitizing materials on a "just in time" basis are more feasible scenarios from an economic standpoint.

fee vs. free   The assumption that everything on the Internet would be free was more prevalent before the growth of online bookstores, shopping malls, and stock brokerages (Borgman 1997c; Miller 1997). Naive statements that "information wants to be free" are gradually being replaced by the recognition that resources available without charge are being paid for by someone: advertisers, governments, universities (as part of grant or research projects), political or religious groups, or public or nonprofit organizations. With the exception of government information, such as the databases of congressional legislation and records maintained by the Library of Congress[3] and reports filed by publicly traded corporations with the Securities and Exchange Commission,[4] or university-supported full-text digital libraries of out-of-print materials, little of the content available without charge on the Internet duplicates content collected by libraries. Libraries deliberately collect materials that are difficult for individuals to acquire on their own. Many items, such as scholarly journals and legal and technical databases, are prohibitively expensive unless amortized over the cost of a large user community. Others, such as unusual items from foreign sources, may be available for a nominal fee but expensive to identify and acquire. Once materials are out of print or otherwise unavailable for purchase, libraries usually are the only place to find them. In assessing the cost of acquiring information, one must take into account the time spent by information seekers as well as the direct costs of the resources and the time spent by librarians and other personnel in making those resources available. Students may place little monetary value on their own time, but spending many hours to discover and acquire "free" resources is rarely cost effective in profit-making environments. Professional assistance in information retrieval is often more cost effective than self-service.

added value   In assessing the tradeoffs between information resources available for purchase and those offered without fee, users need to consider other factors such as the integrity of the source, the reliability and validity of the content, and other intangibles. Commercial vendors of such

3. E.g., Thomas, named "in the spirit of Thomas Jefferson." The URL is www.thomas.loc.gov.

4. E.g., EDGAR (Electronic Data Gathering, Analysis, and Retrieval system). The URL is www.sec.gov/edgarhp.htm.

products add value by ensuring the accuracy of content and quality of reproduction (or other characteristics specific to the format), offering multiple versions or formats of resources, and providing customer support. If users of digital information products have problems implementing them on local systems, questions about searching, or other difficulties, they usually can get assistance from the producer. Similarly, libraries provide support for their services and obtain additional assistance from the producers of the material they purchase. Such support is rarely available with free Internet resources, and thus substantial costs can be incurred in making use of them. The practice of law is especially dependent on information resources that are accurate, authoritative, and current. Cases can be won or lost based on the quality of the information on which legal arguments are founded. Lawyers, law professors, and law librarians are concerned about the integrity of new online resources in comparison to the trusted sources on which they have long relied (Ballard, Spahr, Andrews, and Ingersoll 1999; Edwards 1997; Haigh 1997; Newman 1999; White 1995). Many valuable sources of legal information are appearing on the World Wide Web, both on general subjects and on practice-specific areas such as tax, securities, intellectual property, and anti-trust (Johnson and Krzyminski 1999). Some free sources of case law and statutes are appearing online in direct competition with the established and expensive commercial services provided by Lexis-Nexis and Westlaw. Legal professionals are reluctant to rely on those free resources, however, because neither the accuracy that commercial publishers provide through proofreading and verification of final authoritative versions, nor the persistence of the source, are ensured (Edwards 1997; White 1995). Online sources for treatises and other materials may have comparable content, but some find the analytical capabilities inferior to that of paper (Haigh 1997). The concern for accuracy and authority in online legal resources has spawned a series of articles identifying criteria for evaluation and web sites that evaluate other online sources (Ballard, Spahr, Andrews, and Ingersoll 1999; Edwards 1997; Haigh 1997; Newman 1999; White 1995). All these authors conclude that the onus is on the researcher to evaluate the integrity of the source. To some extent, this always has been true. What is new is the proliferation of self-publishing and the impermanence of online sources. Determining the source and reliability of content is much more difficult in this environment.

The imprimatur of an established publisher who ensures accuracy and assumes responsibility is an intangible value for which it is difficult to assign a price.

Content and Collections

In the eyes of the public, libraries are often synonymous with their collections. What may not be apparent is that collections are much more than the sum of their parts, bringing together disparate items and identifying relationships between them. The world's great collections are known for their depth in particular areas of study, rather than for breadth alone. Digital collections and hybrid collections of materials in many formats raise questions of what it means to "collect," especially when no physical artifact may be associated with a purchase.

Purposes of Collections

Historically, library collections have served four basic purposes: preservation (keeping materials for the future, as they may be unavailable if not collected at the time of their creation), dispensing (providing access to their contents), bibliographic (identifying what exists on a topic), and symbolic (conferring status and prestige on the institution) (Buckland 1992). All these purposes change in character with digital and hybrid collections. When a library acquires access to remote digital libraries on behalf of its user community, is that digital library part of "the collection"? Who is responsible for preserving digital content in distributed environments? What are the boundaries of a library's collection when it dispenses resources that it does not physically house and may not own? When libraries rely on cooperatively maintained digital libraries of metadata to determine what exists, where it exists, and how to acquire access to it, who is responsible for bibliographic control? Does having a large collection of electronic resources confer the same status on an institution as having a large collection of print materials?

Digital Collections

Libraries always have collected materials in a variety of formats, but digital documents are the first to transcend time and place. Digital documents can exist in numerous identical copies, or one copy can be accessed by numerous users, accentuating the tradeoffs between assets and access (Higginbotham and Bowdoin 1993). Collection-development librarians try to spend their funds on the materials judged most likely to be needed by their user communities, and then rely on cooperative agreements to borrow other items on demand. However, in the case of electronic resources it may be more reasonable to acquire items only on demand. For example, journals may cease to exist as volumes of multiple issues, each with multiple articles; they may be replaced by unitary articles that are acquired individually.

Uses of Collections

As Buckland explains in his classic text on library services (1988), many books have been written on how to collect library materials in support of a user community, but little attention has been paid to why libraries collect materials or to how people actually use those materials. In adapting information institutions to new environments, more needs to be known about how people use both printed and digital materials. Information studies research is expanding in scope to encompass the full information life cycle: capturing information at the time of creation, making it accessible, and maintaining and preserving it in forms useful to the user community. Concerns also are expanding to include group processes, rather than viewing individuals as sole actors in information-related activities. The concept of a collection is changing accordingly. Collections are hybrid in form and in scope, linked with other collections internal and external to the organizations that support them.

Preservation and Access

Until recently, concern for the preservation of information resources was relegated to a small cadre of archivists, special-collections librarians, and museum professionals. Public awareness of the fragility of software and of the impermanence of digital data increased substantially because of the "Y2K" problem of converting software to handle dates in the year 2000 and beyond (Chen et al. 1999). Although preservation is a high priority, it must be balanced with access considerations. The best methods for long-term preservation are often poor for access, and vice versa. For example, microfilm is superior for preservation purposes but inferior for access, and digitization is superior for access but inferior for preservation.

A number of factors have made preservation and access pressing matters. One is the concern for preservation of existing print collections, many of which are physically deteriorating because of the fragility of the paper, film, microform, or other materials on which they were created and because of inadequate storage conditions. Another is the lack of means to maintain digital content in a usable form through changes in standards and technology. A third is the difficulty of maintaining persistent access to digital collections. A fourth is the failure to capture and preserve digital content at the point of creation, resulting in the deterioration of public and private records systems.

Preservation of Physical Documents

In a print environment, preserving materials means acquiring them while they are available and then storing them safely for use by present and future generations. Similarly, conservation of print means repairing physical materials to keep them usable, such as patching torn pages and treating brittle paper with chemicals. In most countries, national libraries and archives are charged with preserving and conserving the cultural heritage of their nations. Public libraries and local government archives often have similar responsibilities for their local communities. Special libraries and corporate archives have parallel responsibilities for the records of their parent organizations. These organizations follow accepted practices and standards, which are supported by national and international cooperative relationships, all of which are part of the (often invisible) information infrastructure.

"Brittle books," the crumbling of materials printed on acid paper between the middle of the nineteenth century and the middle of the twentieth, is the most widely known preservation problem. Large portions of the world's collections of print materials from this period are deteriorating, especially those not stored in modern buildings with adequate heating, air conditioning, and humidity controls (Kislovskaya 1996; Lesk 1990; Porck 1996; Sanders 1987). The Commission on Preservation and Access was formed in 1986 "to develop and encourage collaborative strategies for preserving and providing access to the accumulated human record." *Slow Fires*, a video about the deterioration of paper, film, and other physical storage media, was shown widely on television and at public events. The campaign raised awareness inside and outside the library and archives fields, involving historians and other scholars, governments, funding agencies, and the public at large.[5]

International cooperative efforts are underway with the long-term goal of preserving at least one copy of each item deemed of historical significance and providing access to its content (Cook 1997; McClung 1996). No single institution can afford to preserve and conserve all its deteriorating materials; however, by dividing the responsibility, each institution can preserve its share of the world's collection and improve the long-term availability of content for all. Unfortunately, this solution is less simple and complete than it sounds. Preservation and conservation are too expensive to save everything that anyone deems significant, and thus the selection process is often contentious. Underlying the selection process is the difficulty of setting objective criteria for significance, in view of the many social, cultural, and political factors involved. A critical policy challenge lies in determining who decides what is significant.

Preservation of Content

The "brittle books" problem was a catalyst for more general discussion of preservation, conservation, and access to information resources. The first level of preservation decisions is often whether the physical object is sufficiently significant to save and conserve, or whether preserving the content is sufficient. Sometimes both are required.

If items are significant as artifacts, such as manuscripts or first editions of important works, then physical conservation is required. If items are worth saving primarily because of their content, such as classic works that were printed in many copies, then photographing or scanning them may be sufficient. If the content is to be captured and the artifact saved, then the document is handled carefully, turning pages individually and laying the document flat for photography or scanning. This process and some methods of chemical treatment can cause further physical deterioration, so materials are best handled only once (Lesk 1990; Lynn et al. 1990; Porck 1996; Sanders 1997). If only the content is to be preserved, then the object may

5. The Commission on Preservation and Access is now a program of the Council on Library and Information Resources (1755 Massachusetts Ave. NW, suite 500, Washington, DC 20036; http://clir.stanford.edu). Slow Fires (Sanders 1987) is available on video from the Council, as is Into the Future (Sanders 1997).

be dismantled so that individual pages can be stacked in high-speed automatic devices. The latter approach is the least expensive method of preserving content, but it destroys the object in the process. Similar tradeoffs exist in preservation and access for materials other than paper. Film, videotape, and sound recordings are deteriorating too. Sometimes the physical artifact must be conserved and saved, and at other times it is sufficient to transfer the content to another format.

Once the content is captured, it can be stored as a digital document or on microfilm, depending on form and content, and on access and preservation requirements. Microfilm is the most common form for preserving text and still images, as the film is readable for as long as 300 years under optimal conditions. Microfilm is poor for access, however. Pages must be located on microfiche or long reels of microfilm, and most people find the machines unpleasant to use. Digitization is often proposed as an alternative, because it is excellent for access. At present, however, digitization is poor for preservation (Ester 1996; Lynn et al. 1990; Smith 1999; Weber and Dorr 1997).

These decisions about the means by which content is preserved bring issues of form and function into sharp relief. The most cost-effective method of creating a global digital library would be to scan the collections of the world's libraries and archives with fast automatic scanners, destroying the materials in the process. This is not a socially acceptable solution, of course. Not even the most heartless technocrat would destroy the Gutenberg Bible or Shakespeare's First Folio for the sake of cheap digitizing. But where should the line be drawn? There is neither enough time nor enough money to preserve in physical form all the printed materials, films, videotapes, and sound recordings that already exist, much less all the letters, memoranda, reports, and other documentation. Among the most significant—and delicate—decisions that librarians, archivists, museum curators, and other information professionals make is what to select, preserve, and conserve. Lacking adequate funds for preservation, they are faced with difficult choices between saving the content of a large number of objects through inexpensive scanning and saving much smaller number of objects through physical preservation. The fact that these institutions destroy some materials in the process of saving them is neither widely known nor widely advertised. The tradeoffs in preservation and access and the associated economics are difficult to explain to a book-loving public. A major research library recently found itself at the center of public controversy over the destruction of books in the preservation process. Despite following accepted professional practices, the library ceased dismantling books in response to public opinion. As a result, it will be able to preserve the content of far less of its crumbling collection.

Preservation of Digital Documents

Whether materials are "born digital" or digitized from other formats, digital documents must be maintained in a form that continues to be useful and usable to those who may later seek it. In view of the rate of advances in information technology, maintaining content in a continuously viable form is a major challenge. Magnetic media (computer disks, audio, video, and data tapes, etc.) must be copied every few years to maintain the readability of content, and must be stored properly to ensure long-term readability (Hedstrom 1998; Van Bogart 1995). Even if the medium remains viable, it can be difficult to find devices that will read older formats. Already it is difficult to locate operational devices to read media that were widely distributed only a few years ago, such as 5¼-inch floppy disks and 33⅓-rpm phonograph records. Devices to read 8-inch floppy disks, 78-rpm records, Betamax videotapes, and reel-to-reel film are even harder to find. Drives for 3½-inch disks have ceased to be a standard feature of new computers; thus, these disks soon will become obsolete.

Even if the media are readable and devices are available, a user must locate hardware with the necessary operating systems and application software to read older files. Many people have cabinets full of disks containing word processing files created on versions of Microsoft Word or WordPerfect for pre-Windows DOS. Others have files created on Wordstar under the CP/M operating system, which competed with early versions of DOS. Similarly, many people keep files containing spreadsheets, images, sounds, and other content long after they have disposed of the hardware and software on which the files were created. Unless these files are transferred to subsequent generations of hardware and software quickly, they are not likely to be read again.

Various methods have been proposed for dealing with hardware and software obsolescence and with the deterioration of magnetic media. So far, all the proposed methods have significant limitations. The least viable approach is to create a "cybernetic museum" (Cook 1995) containing working models of obsolete hardware and software. This approach has several weaknesses. It is not likely that sufficient spare parts could be acquired and sufficient expertise maintained to make this approach feasible over a long period of time. Obtaining and maintaining all possible combinations of software for each generation of hardware would be difficult. Another weakness of the museum approach is that data created on older devices (e.g., 8-inch floppy disks) will have been transferred to newer media (e.g., CD-ROMs) for which no device drivers exist on the original machine (Rothenberg 1999). A more promising approach for some applications is to emulate software applications and associated operating systems on contemporary systems, thus enabling older software to be run on newer computers (Rothenberg 1995, 1996, 1997, 1999). The most general solution, and one currently in use at large scientific data centers, is to migrate digital content to new media with each new generation of technology (Baru et al. 1998a, 1998b; Foster and Kesselman 1999; Halem et al. 1999; Hedstrom 1991, 1993, 1998; Moore et al. 1999; Rajasekar et al. 1999). The migration approach requires continuous investment in the data to maintain access, but it takes advantage of newer, denser, faster, and less expensive storage technologies as they become available.

All the proposed data-preservation strategies require active efforts to maintain the data in readable form, rather than the passive strategies of putting a book on a shelf or putting paper and microfilm in a storage vault. Many different strategies will be required to address a wide range of circumstances, such as large scientific data centers, corporate archives, faculty research data and teaching materials, and families' digital photographs, genealogical, and tax records.

At this time, we have more questions than answers about how to ensure long-term preservation of digital materials. Awareness of the problem is growing rapidly, which should lead to more research and more policy aimed at solving it (Chen et al. 1999; Hedstrom 1998; Rothenberg 1999).

Persistent Access

In a print environment, libraries hold copies of materials long after their authors are dead and their publishers are out of business. In a digital environment, when the creator of a digital library goes out of business, or decides that providing the service is no longer profitable, or stops supporting the system for any other reason, the content may cease to be available. Digital libraries can disappear without notice, such as when the computer running them crashes and the owners decide not to revive it. Libraries that provide access to commercial digital libraries may do so under lease arrangements that prohibit them from maintaining older materials or converting them to another format when the publisher stops supporting the product. Universities are concerned about the disposition of digital libraries created by their faculty once research funding ends, the course ceases to be taught by that instructor, or the instructor leaves the university. Back issues of electronic journals or other materials may not be available anywhere, to anyone, if those who hold the rights to them have not ensured their preservation.

Capturing Digital Records

Creating records in digital form is introducing a host of unanticipated preservation problems in addition to those outlined above (Cook 1995; Cook 1997; Ester 1996; Kahle 1997; Lesk 1997b; Lynn et al. 1990; Society of American Archivists 1995). When organizations created all their documentation on paper, they had systematic means of controlling it. Most documents were created in multiple copies, with at least one stored in a central place under the control of archivists, records managers, or librarians. When people later needed to find memoranda, purchase orders, contracts, design specifications, correspondence, or other essential documents, they knew where to look. Now most such documents are created on desktop computers, and the "originals" may reside only on local disk drives or on network servers. These documents are subject to purging when the computer user needs more disk space, when the computer system is upgraded, or when a new employee takes over the job. Documents may be password protected and thus under the exclusive control of the individual who created them. Although documents on personal computers may be copied as part of routine network backup procedures, the documents may not be readable by others who do not have the appropriate software or passwords. Further, documents captured in backup procedures may be described only by the file name, lacking other metadata necessary to identify their contents. Few organizations have systematic and effective plans to ensure long-term preservation and access of documents created on personal computers.

Institutional Boundaries

Demands facing libraries, such as the risk of becoming an invisible part of the infrastructure, the changing nature of collections, and preservation and access of content, are also concerns of archives and museums. Rayward (1993, p. 230) notes that libraries, archives, and museums had "an undifferentiated past." Throughout much of the eighteenth and the nineteenth century, books, papers, works of art, specimens of plants and animals, fossils, minerals, coins, and other objects were gathered in common collections. These collections supported broad, multi-disciplinary intellectual interests, without the division between the sciences and the humanities that we take for granted today. The functional differentiation of these three institutions is relatively recent and has resulted in separate physical locations and specialized professional practices. Each takes primary but not exclusive responsibility for a type of material. Libraries mostly collect published materials. Archives mostly collect the records of individuals, organizations, and governments. Museums collect almost anything, organizing it around a general theme (such as art, history, or natural history), a specific theme (such as air and space or automobiles), or a highly specialized theme. Two extremes of specialization (both located in Los Angeles) are the Museum of Jurassic Technology (Weschler 1995), which collects oddities of the natural world, and the La Brea Tar Pits, an active scientific site that displays objects retrieved from the adjacent tar pits.

Partitioning intellectual content among these three sets of institutions is an artificial division of the natural world, and it does not necessarily serve the information seeker well. To study a painter, for example, a student or a scholar ideally should have access to published works about the artist and the artist's work (e.g., books and journals collected by a library), primary materials (e.g., letters and sketches collected by an archive), and the paintings themselves (e.g., the objects collected by a museum). Many information-bearing objects could reasonably be housed in any of these institutions, and indeed ownership is often contentious. Does an important map once owned by a famous person belong with his or her other papers in an archive, or in a library map collection, or framed in a museum? Does a book containing original art works as illustrations belong in a library, in a museum, or in a museum library? Does a bust of a significant author belong in a library reading room, or in a museum? No clear answers to such questions exist for physical objects, and the questions become more complex with digital objects.

Only in recent years have these professional communities started to work together on common standards for description, representation, and organization. Although considerable progress is being made, the digital collections managed by these communities still are far from interoperable. Professional education for libraries and archives is beginning to converge, but libraries and archives maintain large bodies of professional practice distinct to their institutions.

Nor are libraries, archives, and museums the only institutions with their own sets of professional practices related to information. Creators of geographic and spatial data have developed sophisticated metadata standards and are playing a key role in digital library research. Medical records management is a growing area, owing to the sometimes-competing concerns of health-care providers, insurers, patients, and regulators. Similarly, legal informatics is a distinct specialty, in view of the specialized structures and practices of the legal community. Scholarly and professional societies exist to serve these and many other specialties in information science, informatics, librarianship, archives, museums, records management, and related areas. Although multiple societies sometimes cooperate in organizing conferences, meetings, or publications, considerable duplication of effort exists.

As the content of collections and the metadata required to manage those collections are maintained in digital form, the distinctions between libraries, archives, museums, and other information institutions are blurring. In the long run, a holistic approach to information access holds promise for breaking down artificial barriers between disciplines and media, and thus doing a service to the user community. In the short run, these institutions and professions are seeking new niches in which to make unique contributions, sometimes cooperating with each other and sometimes competing.

Summary and Conclusions

Computer networks offer a wealth of new opportunities for providing access to information, so much so that the continuing need for libraries is being questioned. The real question is not whether libraries are needed, but how best to provide access to information in a networked world and how best to support the marketplace for ideas. Libraries in democratic societies are part of a social strategy to promote learning and invention and to ensure an informed citizenry. As methods for creating, seeking, and using information are adapted for digital documents and distributed networks, the means for maintaining these social values are being reassessed. As knowledge becomes a form of capital, principles of open access to information in democratic societies also are being challenged.

Libraries, archives, museums, and other institutions have a long history of theories, principles, and practices for managing information in print. They have adapted their approaches to new media as they are invented. As a result, information institutions are distinguished more by their principles and practices than by the type of materials they manage. Many, if not most, of their approaches for managing physical artifacts can be adapted for digital documents. Libraries in particular play a central role in their countries' information infrastructures, selecting and acquiring resources when they are available, organizing them, preserving and conserving them, and providing access to them for their user communities. They work cooperatively to create "virtual collections," balancing "just in time" delivery with "just in case" collecting.

Relationships between libraries and their user communities also are changing. Public libraries have a broad service mandate and are often in the public eye. They make difficult choices between competing goals, such as print collections vs. online services, physical places vs. virtual spaces, space for people vs. space for books, and buying vs. borrowing. Tradeoffs among competing goals faced by academic libraries are similar to those faced by public libraries. In addition to their traditional responsibilities, many academic libraries are expanding into new areas, such as electronic publishing and tele-learning. Special libraries serve the most clearly defined user communities and provide the most tailored services. They rely heavily on computer networks, digital libraries, and the collections of academic and public libraries to fill the information requirements of their users.

I identified four challenges in rethinking libraries in a digital age. The first is how to maintain visibility while being part of a well-functioning information infrastructure. When people are able to find the information they want, when they want it, and in a useful form, they are often not aware of the effort, expertise, and economic resources involved in providing it. The second is how to manage collections as they become more hybrid and distributed. The third is how to preserve physical and digital materials. Present collections of print, film, magnetic media, and other materials are deteriorating because of the instability of media on which they were recorded and because of poor storage conditions. Future collections are also at risk, because digital media deteriorate and the technology necessary to read and interpret them becomes obsolete. The fourth challenge is how to take advantage of the blurring boundaries between information institutions and information professions. In developing new approaches to managing distributed information resources, it should be possible to draw on the best theories, principles, and practices of libraries, archives, and museums. The fundamental goal is to balance cooperation and competition in implementing social strategies that continue to support cultural values for a digital age.

8

Acting Locally, Thinking Globally

Ideally, a global digital library would provide access to information in all the world's languages, to all people, all the time. Anyone could create information in their native language, yet others could discover that information and have it translated into their preferred languages and formats. The ideal case may be well beyond our understanding of technology or human behavior, but it raises issues worthy of exploration. Generally speaking, the easiest information systems to construct are those with small, consistent collections that serve small and homogeneous user communities. In contrast, a global digital library is the hardest-case scenario: a vast and disparate set of collections intended to serve a vast and heterogeneous user community.

No single collection, user interface, or set of system capabilities will serve young and old, novice and expert, artist and physicist, in Peoria and Prague. Nor will any single system provide adequate access to books, music, movies, and numeric data, much less serve applications as diverse as electronic commerce, weather modeling, census tracking, library catalogs, and virtual classrooms. Yet people with varying backgrounds and skills, speaking different languages, have similar information needs. Content of interest may exist in a wide variety of forms and languages, and the same content and collections may be of interest to a wide range of people, for many different reasons. The prospect of a global digital library presents several opportunities. One is to make information resources accessible to particular user communities while at the same time making those same resources accessible to a broader, ill-defined, and perhaps unknown audience. Another is to enable users to bridge the many formats, representations, and languages of individual digital libraries in their quest for information resources. This chapter explores multilingual data exchange as an example of the tradeoffs between tailoring to local communities and generalizing to a global audience. This particular problem is urgent (in view of the rate at which new text is being created), long-term (in view of the relative stability of languages compared to the transient nature of new media formats), and broad-reaching (in view of the fact that some form of textual content is involved in most forms of electronic communication, whether alone or as descriptions of other media) (Borgman 1997b). Because similar problems are involved in multilingual and multimedia digital libraries, examples are drawn from both areas.

From Local Systems to Global Systems

Systems must be easy to learn and use if they are to support a large and diverse user community. Users of a global digital library will need to follow paths between systems and to exchange content between digital libraries and between applications. At one extreme, a single user interface can be designed for the lowest common denominator of users and content. However, any system that tries to be all things to all people rarely serves anyone well. At the other extreme, a system can provide many user interfaces, multiple sets of capabilities, and multiple ways of representing and organizing content. The latter approach tends to result in excessive complexity that serves few users well. Solutions in the middle range include translating or transferring content on demand between languages, media, and forms of representation.

Medium and Language

Speech carries different meaning than does written text, and photographs convey information differently from movies. Making oneself understood when speaking through a translator is far more difficult than making oneself understood when conversing with a colleague in a common native language. Language translations, whether oral or written and whether manual or automatic, are never full equivalents. Thus, the content and the effect of a message cannot be separated from the form of communication and the language in which it is communicated.

For these and many other reasons, it usually is desirable to capture content in the richest forms possible to ensure the maximum potential for communication. The more accurate the representation of the original form, the less distortion of the creator's (author, artist, film maker, engineer, etc.) intentions, for example. However, the quest to represent unique features of the original (e.g., colors, sounds, typefaces, page layouts, numeric data structures specific to the originating software) may be at odds with the goal of standardizing formats to simplify access. Similarly, although content is most accurate in its original language, translation may be necessary to serve a broader audience.

The paradox of information retrieval is the need to describe the information that one does not have. Searchers must express their information needs by supplying descriptions of information that might solve their problem. People's ability to describe such information is limited by a number of factors, including the degree of problem definition, their knowledge of the problem, their knowledge of the system operations available to solve the problem, and their familiarity with the language(s) in which the desired information exists. An expert on a topic who is knowledgeable about both the terminology and the system's capabilities is better able to describe the information sought than is a novice to the topic and the system. People express themselves in different ways, and their terms often do not match those of the creators and indexers of the information, whether human or machine. Conversely, the same terms may have multiple meanings in multiple contexts. In addition, the same text string may retrieve words in multiple languages, adding yet more variance to the results. An important goal in designing information retrieval systems is to bridge these gaps between the ways that searchers and creators express themselves.

Searching for information in multimedia digital libraries is yet more complex than text-only searching. Many options exist for describing sounds, images, numeric data sets, and mixed-media objects. Sounds can be described with words, or with other sounds (e.g., playing a tune and finding one like it); images can be described with words, by drawing a similar object, or by providing or selecting an exemplar. As Croft (1995) notes, general solutions to multimedia indexing are proving more difficult than originally expected, and solutions that do exist tend to be of limited utility. The most progress is being made in well-defined applications in a single medium, such as searching for music or for photographs of faces. Medium-specific and application-specific searching mechanisms can be combined with textual searching mechanisms, however (Shneiderman 1998).

Design Tradeoffs

In local systems, designers can tailor user interfaces, representation of content, and functional capabilities to the local culture and to the available hardware and software. Input and output parameters are easily specified. If users need to create sounds or to draw images, these capabilities can be provided, along with display, capture, and printing abilities in the matching standards. Keyboards can be set to support the local input language, and screens and printers can be set to support the proper display of local languages.

Designers have far less control over digital libraries destined for use in globally distributed environments. Users' hardware and software platforms are typically diverse and rapidly changing. Designers often must specify a minimum configuration or require a minimum version of client software, making tradeoffs between lowering the requirements to reach a larger population or raising requirements to provide more sophisticated capabilities. The more sophisticated the multimedia or multilingual searching capabilities, the higher the requirements are likely to be and the fewer people that are likely to be served.

Interoperability, Portability, and Data Exchange

Multilingual and multimedia information exchange are not new issues for digital libraries or for distributed computing networks. In 1983, for example, UNESCO released a report on "compatibility issues affecting information systems and services" that reviewed the past 20 years' work in this area and identified new challenges (Lancaster and Smith 1983). In 1994, the (US) National Institute for Standards and Technology, jointly with the Technology Policy Working Group of the Information Infrastructure Task Force, held a workshop on standards policy for the national information infrastructure at which issues of interoperability, data exchange, and open systems, and the mechanisms to achieve them were addressed (Kahin and Abbate 1995). A later research workshop under the aegis of the (US) Digital Library Initiative addressed interoperability and scalability issues specific to digital libraries (Lynch and Garcia-Molina 1995). The joint working groups of the National Science Foundation and the European Union also identified interoperability as a key issue in digital libraries research (Schauble and Smeaton 1998).

Interoperability issues can be divided into three categories (Libicki 1995a,b). The first is *interoperability*, which Libicki defines as getting systems (e.g., telephone systems) to work with one another in real time. Although interoperability failures can prevent communication, systems usually can be patched together to make them interoperate. The second category is *portability*, which enables software to work on different systems (as when a computer language can run on any machine with a certain hardware platform and operating system). When portability failures occur, they usually can be fixed by writing specialized code to accommodate the variations or by dropping functions and working only with a common core of portable functions. The third category is *data exchange* among different systems, such as the transferring of word processing or database files. When data exchange failures occur, they usually can be repaired by writing specialized code to accommodate variations in format, although some data loss may occur. Failures at any point can be expensive to repair in terms of time, effort, labor costs, and accuracy. Incomplete or incorrect data exchange can result in failures to find information, in failures to authenticate identities or content, and in permanent loss of information. All three categories are relevant to digital libraries. Accurate data exchange is a prerequisite for the portability of content-management software and for the ability of distributed systems to interoperate effectively in real time.

Implementing Standards
From a purely technical perspective, the solution appears simple and obvious: everyone should adopt common standards for representing text, images, sounds, languages, etc. This approach is not feasible for practical or political reasons, however, and it is not necessarily desirable. There is far more to standardization than standards. Standards are at the forefront of technology policy because of their strategic importance in economic competitiveness and diplomacy (Hawkins 1995; Kahin and Abbate 1995; Lundvall 1995). Many players and stakes are involved in the standards process. Depending on the situation, some players would benefit by the establishment of a certain standard, others would benefit from the establishment of any standard that addresses the problem, and still others would benefit if no standard were established. If standards are established too early, they can stifle the development of a technology; if established too late,

they can contribute to chaos in the marketplace and to the isolation of parties who chose competing standards (Besen 1995; David 1995).

The political economy of standards is well studied, but not well understood (Agre 1995a; Hawkins, Mansell, and Skea 1995; Lundvall 1995; Mansell 1993). Standards are most likely to be developed and implemented when it is in the interest of many players to do so (Besen 1995). The trend in information infrastructure development is toward open systems that support interconnection, interoperability, and data exchange. Definitions of "openness" abound, as do strategies to implement open systems (Band 1995; Branscomb and Kahin 1995; Libicki 1995a; Wagner, Cargill, and Slomovic 1995).

I raise these issues here to address challenges related to information exchange between digital libraries, rather than to address the standards process per se. However, it must be acknowledged that standards development is itself a social process and that it is subject to a wide range of political and economic factors that often are independent of the technology. As Libicki (1995a) puts it, we are on a "rough road to the common byte."

From Monolingual to Multilingual Digital Libraries

Language is one of the most critical factors in access to information. Information is usable and useful only if it is in a language that can be read or otherwise understood. Communication between people speaking a common language, whether English, Spanish, Hungarian, or Mandarin, is influenced by factors such as subtleties of phrasing, vocabulary, regional accents, and knowledge of the subject matter being discussed. In monolingual information retrieval, some of these difficulties are ameliorated through standardizing forms (e.g., singular/plural, stemming to remove variant word endings), controlled vocabulary (e.g., thesauri that establish preferred terms and make cross-references from synonyms and related terms), and algorithms that employ knowledge of grammatical structure and word frequencies in the language.

People often need information that exists in languages other than those they read or speak, however. Human translators can bridge languages in oral and written communication. They can translate between spoken languages in real time, and they can translate texts. Translation is a challenging intellectual task, as no two languages map precisely onto one another. A word in one language may have several meanings in the other, and the interpreter must determine which is most appropriate. Conversely, one word may incorporate multiple meanings in another language and the appropriate subset must be identified. Often, a narrative explanation is needed in place of a single word. Meaning depends on context as well as on choice of words. Metaphors and idioms are particularly difficult to convey in other languages. Translators are really interpreters of meaning; that is why automatic translation is so limited. Computers can provide approximate translations, particularly of scientific texts, but are far from a reliable substitute for expert human language interpreters.

Providing access to information in multiple languages is a challenge inherent in constructing a global information infrastructure. It is also fundamental to tailoring and interoperability tradeoffs. Given a choice, people generally prefer to communicate in their native language, both online and offline. Communication in international environments frequently involves multiple languages, however, and people often need information written in unfamiliar languages. Multilingual information access is a pervasive problem in automation, and it is of great concern for anyone exchanging information over computer networks. Multilingual access issues affect electronic commerce, information institutions such as libraries, archives, museums, schools, and universities, and those who produce hardware and software for network applications.

Multilingual Information Access
Multilingual digital libraries are being created by countries with more than one national language, by the European Union, and by international research consortia and international businesses. Major scientific, technical, and medical databases, such as INSPEC and Medline, long have contained metadata in English to represent materials in other languages. Monolingual digital libraries also are being created in many different languages. Many of these digital libraries are of interest well beyond the borders of the countries creating them, and to users who are native speakers of other languages. A fundamental challenge of constructing a global information infrastructure and a global digital library is to provide access to these collections, regardless of the language of the content and the language of the information seeker.

Multilingual information access is a complex problem. Peters and Picchi (1997) divide it into two basic parts: (1) multiple-language recognition, manipulation, and display, and (2) multilingual or cross-lingual search and retrieval. The first part involves matters such as encoding character sets and symbols so that they can be exchanged, displayed, and printed accurately, and so that the data can be manipulated (sorted, searched, or otherwise exploited). The second part of the problem is to search for content in other languages, otherwise known as "cross-language information retrieval." Peters and Picchi identify three approaches that are being studied: text translation by machine, knowledge-based techniques, and corpus-based techniques.

Text translation can be divided further: (a) translating the full content of the digital library into another language, or (b) translating only the query (Cross Language Information Retrieval 1997; Frederking et al. 1997; Kando and Aizawa 1998; Kando et al. 1998; Peters and Picchi 1997). Translating the full content is rarely feasible except in very small and specific applications. Oudet (1997) gives the example of meteorological reports, where automatic translation is reasonably successful. For most applications, translating queries appears to be more promising. Queries in English can be translated into Japanese and searched in Japanese databases, and vice versa, for example (Kando and Aizawa 1998; Kando et al. 1998).

Knowledge-based approaches involve multilingual dictionaries, thesauri, or ontologies (Peters and Picchi 1997). In these approaches, searchers can construct a query using terms in their own language. The multilingual thesaurus is then used to translate the terms into the target language; they are then submitted to databases in that language. Thesauri can be translated pairwise(say, between English and Spanish) or among a larger number of languages (say, English, Spanish, French, German, and Russian). In the latter case, a common core of terms would be established, and then the linguistic equivalents in each language would be determined (Soergel 1998).

Corpus-based techniques involve linguistic characteristics of a language and the distribution of terms in a collection of documents. Information retrieval techniques developed for monolingual retrieval, such as vector-space models and probabilistic methods, can be employed for multiple languages (Cross Language Information Retrieval 1997; Frederking et al. 1997; Peters and Picchi 1997). Usually some test databases in each language are required to "train" the algorithms about the relationships between corpora (bodies of text) in each language.

Each of these methods is both promising and problematic. None are complete solutions, and all are under active study. For any of the cross-language techniques to be effective, however, underlying technical issues in managing multilingual text must be resolved.

Character Encoding

Character encoding is at the heart of the data-recognition, data-manipulation, and display components of multilingual information access. The creation of characters in electronic form involves hardware and software to support input, storing, processing, sorting, displaying, and printing. Each character—or ideograph in languages such as Chinese, Japanese, and Korean—needs a unique code to ensure that it sorts, displays, prints, and is matched properly upon searching. Additional codes are required for punctuation, direction of text (left to right or right to left), carriage returns, and line feeds. The internal representation of each character determines how it is treated by the hardware (keyboard, printer, display, etc.) and the application software (sorting, searching, etc.).

To the dismay of those whose languages have far larger character sets, typewriter keyboards were initially designed for the English language; thus, they contain only 26 letters, 10 numbers, basic punctuation, and a few special symbols. Only a few more symbols and function keys were added when the typewriter keyboard (known as the QWERTY keyboard, for the letters in the top row) was adapted to become a computer keyboard. Many versions of the QWERTY keyboard are now in use worldwide, varying by the location of punctuation, symbols, and function keys, and occasionally varying the location of letters. Special characters, such as letters with diacritics, can be generated by programming individual keys or by programming key sequences, often using the escape key. The same key sequence on two different keyboards may produce two different characters, depending on the encoding system employed. Conversely, key sequences required to generate a character vary by keyboard and encoding system.

Effective data exchange is heavily dependent on character encoding. Characters produced from different applications may appear the same on a screen or a printout but have different internal representations. Merging or transferring data between applications requires a common character-encoding standard or software to map variant encoding formats. Searchers need to have the appropriate keyboards and software to generate characters in the encoding standard in which the contents of a digital library are stored, whether locally resident or available through mapping software located at the digital library site or elsewhere. Local printers and displays must have the appropriate software to interpret and produce characters accurately. These factors are not specific to digital libraries; rather, they are issues for all distributed applications on a global information infrastructure.

Monolingual, Multilingual, and Universal Character Sets

Many standards and practices exist for encoding characters. Some are language specific, others are script specific (e.g., Latin or Roman, Arabic, Cyrillic, Hebrew), and some are universal standards that support most of the world's written languages. Digital libraries employ many different character-encoding formats, and this often leads to problems in exchanging data.

After many years of international discussion on the topic, it became apparent that adopting a universal character set offered the best hope for exchanging text in digital form. If data in all written languages were encoded in a common format, then data could be exchanged between monolingual and multilingual applications, whether electronic mail, electronic commerce, or digital libraries. Which common format to accept was a matter of long debate, however. In 1991, the Unicode Consortium and the International Organization for Standardization (ISO) finally reached an agreement to merge the 16-bit Unicode standard and the 32-bit ISO standard into a common 16-bit Unicode standard. Version 1.1 was first published in 1993; version 2.0 is currently the accepted Unicode standard (ISO/IEC 10646) (Libicki 1995b; *The Unicode Standard* 1996).[1]

Unicode can support more than 65,000 distinct characters. To date, the standard provides about 39,000 characters from the world's alphabets, ideograph sets, and symbol collections (The Unicode Standard 1998). It is supported by a growing number of the world's major hardware and software vendors, and it is being incorporated into popular operating systems

1. The URL of Unicode's home page is http://www.unicode.org.

and programming languages. As software for electronic commerce, digital libraries, automated library processing systems, and other applications begins to support Unicode, it will become more widely adopted. As storage costs continue to decline, the storage requirements of Unicode will be less of an issue, particularly for new applications.

In the meantime, massive amounts of text continue to be generated not only in language-specific and script-specific encoding standards but also in local and proprietary formats. Any of this text maintained in digital libraries may become legacy data that has to be mapped to Unicode or some other standard in the future. At present, digital library designers face difficult tradeoffs between the character-set standards in use by current exchange partners and the standard likely to be in international use in the future for a broader variety of applications.

Transliteration and Other Forms of Data Loss

A long-established intermediate approach to character encoding for languages that cannot be typed on a standard computer keyboard is transliteration, which matches characters or sounds from one language to another but does not translate meaning. Languages written in non-Roman scripts, such as Japanese, Arabic, Chinese, Korean, Persian (Farsi), Hebrew, and Yiddish (the "JACKPHY" languages), and Russian, are transliterated into Roman characters in many applications. Transliteration is necessary when mechanical devices such as typewriters and computers do not support the necessary scripts. It also is helpful for people without full competency in the script of the language (e.g., recognition of Chinese or Russian names or terms transliterated in English-language contexts, such as "Beijing" or "Gorbachev"). The transliteration process may be irreversible, and thus some data loss occurs. Despite the existence of an international standards body (ISO/TC46/SC2: Conversion of Written Languages), multiple transliteration systems exist for Cyrillic, Asian, and other character sets. Thus, transliteration can be inconsistent, which is why the same Russian name may appear as "Tchaikovsky" or as "Chaikovskii" depending on which system is used to transliterate Cyrillic characters.

Data also are lost when languages written in extensions of the Roman character set, such as French, Spanish, German, Hungarian, Czech, and

Polish, are stored without the diacritics (accents, umlauts, and other language-specific marks) that form additional characters (e.g., ó, ò, ô, ö, õ, and o are distinct characters, all of which are collapsed into o if the diacritics are omitted).

Data loss is not exclusive to text, however; it is rampant in visual and aural media. Image compression is essential for efficient transmission of either still or moving pictures, and application-specific image-compression standards exist for such applications as fax, pictures, moving images, and high-definition television (Libicki 1995b). Compression algorithms are made more efficient by discarding some of the data to reduce the granularity of the image. Images subjected to "lossy" compression are legible and are suitable for many applications, but the original image cannot be reconstructed. "Lossless" compression retains the full content but requires more storage and more transmission time. Similarly, for music, a popular compression algorithm known as MP3 is used to squeeze digital audio by a ratio of 12:1. MP3 compresses music sufficiently that audio files can be sent via the Internet or stored on a hard disk. Music compressed in MP3 can be expanded and played by an MP3 player with near-CD-quality sound, yet the files are small enough to be attached to an email message. The music industry is promoting another standard, and Microsoft is promoting yet a third standard for music compression and distribution (Chapman 1999). The acceptance of technical standards for music and other audio may be determined as much by the availability of playback devices as by the quality of reproduction.

The amount of data loss that is acceptable varies by application. Far more data loss is acceptable in email and in teleconferencing (where rapid communication tends to be valued over authoritative form) than in financial, legal, or bibliographic records (where authentication is essential). Textual data that have been transliterated or stripped of diacritics are likely to contain variant forms of words that will not match and sort properly, incomplete words that will not exchange properly with digital libraries using complete forms, and incomplete forms that are not adequate for authoritative or archival purposes. In digital libraries, any kind of data loss can result in information retrieval errors (e.g., no matches or wrong matches) and in collection-management errors (e.g., items that cannot be located).

Practices of the Library Community
The international library community began developing large multilingual digital libraries in the 1960s. Language representation is a particular concern for major research libraries, whose collections may include materials in as many as 400 written languages (OCLC 1998b). Standards for record structure and character sets were established long before either Unicode or the Internet was created. Hundreds of millions of bibliographic records exist around the world in variations of the MARC format, although in multiple character-set-encoding formats and multiple forms of transliteration. USMARC was implemented with the American Library Association (ALA) character set, which extends the English language keyboard to include diacritics from major Roman-script languages (Agenbroad 1992; *ALA Character Set* 1989). The ALA character set is used by OCLC and by most American library applications; languages not included in the ALA character set tend to be transliterated. The growing interest in adapting USMARC and other forms of MARC to Unicode reflects the fact that other systems (present and future) will have to accommodate the massive volume of MARC records that already exist in other character-set formats (Agenbroad 1992; Aliprand 1992a; *Beyond the English Catalog* 1997).

The Library of Congress—which contributes its records in digital form to OCLC, to RLIN (the Research Libraries Information Network, the other major US-based bibliographic utility), and to other cooperatives in Europe and elsewhere—has done original-script cataloging for the JACKPHY languages since the early 1980s. RLIN pioneered the ability to encode the JACKPHY languages in their original-script form for bibliographic records, using available script-specific standards (Aliprand 1992b). Records encoded in full-script form are exchanged by the Library of Congress, RLIN, OCLC, and other bibliographic utilities around the world.

Libraries took a long-term view of their data, capturing and representing non-Roman characters in their fullest form many years before search and display technologies were widely available. Full vernacular script in these records can be printed on catalog cards, but until very recently scripts could only be displayed on computers with special equipment. Even though JACKPHY records from OCLC, RLIN, and other sources are loaded into the online catalogs of individual libraries, most applications only support searching the transliterated forms. Integrated library automation software that supports Unicode is becoming more widely available, thus enabling records in non-Roman scripts to be displayed on most terminals and computers. The Library of Congress is implementing a new integrated library system that incorporates Unicode, enabling them to display their JACK-PHY records on public terminals in full form. Previously, these records were viewable only through other systems outside the Library of Congress (Tillett 1999).

The international library community is increasingly concerned about multilingual, multiscript data exchange as new regions of the world come online. The European Union is promoting Unicode and is funding projects to support Unicode implementation in library automation (Brickell 1997). In the mid 1990s, a study of six countries in Central and Eastern Europe (Croatia, the Czech Republic, Hungary, Poland, Slovakia, Slovenia), each with its own national language and character set, found that a variety of coding systems were in use. More than half of the research libraries in the study used Latin2, one used Unicode, and the rest used a national or a system-specific format to encode data; none used the ALA character set (Borgman 1996c).

As libraries, archives, museums, and other cultural institutions throughout the world become more aware of the need to preserve digital data in archival forms, character-set representation becomes a political as well as a technical issue. Many agencies are supporting projects to ensure preservation of bibliographic data in digital forms that can be readily exchanged, including the Commission of the European Communities, the International Federation of Library Associations, the Soros Foundation's Open Society Institute Network Library Program, and the Mellon Foundation (Segbert and Burnett 1997).

Summary and Conclusions

Providing access to information via a global information infrastructure involves many tradeoffs. The overarching goal in constructing a global digital library is to act locally while thinking globally. Designers of each digital library must tailor their systems to the identified needs of their target audience and to the characteristics of content and collections. At the same time, designers should recognize that they are designing a system that will serve as part of a larger entity. By taking into account the needs for data exchange, portability, and interoperability with other systems and services, new digital libraries can serve a broader audience. They also can serve their core user community better by ensuring that their digital library can interact with other systems.

In an ideal world, everyone could create information in whatever language and form they preferred, and everyone could find all desired information regardless of language or form. Technology would exist to bridge the various languages and formats. Though considerable technological progress has been made, true interoperability among languages and forms remains an elusive goal.

Basic data recognition, manipulation, and display factors affect monolingual and multilingual textual exchanges. Textual communication is inherent in virtually all media, as textual metadata are used to describe content in other formats. Effective, efficient, and accurate textual communication is essential to all network applications, public and private, domestic and international, local and global. If the technical problems can be addressed, other aspects of data exchange, portability, and interoperability may become more tractable. Fundamentally, however, access to information in any language is a matter of human communication. Technology is merely a means to assist the process.

9

Toward a Global Digital Library: Progress and Prospects

Thirty years' experience with the Internet has provided a glimpse of what computer and communication networks could do to transform the ways that people communicate, conduct commerce, learn, play, and govern. The twenty-first century promises ubiquitous networks, ubiquitous computing, and ubiquitous information. Dependence on computer networks is increasing dramatically, both for day-to-day communication and commerce and for critical information infrastructure such as electrical power and emergency services. Information technology in general, and the Internet in particular, are contributing to a variety of social transformations, according to the (US) President's Information Technology Advisory Committee (PITAC) (Information Technology Research 1999). These include transforming "the way we communicate," "the way we deal with information," "the way we learn," "the practice of health care," "the nature of commerce," "the nature of work," "how we design and build things," "how we conduct research," "our understanding of the environment," and "government" (ibid., pp. 9–15).

I conclude the book by asking how to get from the Internet of today to the global information infrastructure of tomorrow, focusing on progress and prospects for a global digital library that would improve access to information. Of the many challenges that could be addressed in this context, I select only a few. The first lies in scaling the technology, the economics, and the behavior associated with the Internet to a network that supports several orders of magnitude more users, devices, and capacity while providing new capabilities and services. The second challenge is to provide access to information in this expanded environment. And the third is to transfer the technology and services to parts of the world with different traditions and practices than those of the Group of Seven major industrialized nations that laid the technical and political framework for a global information infrastructure. It remains to be seen whether these challenges can be met. That may be not be possible, realistic, or even desirable.

Scalable Information Infrastructure

"Scalable Information Infrastructure" is a phrase coined by PITAC to address the transformation of the Internet into a national and a global information infrastructure. It is one of four research priorities for information technology identified by PITAC (Information Technology Research 1999). At the core of the scaling problem are the technology issues inherent in expanding the size, scope, and capabilities of computer networks. Scaling involves economic, legal, and political issues, as computer network services become more integrated into society and as they cross jurisdictional boundaries (Kahin and Nesson 1997). Social and behavioral issues also are involved in scaling, since a network originally designed for the technological elite must now serve a broad spectrum of the population. These issues are interdependent, as people will adopt and adapt the technology that is available, with economic, legal, and political considerations influencing their behavior.

Scaling Network Technologies

The Internet was originally intended to support resource sharing between government-funded research sites through basic services such as remote login, file transfer, and email (Quarterman 1990). It has long since expanded beyond this original intent, both in size and capability. By 1985 the Internet supported 2000 computers; by early 1999 it supported 70 million computing and communication devices, with traffic doubling every 100 days. Applications of tomorrow will connect many other types of devices, from credit card readers to home thermostats. The result will be explosive growth in network demand. The projected number of Internet users is expected to grow to a billion or so by early in the twenty-first century, and the number of connected devices is expected to grow exponentially too (Information Technology Research 1999, p. 31).

The predicted growth of computer network connectivity in the twenty-first century is analogous to the expansion of telecommunications in the latter half of the twentieth century. Until telefacsimile (fax) and mobile telephony proliferated, the number of telephone lines per household was a satisfactory measure of telecommunications' penetration. Now the ratio is often greater than 1, as many households and offices have separate lines to handle wired voice telephony, mobile telephony, fax machines, modems, pagers, security systems, and other devices. The available phone numbers within area codes in the United States were consumed years or decades sooner than predicted, so new area codes had to be created. Metropolitan areas such as Los Angeles that had only one area code in the mid 1980s had more than a dozen by the end of the 1990s. Maintaining accurate business cards, stationery, and address directories is only one of many resulting problems. Though online directories can help, businesses and individuals still need to be located on the basis of data in business cards, stationery, and other documents distributed years earlier. Persistent address information is at stake, whether for online resources or for physical or voice contact.

As the long-established model of geographically based telephone numbers breaks down, new models are being introduced. In some regions of the United States, "overlay codes" require callers to use ten digits for all calls. In other regions, mobile phones and pagers have separate "area" codes, thus reserving the geographically based codes for wired telephony. A number of other models exist. In some countries, six-, seven-, and eight-digit local phone numbers co-exist in the same geographic region, for example. The new world of telephony is one of much denser penetration and one where a phone number can no longer be attached to a physical device that stays in a known geographic location. Thus, the system of assigning telephone numbers that scaled up to accommodate the growth of telecommunications over a period of about 50 years appears to have reached its limits. New models based on assumptions of different technologies, applications, and services are needed.

If the predictions of ubiquitous networks, computing, and information are correct, connectivity to the Internet and to the emerging GII will expand at far greater rates than the recent telecommunications expansion. Among the many objects with network addresses will be sensing devices (such as thermostats, security systems, and video cameras) and communication devices (such as credit card readers, badge readers, pagers, and palmtop computers). Already, some child-care centers have networked video cameras that enable parents to observe their children via computers in the parents' offices or their homes. Soon it may be common to check home thermostats and security systems from afar. However, the larger market for network connectivity will involve business and scientific applications. Long-haul trucking relies on communication devices that make it possible to identify a truck's location at all times. The collection of scientific data on weather, earthquakes, and astronomy relies on instruments—some located on the land, some in the sea, and some in orbit—that communicate electronically with data centers.

Associated with the increase in number and variety of devices is an increase in types of content. Text, voice, and numeric data communication are augmented by audio and video content, which increases bandwidth requirements. In turn, these communications are augmented by digital signatures and other means of authenticating sender, receiver, and content. Some of these applications are expected to generate data flows far greater than we now know how to manage. The Earth Observing System–Data Information System (EOS-DIS), part of NASA's "Mission to Planet Earth," is expected to produce more than a terabyte of data per day, for example. The US government is predicting that by about 2004 its large data centers will be accepting 5 terabytes of data per day, maintaining 300 terabytes online (with 15 seconds to 1 minute access time), and archiving 15–100 petabytes of data (Halem et al. 1999).

Much of the data expected to flow through the GII will consist of transactions with only transitory value, such as monitoring the location or condition of sensing devices. Other data will be aggregated, such as credit card transactions and telephone calls being compiled for billing purposes. Some continuous data flows will be collected into digital libraries for primary or secondary uses. For example, meteorological data from satellites have applications throughout the economy, including weather prediction, crop planning, and building codes. These data also are needed for scientific research on long-term weather patterns and environmental changes, and for instruction in geophysics, environmental science, and other topics. Some types of information are compiled solely or primarily for digital library applications, such as legislation, court decisions, patents and trademarks, scholarly publications, and digitized images. These data, in turn, will be retrieved for use in other applications, such as legal cases, grant proposals, dissertations, and advertisements. Some kinds of data, such as movies, music, financial models, and large volumes of text, may be stored in digital libraries and transit the network as a service.

Research is needed to scale the Internet to an information infrastructure that can support this wide variety of concurrent applications and services for many more devices and many more users and at higher speeds, capacity, and capability. Research also is needed on scaling individual applications such as information retrieval to support very large databases of multimedia, with new kinds of services and capabilities, so that they are usable by a much larger and more diverse population. For example, consider that a keyword associated with only five documents in a database of 1000 documents might be associated with 5000 documents in a database of 1,000,000 documents. Finer indexing distinctions, more detailed metadata, more flexible displays, and other types of searching mechanisms will be required by the increases in size and type of material (Lynch and Garcia-Molina 1995; Metadata and Interoperability 1996; Schauble and Smeaton 1998).

Standards to Support Scaling
The integration of hardware, software, systems, networks, and services to form an information infrastructure depends on standards for data exchange, portability, and interoperability and on standards for physical connections among devices. Individual users are concerned with the compatibility of components that are linked on their desktops and between their desktop machines and other information appliances. Institutions care more about knitting all the desktop machines, servers, and other devices into a functioning whole. At the national and international levels, governments construct architectural frameworks to make all these networks function as a whole in the context of political and regulatory considerations. Different standards are required for each of these levels, and somehow they must all interact in predictable and reliable ways (Libicki 1995b). All too often, responsibility for sorting out the complexity of standards and applications that collide at the desktop is left to local network managers and to individual users.

The development of standards for a global information infrastructure involves a complex mix of top-down and bottom-up efforts, national and international management, and competition and cooperation (Kahin and Abbate 1995). Lessons learned from developing standards for information technology and telecommunications are being applied to this environment. Though users might prefer simple, stable, long-term technologies, they also want innovative new products that often require new standards. Much is at stake for the providers. Companies providing information technology frequently engage in "standards wars" to gain market share and dominance (Kahin and Abbate 1995; Shapiro and Varian 1999). At present, for example, users of cell phones are faced with a daunting variety of telephone devices and services, some of which are universal and some of which operate only in cities and regions with compatible technologies. Several technologies are competing to become the accepted international standard for wireless telephony, and each is associated with one or more commercial enterprises. Similarly, technology companies practice "lock-in" strategies to get customers to stay with a particular technology stream (Shapiro and Varian 1999). The most obvious example is the choice of desktop computing platform. A decision to purchase a Macintosh, a Windows, an NT, or a Unix platform is a decision to purchase an array of associated hardware peripherals and software. Changing platforms then becomes very expensive: it involves purchasing not only a new computer but also new peripherals and software, and spending more time on retraining.

Scalable Preservation Strategies

The volume of data in digital form is growing at an exponential rate. Unless active preservation strategies are deployed, these data will become unavailable at a rapid rate because of degradation of storage media or because of obsolescence of the hardware and software used to create them. Many of these data are essential to a functioning society and economy (e.g., national power grids, stock markets), maintaining financial records (e.g., Social Security, taxes, retirement benefits), and maintaining military readiness (e.g., missile launch codes, weapons testing data). Thus, digital data preservation is a component of critical information infrastructure protection as well as of a scalable information infrastructure. We are in the early stages of identifying long-term strategies for digital data preservation.

A recent National Science Foundation workshop on Data Archival and Information Preservation attempted to frame a research agenda for scalable preservation (Chen and Wiederhold 1999). The workshop determined that a variety of strategies will be needed, and that the strategies will vary on the basis of a number of aspects. One aspect is institutional requirements. For example, some data are of cumulative value whereas other data are of incremental value. Large government data centers such as those run by the National Aeronautics and Space Administration (NASA), the National Oceanic and Atmospheric Administration (NOAA), the Social Security Administration, the Internal Revenue Service, and the intelligence agencies acquire massive amounts of data on a continuing basis, aggregate them, and maintain them permanently. The cumulative nature of scientific data is particularly apparent. Climatic data, for example, become more valuable over time, as earlier observations never can be replicated. Longitudinal studies are conducted with data collected on many different instruments over long periods of time, which requires that the data be continually reorganized and restructured for consistency.

In contrast, some institutions retain only a small portion of the data they generate. Decisions about what to keep often are determined by laws and regulations. Government archives are responsible for selecting and maintaining evidence of government activities. Hospitals are required to keep certain patient records. Publicly traded companies are required to maintain certain financial records. Legal records are subject to retention rules. Records and data not retained to meet legal requirements often are discarded on a regular schedule.

In yet other situations, organizations may maintain more of their records than in the past, with the goal of mining these "digital assets" for subsequent applications. For example, the movie industry is actively developing "digital asset management" systems to capture images from film, animation, and computer-generated formats for later use in other products.

Another question about digital preservation is whether data should be continuously available and accessible or whether they are being kept just in case they might be needed later. If continuous availability is the goal, then regular migration to new technologies may be the only feasible approach. However, adequate technology does not yet exist for large-scale migration. Although tape data storage density has increased according to Moore's Law over the last 10 years (doubling every 18 months), data transfer speeds have increased at a proportionately slower rate (Halem et al. 1999). Data should not be read faster than they were recorded; otherwise, transfer errors and physical destruction may occur. Cook (1995) cites a case in which some government departments had not rewound and recopied their tapes regularly, and had stored them in rooms without adequate temperature and humidity controls. The department's data problem was further compounded when these degraded tapes were run on modern tape drives, at about 10 times the speed of the drives on which the tapes were initially created, and some of the tapes melted or caught fire.

Comparing the rate at which NASA generates new data with the rate of technological advances, NASA predicts that it may not be possible to store all the data collected in the future. Halem et al. (1999) write: "Even if the process of migrating key information starts as soon as new storage media become available, the old storage media need to have a life expectancy of at least twice the time needed to transfer data in order to accommodate the explosive growth of our observational and computational systems." Halem et al. conclude, as do others, that substantial research is required both on technology for storing and accessing these massive amounts of data and on strategies for managing and preserving them (Baru et al. 1999; Halem et al. 1999; Hedstrom 1998; Preservation of Digital Information 1998).

If continuous availability is not required, it may be sufficient to store data in a stable form that would enable a "digital archaeologist," with sufficient time and resources, to extract it in a useful form later. These options raise the issue of when it is better to appraise and select the data worth saving for anticipated future needs and when to save everything. In a paper environment, the physical storage requirements prohibit saving everything. Archivists, following accepted professional practices, typically select only a small percentage of all the documents collected by a company or an agency to save. In a digital environment, it may be less expensive to save all the data than to invest the effort in selection. Saving everything raises a host of evidential and privacy issues, however. Only a small amount of electronic mail is worth saving to document the activities of an organization. If everything is saved, personal or confidential information might be revealed unnecessarily, and anything saved could become evidence in lawsuits. Conversely, if everything is destroyed, institutional memory may be lost, making it difficult to reconstruct how and why products were developed or decisions were made. Email-retention policies are a growing concern of managers, lawyers, and policy makers (Bennahum 1999; Meeks 1999).

Digital preservation problems are not exclusive to business and government. Individuals and families are encountering the digital preservation problem as tax records, genealogical databases, and home videos become unreadable. Family photo albums dating from the first days of mechanical and chemical photography are readable; photos from the first days of digital photography may not be.

If digital preservation strategies are to be effective, the tools and the techniques must be easy to use and must not add an undue burden to the processes of data creation and maintenance. Elaborate procedures to add metadata at the time of creation will improve future access, but unless they add value at a rate proportional to their cost such procedures may not be followed. Similarly, data preservation must result in collections that are usable and useful for information access. If a user desiring a single document from a backfile must wait hours or days for the full backfile to be loaded from tape, that data set is likely to go unused. Further, despite containing critical resources, those data may cease to be maintained on the ground of lack of use.

Economics and Politics of Scaling

How network access is regulated and priced will influence what is built, how it is built, the applications and services for which it used, and who has access. Internet services are a commodity already, as are the telecommunications services that support them. Basic network service for email and Web access is relatively inexpensive for most consumer applications. However, basic network services tend to be congested and to have insufficient capacity for advanced applications such as video. Universities, businesses, and governments usually lease higher-speed, higher-capacity lines than those available to individual consumers. The cost for these higher-quality lines is increasing, rather than decreasing as predicted, however (Lynch 1998). A number of pricing models are being proposed that would offer differential services by capacity, by quality, by time of day, and by reservation, rather than the present "first-come, first-served" approach. The technical means by which differential pricing mechanisms might be implemented are not yet clear, in view of the multiple networks and the multiple network owners involved in carrying domestic and international traffic. The pricing mechanisms set by network providers will influence the pricing mechanisms of information service providers, which in turn will influence the choices made by consumers of those services. Conversely, the behavior of consumers (individuals, businesses, universities, governments, and other organizations) will influence the pricing schemes of information service providers and network providers. All these factors will influence domestic and international regulatory approaches to computing and communications media (Kahin and Nesson 1997).

Generally speaking, the Internet of today is available to anyone with a voice-grade telephone line. Voice-grade lines are adequate for electronic mail, searching the World Wide Web, and searching many digital libraries, but are not adequate for high-bandwidth applications such as downloading videos or transferring large volumes of data. Wireless technologies, excellent for voice telephony, are not expected to support high-bandwidth applications either. Fiber optic cables are the most effective technology for advanced applications, but the cables must be laid. The telecommunications industry is laying high-capacity fiber optic lines to upgrade services and is improving the electronics on existing cables to increase capacity (Lynch 1998).

Thus, scaling the Internet from the telecommunications system of today to an advanced information infrastructure of tomorrow is not merely a matter of faster modems. Indeed, the technical limit of modems operating over dialup phone connections appears to have been reached with 56 kilobits per second (although some once predicted that 28.8 kilobits per second was the limit). Higher speed and capacity require connections via fiber optic telecommunications or cable TV lines. Laying new lines is as much a matter of economics and policy as it is of technology. The economics of telecommunications are such that the "last mile" of connectivity is typically the most expensive part of providing access. Bringing telecommunications lines into densely populated urban areas is cost effective because many customers can be served by each main line. Rural areas are another matter. The cost of bringing a line from a main trunk that "last mile" to an isolated farm home is usually prohibitive, if the homeowner must pay the full cost. Universal service policies in the United States and elsewhere amortize the cost of basic telephone service over all customers, making basic service affordable to rural telephone users. As a result, the United States has among the highest rates of telecommunication penetration in the world. In countries with policies that require individual households, businesses, and communities to pay connectivity costs more reflective of the actual cost of providing service, telecommunications penetration tends to be concentrated in urban areas, with rural areas underserved (Mansell 1993; Noam 1992).

The last-mile problem persists in computer networks. Already, metropolitan areas are better served with high-capacity fiber optic lines that can provide video-quality service; rural areas lag behind. Service disparities are even more apparent in countries with minimal telecommunications penetration, where only the major cities may have adequate wiring for advanced capabilities. Many countries have filled the gap in voice connectivity with wireless communications, but wireless is not likely to support high-capacity data transfer in the near future (Lynch 1998). Once high-capacity lines are brought to buildings, they still must be connected to physical devices. The "last foot" of connectivity may be the most expensive part of network access for individuals and organizations, and may vary widely depending on geographic location.

A variety of legal, economic, and policy issues will influence how well the Internet scales to a global information infrastructure. Legal jurisdiction is normally based on territorial boundaries; however, communication and commerce conducted over international computer networks do not respect these boundaries, and this is leading to new models of governance and regulation (Kahin and Nesson 1997). Electronic commerce relies heavily on exchanges between strangers. People never meet, sellers and buyers are in different legal jurisdictions, and identity is an elusive concept. As a result, a new economics of "trust and reputation" is emerging around issues of who will trust whom, for which kind of transactions, under what conditions (Froomkin 1998; Kollock 1999). Public-interest groups, governments, and businesses all are concerned with how to protect privacy online and how to authenticate and verify sources and receivers of information. Closely related are complex topics such as wiretapping and cryptography (Computer Science and Telecommunications Board 1997b; Dam and Lin 1996; Diffie and Landau 1998; Schneier and Banisar 1997; Phillips 1998; Stefik 1997). Many aspects of digital library design also may be subject to regulation, including indexing, reformatting, tagging, filtering, and inter-operating with other systems (Samuelson 1998), as well as broader concepts of privacy, fair use, and rights management.

Technology, standards, and economics are difficult to separate in addressing the problem of scaling the Internet to a global information infrastructure. Issues of information policy are of concern to everyone involved in research and development of information infrastructure and of digital libraries. As Samuelson (1998, p. 13) puts it, "information technology policy is too important to leave entirely to lawyers."

Social Aspects of Scaling

The scalability of information infrastructure has a substantial social and behavioral component. The Internet was initially designed for use by a small cadre of technically sophisticated researchers, and for a limited range of applications. If a global information infrastructure is to serve the general population, it must accommodate a far wider range of computing skills, languages, language abilities, cognitive styles, interests, and aptitudes (Computer Science and Telecommunications Board 1997a). Applications must be relatively easy to learn and use if they are to support diverse communities of users, yet the growth in applications also means a growth in complexity. Much more is known about how to construct information technologies than about how people use them, as has been noted throughout this book. People are easily overwhelmed by many of today's information systems and by the complexity of maintaining an operational desktop computing environment. The challenge is to make systems simple to use while expanding their capabilities.

Technology and behavior evolve together, which is why it is so difficult to anticipate second-level effects on organizational behavior and on lifestyle (Sproull and Kiesler 1991). Electronic mail was initially intended as an ancillary communication mechanism to coordinate the sharing of computer time (Quarterman 1990). Who could have anticipated the volume and variety of today's email traffic, that family members would communicate online, or that email backup tapes would become legal evidence in court cases? Similarly, pocket pagers were initially a useful technology for contacting service and marketing people on the road and later for keeping executives in touch with their offices. Who anticipated parents' use of pagers to stay in contact with their children, or teenagers' use of pagers to pass notes to their friends? As more devices are networked, as wireless or "untethered" nomadic computing becomes more widespread, and as more applications support cooperative and collaborative activities, uses of these technologies will change in unanticipated ways. Our understanding of how people use desktop computers is inadequate, and what we do know does not scale to a world of ubiquitous computers, networks, and information.

The Global Digital Library Revisited

In chapter 2 I proposed the concept of a "global digital library" as a means of exploring the role of a global information infrastructure in providing access to information. Mine is hardly the first proposal for a mechanism to identify and locate the world's stores of knowledge, however. Neelameghan and Tocatlian (1985) date the idea of a "global information system" to the fifteenth century, with the invention of movable type and the opening of intercontinental sea routes. Otlet (1934, 1990) promoted similar ideas in Europe early in the twentieth century. The International Federation of Library Associations and Institutions has been promoting programs on "universal access to publications" and "universal bibliographic control" for several decades (IFLA 1998). In 1982, UNESCO established a working group on a "Global Network of Scientific and Technological Information" (United Nations 1982). Many other such programs exist to coordinate international information activities so that published materials, "gray literature" (e.g., technical reports and other materials that are produced in few copies, often outside mainstream publication channels), unique archival collections, and museum objects can be identified and located.

In several respects, the concept of a global digital library is qualitatively different from earlier views of a global information system. The digital aspects are one obvious change. Descriptions of materials (metadata) have been available online since the early 1970s; the full content of many documents is now online too. Instead of multiple independent networks for a select few, a constellation of interconnected networks is widely available in developed countries.

Another qualitative change is in the scope of content available. Efforts by UNESCO, IFLA, and other international organizations are aimed at collecting, organizing, preserving, and providing access to information resources that are expected to be useful to many people for the foreseeable future. These efforts are needed more than ever, in view of the difficulties of preserving access to print and digital resources. A global information infrastructure also can provide access to resources that are not intended for indefinite availability or for large audiences. These include personal and corporate web sites, working documents, electronic magazines ("ezines"), discussion groups, and many other resources that may exist online only for hours, days, or weeks.

International Development
More-developed countries often provide less-developed countries with economic, technical, military, and humanitarian assistance. Information plays a key role in most forms of development assistance and cooperation between countries (Arrow 1969; Eres 1981, 1985, 1989; Neelameghan 1997; Neelameghan and Tocatlian 1985). Countries vary widely on traditions, practices, policies, and behavior related to information, however. Any kind of development assistance tends to be an idealistic undertaking and a volatile political tool (Dosa 1985). The literature abounds with cautions about considering the complex mix of social, economic, political, and cultural factors specific to the situation under study. A few general observations from the literature on information development are useful to set the context for the challenges involved in creating a global digital library.

Great differences exist between countries in the availability of information resources. Developed countries have in place sophisticated infrastructures for creating, producing, managing, and disseminating information resources, whereas less-developed countries typically do not (Dosa 1985; Eres 1989; Meadows 1991; Sussman and Lent 1991). Information about local conditions that people need for economic, educational, or other forms of development may not exist in local languages. If it does exist, the means to transfer it within the country may be inadequate. Information produced elsewhere may not be applicable, or it may be unusable as a result of language or format constraints.

Regional cooperation in information transfer is growing, particularly on topics such as agriculture and the environment. In some cases these are centralized collections, and input may be either centralized or decentralized;

in others they are independent but linked collections; and others involve coordination of information activities of multiple types. Many agencies are participating, including the European Union, UNESCO, private foundations such as Mellon and Soros, an assortment of governmental, non-governmental, and quasi-governmental organizations, and professional organizations (Dempsey 1994; Neelameghan 1997; Smith 1992).

The relationship between information supply and demand differs in developed and developing countries. As UNESCO and other agencies have found, increasing the information supply does not necessarily increase demand. In the 1980s, UNESCO made a strategic decision to shift its emphasis from increasing the supply of development-related information to stimulating demand (Neelameghan and Tocatlian 1985; UNESCO 1981). Unless people know what to seek and what to do with information once they have it, information may have little value. Many development efforts now focus on enabling countries to take advantage of these technologies for acquiring and managing information, rather than simply increasing the supply (Lass and Quandt 1999a; Neelameghan 1997; Soros Foundations 1995).

Politics of Access

Even in the most democratic of countries, governments place some restrictions on freedom of speech, and thus on the free flow of information. Mayer-Schonberger and Foster (1997) identify four types of speech that countries commonly regulate within their borders and which they may attempt to regulate online: pornography, subversive information (e.g., that promulgated by anarchist groups or others deemed dangerous), hate speech (e.g., strong racist, sexist, or political speech, such as that of neo-Nazi groups in Germany and Austria), and privacy. Paradoxically, the international dimension of information infrastructure both strengthens and weakens speech regulation and speech protection. Mayer-Schonberger and Foster (ibid., pp. 242–243) comment that "an escalating national de jure regulation of speech meets a similarly pervasive de facto futility of enforcement."

The relationship between democracy and the flow of information is complex, although Kedzie (1997) does find a strong correlation between measures of democracy and measures of Internet penetration, using 1993 data.

The relationship between democracy and information flows is particularly complex. The Internet is often viewed as a democratizing technology, because control is largely decentralized. In contrast, print and broadcast media are often seen as a negative influence on democracy and on equity, because control can be centralized and power concentrated (Beniger 1986; Gillespie and Robins 1989; Innis 1951; Mansell 1993; McChesney 1996; McLean 1989; McLuhan 1964; Melody, Salter, and Heyer 1981; Mitchell 1995; Reich 1992; Toffler 1981).

Control over computer networks can be centralized, however. China, for example, requires users to register with the government. China, Singapore, Saudi Arabia, Iran, Vietnam, and other countries have established filters, firewalls, and other controls at a national level to restrict access to specific sites deemed offensive (Jehl 1999; Kessler 1996; Mayer-Schonberger and Foster 1997; Tan, Mueller, and Foster 1997). In many respects, these controls are extensions of regulation of print and broadcast media (Volkmer 1997). In sum, the availability of a global information infrastructure does not guarantee freedom of speech or access to information. Rather, access may be determined by a complex mix of domestic and international laws, and by technical means of enforcing and undermining those laws.

Individuals, Institutions, and Access

One of the promises of a global information infrastructure is for individuals to have direct access to information resources located anywhere on the network, so that they can seek and use information on their own and can create new resources for others to use. In many respects, however, individuals are becoming more dependent on institutions for information access, rather than less dependent as predicted.

To illustrate these relationships, let us compare access models for the physical world to those of the online world. In the world of print, individuals can gain access to many libraries, public and private, at home and abroad. Depending on local practices, prospective users may or may not need an affiliation with the institution to gain access, may or may not be required to identify themselves to gain entry, and may or may not be allowed to browse shelves or borrow materials. Normally users can browse catalogs and indexes once they have been admitted to the library. Even if they are not allowed to browse shelves, they will be able to request specific items to be retrieved on their behalf.

In an online world, more credentials are being checked and fewer resources are available without authorization. Because of intellectual property rights and contractual arrangements, institutions are placing more stringent controls on access than would be necessary or practical with print materials. In a print world, access is largely controlled through entry to the building. In the online world, access rights often are resource specific. In the hybrid libraries of today, the result is an odd mix of privileges that vary between on-site and off-site use.

American public libraries and libraries in public universities, for example, typically allow anyone to enter their buildings. Once inside, anyone usually can use materials on open shelves or use computer terminals. Borrowing privileges, special collections, interlibrary loan, and other services may be restricted to members of the local community, however. Different access restrictions apply when one is entering the same library institution through an online connection, however. Many of the digital resources freely available in the building may be available online only to authorized members of the community. Digital library contracts typically define the user community as institutional affiliates (e.g., employees; university students, faculty, and staff; residents of the jurisdiction of a public library) plus those physically present in the building, owing to the impracticality of controlling physical access on a resource-by-resource basis, each governed by a different contract. Defining institutional affiliation for national libraries is especially problematic, as national libraries typically are open to all residents of the country and to foreign visitors. With regard to the use of digital materials, many national libraries are defining the user community as those people physically present in the building. Electronic documents acquired by the Library of Congress as materials deposited under copyright law, for example, are available only within the Library's buildings. Thus, in an ironic twist, individuals may now have less access to information resources via a global digital library than they have in a physical library.

The access situation is becoming more complex, and all the proposed approaches have drawbacks. Providing every user with an individual password for each resource is not feasible. The overhead of assigning and maintaining such a password database is untenable, to say nothing of the burden on users of keeping track of them all. Alternatively, credentials can be checked unobtrusively by verifying that the user's domain name or Internet protocol (IP) address is affiliated with the institution providing the services. Controlling access through IP addresses is feasible only when users are connecting by means of institutionally provided computers or servers, however. Under the IP-address-verification approach, authorized users cannot gain access by means of other accounts they may hold, such as those on commercial Internet service providers (e.g., America Online, CompuServe). The IP-address approach also keeps universities and other organizations in the business of providing Internet services when they might find it more economical to outsource Internet access. Another approach is for authorized users to log onto a "proxy server" by name and password. Once authenticated, users have access to institutional resources. This approach requires organizations to maintain a secure proxy server and to maintain a database of authorized users. It allows users access by means of other accounts, and it gives organizations the choice not to be Internet service providers.

All these authentication approaches have privacy implications. The "right to read anonymously" (Cohen 1997) is more easily protected with print materials than with electronic materials. In most cases, people can read books in a library or borrow them without leaving a permanent trace of their reading habits. However, purchasing books from commercial bookstores, whether online or offline, may leave a permanent record that is not subject to privacy protection under US laws. Conversely, records of materials purchased in the European Union would be subject to privacy protection under EU data protection laws. Complicating matters further, records can be kept within the United States on Europeans who purchase materials from US-based suppliers.

The situation is even more complex with electronic materials. Many publishers of electronic resources would like to authenticate use by tracking who is using what materials, even to the level of what parts are read or used and how much time is spent with each (Cohen 1997). Libraries, businesses, governments, and others who acquire access to these resources on behalf of their user communities generally do not wish to provide these data, nor do most users, if they are aware of the tracking. An intermediate approach is to "anonymize" the data in such a way that the user's authorization can be confirmed without revealing the user's personal identity. No simple solution exists for these contentious issues. A wide range of contract negotiations, policies, laws, practices, and system designs will be involved in resolving them (Agre and Rotenberg 1997; Cohen 1997; Samuelson 1998).

Institutional Roles and Responsibilities

Cultural differences often come to the fore when cooperative efforts are undertaken. One cultural difference that is of particular relevance to the design of a global digital library is the tradeoff between preservation and access. Libraries are concerned with both, but to varying degrees. Historically, libraries in Europe, as in much of the rest of the world, emphasize preservation. Their orientation follows from monastic traditions and their responsibilities for the preservation of cultural heritage. France, for example, is providing digitized resources from its collections more for the sake of promoting its cultural heritage than for the sake of providing access to information (Kessler 1996). American libraries, though concerned about preservation, tend to place more emphasis on assisting their users in solving information-related problems, providing resources from their own collections and acquiring materials from elsewhere as necessary. Compared to libraries on the European continent, American libraries provide more user services, provide open-shelf access to most of their collections, and offer greater borrowing privileges, longer hours, and more outreach programs (Buckland 1988, 1992; Lass 1999a–c; Lass and Quandt 1999a; Maack 1993). Libraries in the United Kingdom fall somewhere in between, but their services overall are more in line with American than with Continental traditions. Though these are broad generalizations, and considerable variation exists within and between countries, they suggest some of the differences in practices that determine what gets cataloged, what gets digitized, and what is provided on public computing networks.

A number of factors are contributing to the shifting balance between preservation and access, and to changes within and between countries. One factor is the rising cost of information resources, which is resulting in slower growth of library collections despite the increase in amount of materials published (Pew Foundation 1998). Libraries, archives, museums, and other agencies with substantial collections of information resources have incentives to do more with the collections they have. They can provide a variety of new services with digitized materials, from document delivery to distance-independent learning.

Individual access to content depends on institutions' abilities to make the content they hold available, whether online or offline. In turn, institutions' capacity to provide their own resources online is increasingly dependent on their ability to broker agreements with other institutions—fellow libraries, archives, or museums, the government agencies or other parent organizations that fund them, or external funding agencies. This process often creates strange bedfellows, especially in an international context. Although libraries in some parts of the world have long histories of cooperation, others have a history of direct competition for scarce resources (Higginbotham and Bowdoin 1993; Pafford 1935). Many political and cultural factors are involved in cooperation, and only a few are specific to libraries. In many respects, these are the same concerns that constrain international business relations.

Case Study: Central and Eastern Europe in Transition

The situation in Central and Eastern Europe (CEE) offers a rare opportunity to study the relationship between political, economic, and cultural traditions related to information and the use of information technologies for access to information. In the period between the Second World War and the fall of the Berlin Wall, information technology was largely unavailable and unaffordable in this region, and its use was discouraged. Almost immediately after the political changes of 1989–90, however, these countries began large-scale investment in telecommunications and computer networks. The European Union, the United States, Japan, the World Bank, the Mellon and Soros Foundations, and other countries and agencies assisted the CEE countries in developing their information infrastructure through monetary grants and loans and contributions of technical expertise. Why the rapid shift? What was the motivation for these countries to invest so much of their scarce resources in information technologies and services? What is the motivation of other countries to assist them? How will they implement these technologies? How quickly can the CEE countries adopt and adapt new technologies? To what extent will their choices be similar to those in other countries and to what extent will they be adapted to local circumstances? To what extent will their systems be interoperable with those elsewhere in the global information infrastructure?

The case study presented here is based on my research in Croatia, the Czech Republic, Hungary, Poland, Slovakia, and Slovenia (Borgman 1995, 1996a,c,d, 1997a–c; Borgman and Caidi 1999). About 300 people were interviewed in 1993 and 1994 to provide a baseline for developments since 1989; most of these interviews were conducted while I was living in the region and teaching at two universities in Budapest. Those interviewed include heads of national computer networks, government ministry officials, directors of research libraries, information technology managers, and professional staff of major libraries in the region. A survey of research libraries in these countries conducted by mail in 1994–95 provided responses from a larger number of institutions, as well as quantitative data on the implementation of automated systems (Borgman 1997b). These data are supplemented by subsequent visits to these and other countries in the region (Lithuania, Russia, Ukraine), continuing contacts with key respondents, and reviews of related work. Further data are being collected in 1999 on information infrastructure developments in Hungary, in the Czech and Slovak Republics, and in Poland (Caidi, in progress).

In both literature and politics, "Central and Eastern Europe" sometimes includes the entire former Soviet Bloc and the former Yugoslavia and sometimes refers to a subset, distinguishing former Soviet satellite states in the Western part of the bloc from "the former Soviet Union," the Commonwealth of Independent States, the present and former Yugoslav republics, or other subsets such as the Baltic States or the Caucasus. In this book, "Central and Eastern Europe" refers to the region of Europe that was under Soviet control until 1989, plus Yugoslavia, which was a non-aligned nation. Poland is among the larger countries in this region, with about 40 million people; Hungary, the Czech Republic, and Slovakia each have 10 million or fewer; Croatia has about 41/2 million; Slovenia has about 2 million. Each of the six countries studied has a different national language.

The case study begins with a brief overview of the state of information infrastructure in the region before and after the political changes, with respect to the global digital library issues identified earlier. The latter half of the case study is an historical comparison of developments in the United States and the United Kingdom with those in Central and Eastern Europe.

Information Infrastructure in Central and Eastern Europe

The countries of Central and Eastern Europe included in the study entered the 1990s with telecommunications penetration of about fifteen telephones per hundred persons and a weak technical infrastructure based on pre-Cold War mechanical switching technology. They lacked digital transmission systems, fiber optics, microwave, and automated systems control and maintenance (Zonis and Semler 1992). Until 1990, business, government, and education made little use of computers, although some mainframe-based data processing centers handled scientific military applications. Communication technologies such as typewriters, photocopiers, and fax machines were registered and controlled to varying degrees in each country. The CEE countries could not legally make connections between their computer networks and those of countries outside the Soviet Bloc owing to the Coordinating Committee for Multilateral Export Controls (COCOM) regulations and other embargoes imposed on the region by the West (Heinz 1991; Lavigne 1992; Mastanduno 1992), although clandestine network connections were widely known to exist. Almost immediately after the political changes, the Vienna Computer Center provided external connections to the Internet, and network access for these countries expanded quickly thereafter (Rastl 1994). However, network growth in the region continues to be constrained by the lack of high-capacity telecommunications lines.

The economic motivations of the European Union, the United States, Japan, and other trading partners to invest in telecommunications and computer networks in Central and Eastern Europe are fairly obvious. Not only does this region represent a substantial new market for information technology per se, the implementation of technology is seen as a necessary prerequisite for business development. Doing business with people who lack telephones, fax machines, photocopiers, and electronic mail is difficult and inefficient. In theory, an improved internal information infrastructure will assist these countries in marketing their own products domestically and internationally, which in turn will provide them with capital to purchase goods and services from abroad.

An information infrastructure is far from a "plug and play" technology, however. Rather, it is a complex social and technical construct (Star and Ruhleder 1996). The countries of Central and Eastern Europe differ on key factors influencing information infrastructure development from the United States (where computing and communications technology were first developed) and from the European Union countries (from which they were politically isolated for 40 years). Some of the more apparent differences involve politics and economics. The CEE countries within the Soviet Bloc operated as command economies under central planning. In contrast, the European Union countries and the United States are market-based demand economies, with varying degrees of government regulation. The organization of work and the day-to-day practices of commerce are very different under these systems, often in subtle but important ways. The countries of Central and Eastern Europe are in varying states of transition toward market-based economies. The transformation is not complete, nor may it ever be. Some scholars expect these countries to develop some hybrid form of political economy (Berend 1998; Schopflin 1994). These are deep structural changes that will evolve over several decades.

This study explored the development of information infrastructure by focusing on the relationship among libraries, computer networks, and the government ministries that oversee libraries and networks. One of the first investments in information infrastructure in the region was to automate the internal processes of selected research libraries. Automation enabled these libraries to provide services over the Internet and made their holdings more widely known and available. These were national efforts, requiring the approval and support of government ministries and coordination with national computer networks. In most cases, private foundations provided additional funding to seed these projects.

Libraries reflect cultural and political traditions of their societies. In this region, as elsewhere, libraries are the primary social institution providing access to information. As government bodies (e.g., national libraries, national academies, national centers for scientific, technical, and medical information) and as components of the higher education system (e.g., university libraries), research libraries were among the first institutions in their countries to be connected to computer networks. They also had more experience with automation than most other sectors except the military, whether with small local databases or with the products of centrally managed scientific, technical, and medical databases—although far less experience than libraries in countries to their west. Thus, library comparisons may identify significant international and cross-cultural differences in practices and assumptions related to information infrastructure. Research libraries in the region also may be a bellwether for other economic sectors that are adopting and adapting information technologies.

The Mellon Foundation and the Soros Open Society Institute began library development programs in the region early in the 1990s. For Mellon and Soros, funding for automated library systems was a means to improve access to information and to promote cooperation within and between countries. Improving information access also was seen as a means to hasten the process of democratization (Lass 1999a–c; Lass and Quandt 1999a; Segbert and Burnett 1997).

Traditions and Practices

A global digital library would bring together institutions with very different histories. Library services in CEE reflect the combined influence of European library traditions and socialist philosophy (Krzys, Litton, and Hewitt 1983; Price and Price 1985; Simsova 1968; Vosper 1989). As noted earlier, libraries in this region are oriented more toward preservation of cultural heritage than toward access to information. Of central interest in this research is the degree to which these libraries would take advantage of the improved access made possible by computer systems and networks. A related issue is the amount and type of cooperation between institutions necessary to improve access to their respective collections.

The CEE countries have national copyright deposit laws, national bibliographies, and other means of managing domestic information, but persistent problems with information dissemination. Under the previous political system, national library laws created national networks and specified some cooperative activities, but they also created structural barriers to cooperation. For example, subcommunities of libraries report to different government ministries, divided both by type of library and by subject area (Davies 1992; Rozsa 1992; Segbert 1996). As a result, each country has one national library that is responsible for producing the national bibliography and other national libraries or information centers in subject areas.

Some of the subject-based national libraries cover broad areas, such as science and technology, medicine, agriculture, and education; others are responsible for collecting materials in specialized topics, such as horticulture or botany. Within universities, from dozens to over 100 individual libraries report to the heads of departments and faculties, with minimal coordination of services. Cooperation among the libraries within a university is an issue, as are cooperation between universities and cooperation between countries. The relationship between cooperation and automation is a recurrent theme in studies of libraries and information access in the region (Davies 1992; Lass 1999a–c; Lass and Quandt 1999b; Meadows 1991; Roberts 1994; Segbert 1996; Segbert and Burnett 1997).

Public libraries in the region also consist of a few large collections and thousands of small collections, managed under a complex mix of centralized and decentralized control. A number of interviewees mentioned that the Soviet formula for public libraries was one library per 1000 population, providing at least a small reading collection for each community. During the period of Soviet control, Hungary, with a population of about 10 million, had about 10,000 public libraries (Kiss 1972); the Ukraine, with a population of about 52 million, had more than 50,000 public libraries (many of which have been closed or combined into larger collections).

Computer Networks

The Central and Eastern European countries began experimenting with computer networks in the mid 1980s, with computer science departments in universities or academies of science establishing the first networks. In 1993 and 1994, when the initial data were collected, these countries were in the process of establishing or revising management structures for Internet service provision. At the time, governments were the only network service providers. The heads of these new or restructured agencies represented their countries in the organizations responsible for international connectivity.

Generally speaking, a symbiotic relationship existed between the research libraries and the network agencies. The libraries needed the networks as a means to provide access to their own content and to gain access to resources elsewhere. The networks needed the libraries both as a customer base and as sources of content and services they could deliver to others. Networks also needed libraries as a means to promote the value of computer networks to the higher education, government, and business sectors. Although higher education and government were consuming network capacity as quickly as the networks could provide it, the network providers also wished to create demand in the newly privatized business sector. These countries are in transition from a command economy to a demand economy, and predictable tensions existed between those who preferred centralized control and planning for information infrastructure and those preferring decentralized approaches (Borgman and Caidi 1999).

In the mid 1990s, the CEE countries were among the fastest growing in Internet penetration (Volkmer 1997). Email was especially attractive in this region because of the weaknesses of voice telephony and postal services. For those with email access in CEE countries, sending messages online can be faster, cheaper, and more reliable than telephone calls, faxes, or postal mail.

Information Flows

The supply of and the demand for information resources are changing in subtle and profound ways in the region. Under the previous political system, information flows were controlled and censored to varying degrees in each of these countries. Most access to foreign materials was limited to state planning, research, and development. Access to foreign literature on business, finance, social sciences, or humanities was minimal (Meadows 1991). Gifford (1993) describes the "bibliographic blackout" from 1948 to 1988, during which people in these countries had little access to scholarship about their countries or neighboring countries. A substantial flow of underground literature, known as *samizdat,* took place during this era. Samizdat, a clandestine form of self-publication, included domestic materials banned by the government, translations of foreign materials, and other documents that were critical of official policies and practices (Rupnik 1991; Shane 1994; Skvorecky 1991; Z 1991). The fact that much of the long-suppressed samizdat literature is now available in libraries exemplifies the sea change in official attitudes toward access to information. Indeed, political analyses of the challenges inherent in the transition toward democracy in Central and Eastern Europe emphasize the need for freer flow of information and for informed public debate (Hankiss 1994; Havel 1985; Schopflin 1994).

In the past, publicly available information in CEE was mixed with propaganda to such a degree that it was not trusted (Gifford 1993). The CEE countries did not develop an information society in which information is highly valued; who you knew tended to be more important than what you knew (Gifford 1993; Shane 1994). Comparing infrastructure requirements in the United States to those in the region, Gifford (1993, p. 103) comments that "in the United States, a major task is to design systems to sift intelligently through an information overload, whereas in the societies of Eastern Europe the task is to educate people about the value of information and the need to make informed decisions." Shane (1994) makes a book-length argument that the liberalized information policies of *glasnost,* including more freedom of the press, led directly to the downfall of the Soviet Union. People gained access to information about events internal to their country as well as events elsewhere for the first time in many decades, and became dissatisfied with their circumstances as a result.

Negotiations between Western countries and the Soviet Bloc on information and media policy in 1955 shed some light on official attitudes toward information access (Ropers 1989). While the Western countries stressed "free flow of information" as an inalienable human right (see Information Freedom and Censorship 1991) and as a condition for improved relations, the Soviet Union saw economic relations as a precondition for any liberalization in information exchange. As Ropers explains, because the Soviet Union viewed Western media as promulgating a distorted view of their countries, they required state control of information flows as a condition of liberalization. The West viewed this requirement as a pretext for protecting the government from both internal and external criticism. Similarly, the West emphasized individual rights and freedoms, while the Soviet Union was concerned with agreements between official bodies such as publishing houses, radio and television, and related scientific and technical organizations. Thus, the two sides interpreted the concept of information exchange in much different terms.

Goals for Information Technology

Establishing computer networks and automating library operations are means to ends. The most interesting questions in this study involve what those ends are and how they compare to those of other countries. Comparing the goals for information technology between this region and other, more-developed regions will aid in determining how portable information systems are and in identifying challenges inherent in creating a global digital library.

The study focused on the automation of research library operations as an essential component of information infrastructure for these countries. Library automation in the United States and the United Kingdom, beginning in the 1960s, has led to operational efficiencies, economies of scale through cooperation, increased access to library collections, and a wide range of new information services (Borgman 1997b). The Central and Eastern European countries are implementing integrated library systems that were developed in the United States, the United Kingdom, Western Europe, and Israel. If the CEE countries implement these systems in ways similar to how they are used in the originating countries, the potential exists for the CEE countries to create similar information infrastructures quickly, "leapfrogging" over several generations of technology. Yet to do so would mean that these countries adopt the technology and associated practices as a whole, rather than adapting them to their own traditions and practices. Full, unaltered adoption of these systems is unlikely, in view of the fact that the technology originated in countries with more advanced information infrastructures, different work practices, different attitudes toward information, different traditions in preservation and access, and different political and economic systems, and was designed by people trained in different educational systems. These differences will influence how these countries participate in a global information infrastructure and a global digital library.

As a means to assess what those differences and influences might be, let us compare goals for library automation in CEE to those of the United States and the United Kingdom. This is not to claim that the CEE countries should adopt these models from abroad. Rather, the purpose is to explore the portability of the models of a global information infrastructure set forth by the United States and the other Group of Seven nations. For a global digital library to be effective, it must somehow build upon existing infrastructure and investments.

Libraries in the United States and the United Kingdom laid a framework of standards and practices for library automation that has been widely adopted. The USMARC and UKMARC standards for representing cataloging data spawned UNIMARC and various related MARC formats. The

Anglo-American Cataloging Rules have been translated into many languages because they support the MARC formats used in automated cataloging systems. Similarly, US and UK practices for resource sharing, cooperation, and data exchange are embedded in the integrated library systems developed in these countries, and these systems are being implemented in many other countries.

Thus, an infrastructure exists for library automation. This infrastructure evolved over several decades and has its roots in traditions and practices that long preceded modern computing and communications technologies. The case study explores the evolution of library automation infrastructure through four overlapping phases, comparing developments in the United States and the United Kingdom to those in Central and Eastern Europe. The phases are operational efficiency, access to institutional resources, access to external resources, and interoperability of information systems. These phases are cumulative; new goals emerge, while prior goals still must be met.

Operational Efficiency

Efficiency of internal operations marked the first stage of library automation in the United States and the United Kingdom, beginning in the 1960s. Libraries were overwhelmed with the manual processing of acquisitions and cataloging resulting from the growth of higher education and the scientific enterprise. Similar to practices in other sectors of the economy, libraries began with locally developed mainframe systems and took a systems-analytic approach to improving internal work flows. Online shared cataloging systems were developed in the late 1960s to reduce transaction costs in creating catalog records. Libraries reduced the number of staff through the cooperative use of these systems, and shifted labor-intensive processing from professional to paraprofessional and clerical staff.

Thus, a starting point is to ask whether the first stages of automation in Central and Eastern European libraries were marked by operational efficiencies and increased cooperation among libraries for mutual benefit. The answer appears to be no, owing to a variety of structural characteristics (Borgman 1996c, 1997b). Our survey found that reducing staff costs was the lowest-ranked reason to automate. Under the previous political system, these countries had a "full-employment" model in which a certain number of workers were assigned to an organization. Labor was a fixed commodity that could not be traded for capital expenditures. In government-funded bodies such as research libraries, labor remained a fixed commodity at the time of this study. Managers reported few incentives or options to reduce their labor force. Although management practices are changing in the transition toward democracy and market economies, libraries are public agencies and change is slower than in the private sector.

Despite the fixed numbers of staff, CEE libraries are experiencing a severe labor problem in recruiting, retraining, and retaining people with the skills necessary for automating their operations and services. They need people with technical skills who speak English. Technical and language skills are coupled for several reasons. One is that these libraries are purchasing hardware and software for which the original documentation is written in English. Though translated documentation may be available, it tends to be less accurate. A number of technical staff reported that their initial motivation to learn English was to read documentation and related technical materials. They also need English to communicate with technical support, customer service, and marketing staff of most hardware and software vendors. Yet another reason for the coupling is that English has supplanted Russian as the common language for communicating across borders. CEE regional conferences on computer networks and on library automation are now conducted in English. English is a prerequisite for participation in most conferences and training workshops and is necessary to read most of the current technical literature.

People with technical and language skills command higher salaries than most libraries can pay, and they are highly sought in the growing private sector. In interviews, concerns were frequently expressed about the shortage of qualified technical people. Several library directors commented that they would prefer to have fewer staff and pay them more, but that they were not allowed to do so. Libraries are concentrating on retraining the staff they have and universities are incorporating more technical training in education for the field.

Another component of operational efficiency in the United States and the United Kingdom is cooperative cataloging, which builds upon Anglo-American traditions that long predate automation. By now, US and UK libraries obtain catalog records (metadata) from external sources for the vast majority of their domestic materials and for a substantial portion of foreign materials (Chapman 1999; Leazer and Rohdy 1994). In the CEE countries studied, national libraries create catalog records for domestic materials and distribute them to libraries throughout their countries. Despite the fact that these libraries' collections consist primarily of domestic materials (Gifford 1993; Meadows 1991; Roberts 1994), they make little use of those records. On average, research libraries in CEE utilize records from their national libraries and other sources for only 17 percent of new materials; they create original records for the remaining 83 percent. These figures exclude the national libraries that create the records for distribution (Borgman 1996c). One explanation that librarians gave for not using national library records was that their countries' national bibliographies were several years behind schedule. In these cases, libraries created their own records rather than hold the materials until national records became available. Lass (1999b) found similar results in his study of library automation in the Czech and Slovak republics. Some productivity improvements were gained at first through automating work flows, but they were not sustained.

Some of these differences can be attributed to the early stage of automation development in CEE, some to economics, and some to attitudes toward cooperation. Libraries in the United States and the United Kingdom have had several decades to build a critical mass of records in shared systems such as OCLC, RLIN, and CURL and enjoy extensive connectivity with computing networks. In theory, CEE libraries could obtain records for their foreign materials and some of their domestic materials through the same shared systems. In practice, the costs are prohibitive for most CEE libraries, although some are making limited use of these systems, either online or through subsets on CD-ROM.

Automation in CEE libraries began on a small scale in the 1970s but was not widespread until the 1990s (Borgman 1996c). Computer network penetration also was minimal until the 1990s, so the transition from manual distribution of catalog records to online shared systems was not technically feasible until very recently. Slovenia is the most advanced, having begun a shared national catalog in the 1980s to serve all of Yugoslavia. The system now serves Slovenia for shared cataloging, interlibrary lending, and common purchase agreements (Institute of Information Science 1993a,b).

Hungary is building a shared national database, known as MOKKA (an acronym in Hungarian) (Borgman 1996d; Lass and Quandt 1999b). Libraries in the Czech and Slovak Republics began constructing a common database under the CASLIN (Czech and Slovak Library Information Network) project funded by the Mellon Foundation (Lass and Quandt 1999b).

Access to Institutional Resources

Putting an institution's resources online, or at least the metadata that describe those resources, is a necessary step toward creating national and global digital libraries. Online catalogs were the focus of the second phase of automation development for libraries in the United States and the United Kingdom after addressing operational efficiency. They became available in the early 1980s, and they moved onto the Internet later in the 1980s as computer networks expanded. Many research libraries provide digital libraries of full text, images, and other local resources too. Online catalogs are now but one component of "online public access systems."

Integrated library systems enabled American and British libraries to improve existing services and to offer new services. Online catalogs provide more powerful searching capabilities than do card catalogs, such as enabling users to search for keywords in titles and subject headings, and to constrain their topics by dates, languages, type of material, or combinations of features. Acquisition and circulation data can supplement cataloging records, showing not only what a library owns but also what is available for loan and what is on order. Most systems now allow users to email or print search results, which then can be used for browsing in open-shelf libraries. Some closed-stack libraries speed book delivery by linking the online catalog to the book paging system so that users can order materials directly from the catalog terminals. (An example of the latter can be found in the British Library's new building in London.) Some integrated library systems enable users to place requests for materials that are on order or currently on loan to others, to place document-delivery requests, or to renew materials. Online catalogs in the United States and the United Kingdom typically provide access to the holdings of all the libraries at a university or other institution and often to those of multiple participating institutions.

Although CEE respondents stated that putting local resources online was the top priority for automation, the process appears to be proceeding somewhat differently than it did in the United States and the United Kingdom (Borgman 1996c). Much of the difference may be due to a greater emphasis on preservation of materials than on access to information. Most CEE libraries maintain closed stacks and loan few of their materials, for example. Students, faculty, and staff of a CEE university typically have use and borrowing privileges only at the central university library and at one or more department or faculty (college) libraries with which they are affiliated. Online catalogs in CEE universities often contain only the holdings of the central university library, leaving users dependent on manual access to the catalogs of departmental libraries. Automation was not typically associated with consortia of libraries within universities, nor did extended university-wide library privileges appear to result from automation. In some cases, automation projects linked multiple research libraries in a geographic region, however. Mounting online catalogs was the top priority for these libraries, and little progress had been made in automating acquisitions, serials, or circulation. Thus, the service improvements gained by US and UK libraries through combining these functions were not evident in CEE libraries.

The relative lack of emphasis on service or access in these automation projects also is evidenced by the fact that in about 20 percent of the libraries studied computer workstations for online catalogs or for CD-ROM databases were for staff only (Borgman 1996c). In these cases, users were dependent on staff to conduct searches on their behalf.

Closed stacks persist throughout Europe because of architecture and because of tradition. Libraries occupy old buildings with large public reading rooms that are separate from dense storage areas for the collection. Books often are stored by size or date of acquisition, for efficiency of storage and ease of retrieval by trained staff. Shelving areas are too narrow and too poorly lit to make public access practical. Placing large portions of collections on open shelves for browsing usually requires new construction or substantial renovation to existing buildings. In the rare cases of new construction, CEE libraries are providing more open stacks for public access.

Closed stacks make users dependent on the metadata in catalogs to identify items of interest, and reduce anonymity by linking user names to requested items. Elapsed time from requesting an item from the stacks to delivery to a reader's station in the library ranges from under an hour to overnight. Closed-stack libraries suffer fewer losses of materials than do open-stack libraries, thus improving the preservation of materials for readers of the future, but at the cost of convenience for readers of today.

Access to External Resources

Once US and UK libraries had automated basic operations and put their catalogs online, they turned their attention to providing access to resources outside their institutions. This endeavor involves several related goals. One goal is access to cataloging data (metadata) of other institutions as a means to convert manual backfiles to computer-readable form. Another is to identify materials available for lending or document delivery on behalf of the library's users. A third goal is to provide access to online resources held elsewhere.

The large shared cataloging utilities, such as OCLC, RLIN, and CURL, have enabled US and UK libraries to meet the first two of these goals. Online catalogs of recent materials are useful finding aids, but until all records have been converted to computer-readable form the full benefits of integrated library systems cannot be realized. If catalog records for most of a library's holdings exist in a large shared database, the least expensive and most efficient method of data conversion is to extract the matching records for the local online system (Schottlaender 1992).

The matching approach offers several advantages over keying records from card catalogs or other sources of legacy data. One is that the work can be outsourced so that project staff do not need to be hired, housed, or supervised. Another is that shared records are usually of better quality because they meet modern cataloging standards. Records in card catalogs that were created over many decades tend to be highly variable in form and quality, reflecting historical changes in policies, practices, and cataloging rules. A third advantage is that the library contributes new records to the database for those records that could not be matched. As a result, the database grows and becomes more valuable to other libraries. A fourth advantage is that the library's holdings are identified in the shared database. These holdings records can support interlibrary lending and document delivery.

To date, libraries in CEE lack shared databases with a critical mass of catalog records on domestic materials that can be used for converting records or for document delivery. This appears partly to be a problem of the early stages of development and partly a problem of willingness to cooperate toward these goals. Slovenia is the only country studied with a functioning shared system that serves these purposes. Hungary is in the early stages of constructing such a system, as are the Czech and Slovak Republics. However, Czech and Slovak libraries have not continued the CASLIN project beyond the end of the Mellon funding, although some aspects of cooperation appear to be continuing (Lass 1999a–c; Lass and Quandt 1999a).

Progress toward reaching the volume of records necessary to reap these benefits is slow. CEE libraries that are converting their backfiles of catalog records appear to be doing so by in-house keying or scanning of records from card catalogs or other legacy data. This is a slow and cumbersome process, although if the records later are contributed to a shared database they can contribute to achieving the necessary mass. Similarly, interlibrary lending and document delivery in the region, with the exception of Slovenia, continue to rely on manual methods. Each library sends catalog cards of its new holdings to the national library, which files them in a central holdings list. Our respondents commented on the process as being slow, cumbersome, and inaccurate. Libraries throughout the region rely heavily on the British Library, OCLC, and commercial services for borrowing foreign materials.

Although shared national or international cataloging services have been the preferred approach to resource sharing and document delivery in many countries (Day, Heery, and Powell 1999; Dempsey 1990; Hein 1991; Holley 1993; Rau 1990), they are not the only solution. As technology improves, federated approaches to creating a "virtual shared catalog" may become more feasible. Technical problems remain to be solved, such as reconciling varying forms of metadata and data structures at the time of retrieval. More problematic are the underlying challenges of cooperation among institutions.

The third goal in access to resources external to the institution is to provide direct links to indexing and abstracting databases (e.g., Medline and Current Contents), full text and multimedia databases, electronic journals, and other online resources. In the early days of online public access systems (late 1980s), some US libraries purchased databases on tape and mounted them on local networks. The United Kingdom took a different approach, mounting databases nationally on JANET, the Joint Academic Network, which is their Internet service for higher education. With the advent of higher-capacity networks and the World Wide Web, libraries now are able to offer services to their users without mounting databases on local or national networks. Rather, they can contract for services and provide a link from their home site. Increasingly, these are cooperative ventures. One is the California Digital Library,[1] which provides services to all nine campuses of the University of California (with about 180,000 students) and to a growing number of other institutions.

CEE libraries never had the resources or the technical infrastructure to purchase commercial services and mount them locally, although national technical information centers provide some scientific and technical databases. However, CEE libraries began building databases of local materials (such as journal articles, theses, special collections, and government documents) long before they undertook automating their catalogs. They are providing some of these resources online. Providing access to commercial services on behalf of their user communities probably will require cooperative ventures, in view of the small size of CEE institutions. The Soros Foundation's Network Library Program is brokering a multiyear, multinational contract for online access to a set of commercial databases of scholarly materials. If successfully implemented, this program could substantially improve access to scholarly information resources in the participating CEE countries.

Interoperability of Information Systems

Having made considerable progress in operational efficiencies, in improving access to resources held by their institutions, and in gaining better access to external resources, libraries in the United States, the United Kingdom, and elsewhere are working toward interoperability between systems. The trend from independent to linked systems is exemplified by this phase of library automation. Research libraries maintain online links to most of their partners. Links to suppliers enable them to place orders for print materials and receive invoices online. Links to shared databases enable them to

1. The URL is www.cdlib.org.

exchange and update records in real time and to place interlibrary lending and document-delivery orders. Direct links to digital resources elsewhere enable libraries to provide a variety of online services without the overhead of mounting databases on local systems. The online public access systems managed by libraries are linked to systems and services managed by other units of their parent institutions. From the users' perspective, the array of services provided by the library or university may appear as a unified whole. Users need not be aware that these resources actually exist in multiple locations throughout a globally distributed network.

The trend toward interoperability can be attributed partly to advances in technology and partly to changes in policy. Technological advances have simplified and encouraged interoperability and open systems. The World Wide Web now provides a familiar and common framework for linking systems. Standards such as Unicode (which supports a common means of encoding characters in the world's written languages) and Z39.50 (which supports client-server relationships for information retrieval) also are steps toward this goal. These technical advances have supported a growing market for online information resources, at the same time that print materials are becoming more costly. In addition, a growing proportion of the user population has Internet access, enabling them to use library services online. All these factors have contributed to the access orientation of US and UK libraries, and to the determination that they could not sustain an adequate level of services by operating as isolated institutions. By working together, they can share resources with other institutions, collectively providing more resources and services to their user communities. American and British libraries thus have adapted the available technology to suit their goals.

Central and Eastern European research libraries are at a much earlier stage of development. They are still struggling with implementing the technology per se, and are just now beginning to reckon with the organizational and policy changes that result (Lass and Quandt 1999b). CEE libraries are addressing issues that American and British libraries resolved years ago, such as which cataloging rules and MARC formats to follow. US and UK research libraries have amassed data in USMARC and UKMARC formats, following the Anglo-American Cataloging Rules (AACR), for more than 30 years. The CEE countries established national formats in the 1970s, most of which were variants of MARC. Generally speaking, the formats were not widely implemented, owing to the low level of automation. Further, these formats were based on national cataloging rules that did not adapt well to automation. CEE libraries now are implementing USMARC, UKMARC, or UNIMARC formats, as these are the formats supported by commercially available integrated library systems. In turn, most CEE libraries are finding these formats easier to implement by translating AACR than by adapting national cataloging rules.

These are wrenching changes in an organization. Cataloging rules and practices are based on traditions that may date back hundreds of years. Embedded in these rules are cultural perspectives on such matters as the role of individuals vs. groups in society, the nature of credit for work, and assumptions about how users will seek the information represented by these records. These changes in rules and practices are profound. Work is done in much different ways, and the old data models cannot simply be mapped onto new ones. Records must be transferred from manual to automated formats, and between automated formats. The complexity of mapping between MARC formats illustrates the complexity of this process. IFLA, the European Union, and other agencies are working on effective mappings among the MARC formats that will simplify the process of international data exchange and interoperability (Metadata and Interoperability 1996; Segbert and Burnett 1997; Smith 1992).

Mappings are difficult to accomplish because one-to-one relationships rarely exist. More often, one-to-many or many-to-many relationships exist. For example, AACR makes fine distinctions between the roles that individuals play in the creation of a document. Authors, editors, compilers, illustrators, composers, and other participants are identified separately. Other cataloging rules may group all the personal names associated with a document into a common field. In these cases, all the personal names from a record created under AACR could be mapped to a single name field. Similarly, records cannot easily be mapped from a format with all the names in one field to a format where role distinctions are made. Mapping subject headings between formats is even more complex. Some rules have one type of subject heading; others employ categorical structures, and these structures vary. Common types of subject headings include author, topic, geographical region, and historical period. Even if a mapping can be made in one direction, it may not be reversible without losing data.

CEE libraries are learning that decisions as basic as the choice of cataloging rules, formats, and standards for character representation determine the ease of interoperability with other systems. Following current national standards will ease interoperability with other systems within that country, but it may complicate international data exchange. Should a newly automating library follow the practices of the national library or those of OCLC, for example? Should a library that collects a substantial portion of foreign materials follow the practices of foreign partners or those of domestic partners, if the practices conflict? Libraries in Central and Eastern Europe are facing the standards challenge common to any new form of technology—the need to gamble on which standards and practices will serve them best in the long term.

From Interoperability to a Global Digital Library

The larger questions involve how well the existing infrastructure for libraries will serve new participants in a global information infrastructure and whether the GII will form an adequate foundation for a global digital library. The case study focuses on cataloging data as the core of a global digital library. These are the metadata that describe collections of materials gathered over a period of centuries. Along with the contents of archives and museums, these materials represent the cultural heritage of nations, countries, and peoples. Libraries devote substantial effort to creating metadata as a means to ensure the preservation and continued accessibility of materials for future generations. Cataloging data are expensive to create, but they are amenable to sharing because only one record needs to be created for each unique work. Any library holding a copy of that work can use the same record to describe it, at least in theory.

The creation and sharing of cataloging data via computer networks is one of the success stories of a global digital library, with a 30-year history already. Success is far from complete, however, nor has the road always been smooth, as we have seen. Libraries around the world are struggling to balance local traditions with international standards and practices, bringing the local-global tradeoffs into sharp relief. Nor are the standards and practices stable. IFLA is actively engaged in revising rules and practices to reflect the needs of a larger constituency and to make them applicable to new media. Current efforts are aimed at making cataloging rules and the associated standards for machine-readable records more compatible with encoding standards such as SGML and XML and with metadata models such as the Dublin Core.

Another question is how far the standards and practices for cataloging data can be stretched to other media. Electronic publications rarely follow the "one work, many copies" rule, for example. Is it productive to share records when all point to a common network resource rather than to locally held physical copies? Perhaps. Despite the efficiencies achieved through technology and cooperation, cataloging remains an expensive and labor-intensive process. The process can be justified for materials that will be retained and preserved for decades or centuries. It cannot be scaled up to accommodate the mass of electronic publications, many of which have short life spans. Automatic indexing of digital documents provides some access, though less comprehensive than that provided through manual means. A common gateway to distributed resources, each of which has its own metadata and search mechanisms, is another approach to providing access to heterogeneous resources. Many approaches are being tried, and more explorations, experiments, and evaluations are needed.

An issue central to the development of a global digital library is how well the cooperative relationships formed for sharing cataloging data, document delivery, and resource sharing will adapt to an environment of distributed access to information with many new players. Libraries are both cooperating and competing with many other organizations involved in providing information services. The process of negotiating new models for commerce, intellectual property, and privacy is straining relationships among players, however. Cooperation among institutions involves a considerable amount of overhead, as Central and Eastern European libraries are learning. New organizations must be formed, staffed, and maintained; more meetings must be attended. Dues often must be paid. Isolationism may appear easier, at least in the short term.

Cooperative organizations are sustainable only so long as the participants are receiving mutual benefits, whether in the form of cost savings, improved services, or intangible political advantages. In many cases, library cooperatives are a component of larger cooperative relationships among parent institutions. In the United States, these may involve student exchanges, shared purchase agreements, sports competitions, and other benefits. When organizations have many reasons to work together, they are more resilient to changes as substantial as those taking place in information infrastructure. The challenges may be even greater for libraries in regions such as Central and Eastern Europe, where cooperation was established primarily for library services, lacking larger institutional histories of cooperation.

The portability of technology and the sustainability of cooperation is a concern in Central and Eastern Europe. Underlying the rules, standards, and practices necessary for interoperability are a set of agreements for deploying them in a mutually beneficial manner. Lass, in his anthropological study of the Mellon-funded CASLIN project (1999a–c), found that the libraries and funders interpreted project goals much differently. The Mellon Foundation funded library automation as a means to promote cooperation between libraries, the end goal being improvements in access to information in these countries. Mellon intended CASLIN to be a consortium of libraries that would build a network of local automated systems and a common shared cataloging resource, and ultimately be self-sustaining. The libraries saw automation as an end in itself, according to Lass. As a result, they automated their cataloging processes without establishing a functioning consortium. Most of those involved in the project are more positive about their achievements, but they too acknowledge that CASLIN no longer exists as an entity (Balik 1998). Balik, who is the National Librarian of the Czech Republic, proposes that the CASLIN framework still could be used as a general model for cooperation.

With the benefit of hindsight, Lass attributes the CASLIN project's failure to establish a sustainable shared system to an attempt at technology transfer without the prerequisite "vision transfer" of common goals for mutual benefit. Our study found similar evidence of differing visions between CEE librarians and Western funding agencies. For example, a number of librarians viewed automation more as a means to "modernize" and to "rejoin Europe" than as a means to establish sustainable models for providing information services. Only time will tell whether these are painful first steps toward an information society or whether they foretell longer-term trends in the region.

The real world is messy. An American or a British or any other world view cannot be imposed on these institutions any more than their traditions and practices can be imposed on others. As Lass (1999b, p. 13) observes:

Rather than thinking of the library as an institution with a definable organizational structure, a mission, and a set of rules that help fulfill it—in other words, as a local tradition into which a new and different tradition is being introduced—it seems more productive to view the library, together with its history, as a confluence of complex interlocking networks of books, religious wars, world views, political agendas, and influential individuals, and as being essentially porous and unbounded.

Summary and Conclusions

Information technologies are converging, computer networks are extending their reach, digital libraries are proliferating, and the user community is growing exponentially. These developments combine to make vastly more information resources available to many more people in many more places. Some predicted that computer networks and digital libraries would lead to the end of books, bookstores, libraries, and archives, to a proliferation of virtual classrooms, and to employees working great distances from their employers. Although profound social changes are taking place, few of these effects have occurred to the extent predicted or in the ways anticipated. Book publishers and bookstores are thriving, online and off. Libraries, archives, and museums are taking leading roles in providing access to their resources in digital forms. Distance-independent learning is still in experimental stages as its providers try to find the combination of content, delivery mechanisms, and students most amenable to new forms of instruction. Meanwhile, admission to "traditional" colleges and universities remains as competitive as ever. Telecommuting is an established employment model, but only for certain jobs, employees, and employers. These new technologies are being adopted, but they are continually being adapted to suit the needs of individuals and organizations.

The first-level effects (Sproull and Kiesler 1991) of information technologies on access to information already are apparent. Methods for capturing and organizing information have improved substantially, leading to the development of more and better digital libraries. The fact that less progress has been made in techniques for searching and managing information resources is largely attributable to the human communication aspects. Technologies for scanning photographs, for example, are far more advanced than are techniques for describing those images so that they can be found again later. Second-level effects on behavior and organizations are becoming apparent. People are integrating computers, telephones, and other information appliances into their lives in unanticipated ways. These technologies can be employed to work more efficiently, to learn and play more creatively, and to stay in touch with far-flung friends and colleagues. They also can be used to disrupt communication and commerce, to violate privacy, and to gather evidence.

The technical and political framework for a global information infrastructure, laid by the Group of Seven nations, continues to evolve through the efforts of many players around the world. Among the greatest challenges faced in realizing a GII is to scale the present-day Internet to a much larger, more complex, and more diverse information infrastructure that will support many more users. It must be robust, reliable, and relatively easy to use. Neither the technology nor the knowledge of how to build such a network yet exists. Scaling up to a global information infrastructure will require much more than higher-capacity telecommunications lines and faster connections. It will also require techniques for managing several orders of magnitude more devices and users. Scaling requires new methods for seeking, creating, using, managing, preserving, and delivering information. It requires new economic models for allocating network resources. New policy models are needed for protecting and managing intellectual property, privacy, and security, both domestically and internationally. Also required are methods for authenticating users, documents, and transactions, and means for assessing liability for failures of authentication that lead to fraud or financial losses. These are prerequisites both for electronic commerce and for a global digital library.

As a global information infrastructure becomes truly global, differences in culture and in stages of technological development will have to be accommodated. Access to information is an issue that is particularly sensitive to these factors. Countries already reached by the Internet have widely differing degrees of telecommunications and computer network penetration. Laws that govern access, intellectual property, privacy, and security differ by political, cultural, religious, and other aspects of nations and societies. In some parts of the world, increasing the supply of information is the problem; in others, it is increasing the demand for information. In countries where information is in oversupply, the problem is human attention. The difficulty often lies in finding the right information, at the right time, with reasonable effort and expense.

I posed the construct of a "global digital library" as a way of thinking about access to information in an internationally distributed computer network. The global information infrastructure presents a wealth of opportunities for providing information resources to people around the world. At the same time, it poses a daunting array of technical, social, and policy challenges. Four trends in the design of digital libraries were identified: from metadata to data, from independent to linked systems, from searching to navigation, and from individual to group processes. These trends emerge from the larger framework of information technology development and from new ways of thinking about relationships between people and technology.

Research on digital libraries and on access to information has moved from computer and information science into the physical and life sciences, the social sciences, and the humanities. Concurrently, research questions have expanded from technical concerns for information retrieval and content representation into social aspects of digital libraries and across all phases of the information life cycle. Scholars in the disciplines are working with computer and information scientists to construct and study digital libraries tailored to their information needs and practices. Researchers are partnering with information professionals such as librarians, archivists, curators, and records managers to address pragmatic technical issues, management questions, and preservation and policy concerns.

Information can be empowering, but it also can be overwhelming. Information overload resulting from the proliferation of online resources will only get worse unless the technical, social, and policy issues associated with access to information are addressed in these early stages of constructing a global information infrastructure. The focus of this book is on improving access to information in a networked world. Yet we recognize that access to information is not a universally held value. It is a value embedded in cultures and traditions, in institutions and individuals, and in technology, economics, and policy. To paraphrase Pamela Samuelson's (1998) comments on information technology policy, access to information is too important a problem to leave entirely to government officials, corporate policy makers, librarians, archivists, computer scientists, or lawyers. Rather, it is a problem faced by people in all walks of life, at most stages of life, in all parts of the world. I hope this book will stimulate discussion of these issues among users and designers, individuals and organizations, creators and suppliers, workers and learners, young and old, in all walks of life, and in all parts of the world.

References

Bibliographic references serve an important role in providing access. The two primary functions of references are to document the author's sources and to provide further background information for the reader. To serve both functions, the references must be sufficiently complete that the reader can locate them. I always err in the direction of providing more detail to assure that the source can be found. —CLB

In keeping with the author's comments and in recognition of the unusually wide variety of documents listed, these references have not been edited in detail. —ed.

Adler, M. J. 1940. How to Read a Book: The Art of Getting a Liberal Education. New York: Simon and Schuster.

Agenbroad, J. E. 1992. Nonromanization: Prospects for Improving Automated Cataloging of Items in Other Writing Systems. Cataloging Forum, Opinion Papers, No. 3. Washington, DC: Library of Congress.

Agre, P. E. 1994/1995. From high tech to human tech: Empowerment, measurement, and social studies of computing. Computer Supported Cooperative Work 3 (2): 167–195.

Agre, P. E. 1995b. Institutional circuitry: Thinking about the forms and uses of information. Information Technology and Libraries 14: 225–230.

Agre, P. 1996. Libraries and communities. The Network Observer 3 (5). http://dlis.gseis.ucla.edu/people/pagre/tno/may–1996.html#libraries.

Agre, P. E. 1998. Designing genres for new media, in Steve Jones, ed, CyberSociety 2. 0: Revisiting CMC and Community, Sage. http://dlis.gseis.ucla.edu/people/pagre/genre.html

Agre, P. E., and Rotenberg, M., eds. 1997. Technology and Privacy: The New Landscape. MIT Press.

The ALA character set and other solutions for processing the world's information. 1989. Library Technology Reports 25 (2): 253–273.

Aliprand, J. M. 1992a. Nonroman scripts in the bibliographic environment. Information Technology and Libraries 11 (2): 105–19.

Aliprand, J. M. 1992b. Arabic script on RLIN. Library Hi Tech 10 (4): 59–80.

Allen, B. L. 1991. Cognitive research in information science: Implications for design. Annual Review of Information Science and Technology 26. Medford, NJ: Learned Information, 3–37.

Allen, T. J. 1969. Information needs and uses. In Cuadra, Carlos A. and Luke, Anne W., eds. Annual Review of Information Science and Technology 4. Chicago: Encyclopaedia Britannica, 3–29.

Andersen, D. L., Galvin, T. J., and Giguere, M. D. 1994. Navigating the Networks: Proceedings of the ASIS Mid-Year Meeting, Portland, Oregon, May 21–25, 1994. Medford, NJ: Learned Information.

Anderson, J. R. 1990. Cognitive psychology and its implications. San Francisco: W. H. Freeman.

Anderson, R. H., Bikson, T., Law, S. A., and Mitchell, B. M. 1995. Universal Access to E-mail: Feasibility and Societal Implications. Santa Monica, CA: Rand. Available at http://www.rand.org/publications/MR/MR650/

APA Manual. 1994. Publication manual of the American Psychological Association (4th ed.). Washington, DC: American Psychological Association.

Arms, W. Y. 1995. Key Concepts in the Architecture of the Digital Library. D-Lib Magazine. http://www.dlib.org/dlib/July95/07arms.html.

Arrow, K. 1969. Classification notes on the production and transmission of technological knowledge. American Economic Review, Papers and Proceedings 52: 29–35.

Atkins, T. V., and Ostrow, R. 1989. Cross-reference index : a guide to search terms (2nd ed.). New York, NY: Bowker.

Avram, H. D. 1972. Library automation: A balanced view. Library Resources and Technical Services 16 (1): 11–18.

Avram, H. D. 1975. MARC, Its History and Implications. Washington, DC: Library of Congress.

Avram, H. D. 1976. International standards for the interchange of bibliographic records in machine-readable form. Library Resources and Technical Services 20 (1): 25–35.

Avram, H. D., and Markuson, B. 1967. Library automation and Project MARC. the Brasenose Conference on the Automation of Libraries. London: Mansell.

Baca, M., ed. 1998. Introduction to Metadata: Pathways to Digital Information. Los Angeles: Getty Information Institute.

Baker, N. 1994. Discards. The New Yorker, April 4, 1994: 64–86 passim.

Baker, N. 1996. The author vs. the library (San Francisco, California, Public Library) The New Yorker 72 (31), Oct 14, 1996: 50–61.

Baker, T. 1998. Languages for Dublin Core. D-Lib Magazine. Http://www.dlib. org/dlib/December98/12baker.html

Baker, B. B., and Lysiak, L. D., eds. 1985. From tape to product: Some practical considerations on the use of OCLC-MARC Tapes. Ann Arbor: Pierian Press.

Baldwin, T. F., McVoy, D. S., and Steinfield, C. 1996. Convergence: Integrating media, information and communication. Thousand Oaks, CA: Sage.

Balik, V. 1998. The national electronic library: The situation in the Czech Republic. Liber Quarterly 8 (1): 7–14.

Ballard, Spahr, Andrews, and Ingersoll, LLP. 1999. Information Quality: A checklist for determining the value of information retrieved from the Internet. The Virtual Chase: A Research Site for Legal Professionals. Http://www.virtualchase. com/quality.html.

Band, J. 1995. Competing definitions of "openness" on the NII. In B. Kahin, and J. Abbate, eds. Standards policy for information infrastructure. MIT Press, pp 351–367.

Bangemann Report. 1994. See Europe and the Global Information Society. Recommendations to the European Council, 1994.

Barnes, M. 1997. The costs of systems: What we're spending. Bobbin 38 (11): 25–26.

Barlow, J. P. 1993. A plain text on crypto policy (the U. S. government's policy on cryptography) (Electronic Frontier). Communications of the ACM 36 (11) (Nov 1993):21–26.

Barry, J., Bilal, D., Penniman, D. 1998. Automated System Marketplace 98. The competitive struggle. Library Journal 123 (6): 43–52.

Baru, C., Moore, R., Rajasekar, A., Wan, M. 1998. The SDSC Storage Resource Broker, Proceedings of CASCON'98 Conference, Nov. 1998, Toronto, Canada.

Baru, C. K., Moore, R. W., Rajasekar, A., Schroeder, W., and Wan, M. 1999. A data handling architecture for a prototype federal application. IEEE Conference on Mass Storage Systems, MSS'98, March 1998, Silver Spring, MD. Http:// www.npaci.edu/DICE/Pubs/ieee_mss.htm.

Bates, M. J. 1977. Factors affecting subject catalog search success. Journal of the American Society for Information Science 28 (3): 161–169.

Bates, M. J. 1979. Information search tactics. Journal of the American Society for Information Science 30 (4): 205–214.

Bates, M. J. 1981. Search techniques. In M. E. Williams, ed. Annual Review of Information Science and Technology 16. New York: Knowledge Industry for American Society for Information Science, 139–169.

Bates, M. J. 1984. The fallacy of the perfect thirty-item online search. RQ 24 (1): 43–50.

Bates, M. J. 1986. Subject access in online catalogs: A design model. Journal of the American Society for Information Science 37 (6): 357–376.

Bates, M. J. 1989. The design of browsing and berry-picking techniques for the online search interface. Online Review 13 (5): 407–424.

Bates, M. J. 1990. Where should the person stop and the information search interface start? Information Processing and Management 26 (5): 575–591.

Bates, M. J., and Lu, S. 1997. An exploratory profile of personal home pages: Content, design, metaphors. Online and CDROM Review 21 (6): 331–339.

Bates, M. J., Wilde, D. N., and Siegfried, S. 1993. An analysis of search terminology used by humanities scholars: The Getty online searching project report no. 1. Library Quarterly 63 (1): 1–39.

Battin, P. 1998. Leadership in a transformational age. In B. L. Hawkins and P. Battin, eds. The Mirage of Continuity: Reconfiguring Academic Information Resources for the 21st Century. Washington, DC: Council on Library and Information Resources and the Association of American Universities. pp. 260–270.

Battin, P., and Hawkins, B. L. 1998. Setting the stage: Evolution, revolution, or collapse? In B. L. Hawkins and P. Battin, eds. The Mirage of Continuity: Reconfiguring Academic Information Resources for the 21st Century. Washington, DC: Council on Library and Information Resources and the Association of American Universities. pp. 3–12.

Batty, D. 1998. WWW—Wealth, Weariness, or Waste. D-Lib Magazine 4 (11). http://www.dlib.org/dlib/november98/11batty.html.

Bazerman, C. 1988. Shaping Written Knowledge: The Genre and Activity of the Experimental Article in Science. Madison: University of Wisconsin Press.

Beck, E. E. 1995. Changing documents/documenting changes: using computers for collaborative writing over distance. In: S. L. Star, ed. The Cultures of Computing. Oxford, UK: Blackwell, pp. 53–68.

Becker, P. A., Dodson, A. T., comps. Yoakam, L. L., ed. 1984. Collected papers of Frederick G. Kilgour, OCLC years. Dublin, OH: OCLC Online Computer Library Center.

Belkin, N. J., Oddy, R. N., and Brooks, H. M. 1982a. ASK for information retrieval: Part I. Background and theory. Journal of Documentation 38 (2): 61–71.

Belkin, N. J., Oddy, R. N., and Brooks, H. M. 1982b. ASK for information retrieval: Part II. Results of a design study. Journal of Documentation 38 (3): 145–164.

Belkin, N. J., and Vickery, A. 1985. Interaction in information systems: A review of research from document retrieval to knowledge-based systems. London, UK: British Library. Library and Information Research Report No. 35.

Beniger, J. 1986. The control revolution: Technological and Economic Origins of the Information Society. Cambridge: Harvard University Press.

Bennahum, D. S. 1999. Daemon seed: Old email never dies. WIRED 7 (5): 100–111.

Benton Foundation. 1996. Buildings, Books, and Bytes: Libraries and Communities in the Digital Age. http://www.benton.org.

Berend, I. T. 1998. Decades of Crisis: Central and Eastern Europe Before World War II. Berkeley: University of California Press.

Berger, M. G. 1994. Information-Seeking in the Online Bibliographic System: An Exploratory Study. PhD dissertation, University of California, Berkeley, School of Library and information Studies. UMI #AAI9504745.

Berghel, H. 1997a. Cyberspace 2000: Dealing with information overload. Communications of the ACM 40 (2): 19–24.

Berghel, H. 1997b. Email—the good, the bad, and the ugly. Communications of the ACM 40 (4): 11–15.

Besen, S. M. 1995. The standards processes in telecommunication and information technology. In R. Hawkins, R. Mansell, and J. Skea, eds. Standards, innovation and competitiveness: the politics and economics of standards in natural and technical envrionments. Aldershot, Hants, England: Gower. Pp. 136–146.

Beyond the English Catalog: Unicode and You. 1997. American Library Association Annual Conference, June 28, 1997, San Francisco. Audiotape available from ALA, Chicago.

Bilal, D. 1998. Children's search processes in using World Wide Web search engines: An exploratory study. In R. Larson, K. Petersen, and C. M. Preston, eds. ASIS '98: Proceedings of the 61st American Society for Information Science Annual Meeting 35. October 24–29, 1998, Pittsburgh. Medford, NJ: Information Today, pp. 45–53.

Billington, J. H. 1996. Libraries, the Library of Congress, and the information age. In Books, Bricks, and Bytes, Daedalus, Journal of the American Academy of Arts and Sciences; Proceedings of the American Academy of Arts and Sciences 125 (4): 35–54. Republished in S. R. Graubard and P. LeClerc, eds. 1998. Books, Bricks, and Bytes: Libraries in the Twenty-First Century. New Brunswick, NJ: Transaction Publishers.

Birnbaum, J. 1997. Pervasive information systems (The Next 50 Years: Our Hopes, Our Visions, Our Plans). Communications of the ACM 40 (2): 40–41.

Bishop, A. P., and Star, S. L. 1996. Social informatics for digital library use and infrastructure. In M. E. Williams, ed. Annual Review of Information Science and Technology 31. Medford, NJ: Information Today, pp. 301–401.

Bits. 1998. Eye-opening reports about desktop computing costs. http://www.lanl.gov/Internatl/divisions/cic/bits/archive/98june/Marcia_REDI.html.

Bits of Power: Issues in Global Access to Scientific Data. 1997. Committee on issues in the transborder flow of scientific data, U. S. national committee for CODATA; Commission on physical sciences, mathematics, and applications; National Research Council. Washington, DC: National Academy Press.

Blair, D. C., and Maron, M. E. 1985. An evaluation of retrieval effectiveness for a full-text document retrieval system. Communications of the ACM 28 (3): 289–299.

Books, Bricks, and Bytes. 1996. Daedalus, Journal of the American Academy of Arts and Sciences; Proceedings of the American Academy of Arts and Sciences 125 (4).

Borgman, C. L. 1984. Psychological research in human-computer interaction. In M. Williams, ed. Annual Review of Information Science and Technology, Vol. 19 (pp. 33–64). White Plains, NY: Knowledge Industry Publications.

Borgman, C. L. 1986a. The user's mental model of an information retrieval system: An experiment on a prototype online catalog. International Journal of Man-Machine Studies 24: 47–64.

Borgman, C. L. 1986b. Why are online catalogs hard to use? Lessons learned from information retrieval studies. Journal of the American Society for Information Science 37 (6): 387- 400.

Borgman, C. L. 1989a. All users of information systems are not created equal: An exploration into individual differences. Information Processing and Management 25 (3): 237–252.

Borgman, C. L. 1989b. Bibliometrics and scholarly communication: Editor's introduction. Communication Research 16 (5) (Special issue on bibliometric techniques for the study of scholarly communication): 583–599.

Borgman, C. L. 1990a. Editor's introduction. In C. L. Borgman, ed. Scholarly Communication and Bibliometrics, pp. 10–27. Newbury Park, CA: Sage Publications.

Borgman, C. L., ed. 1990b. Scholarly Communication and Bibliometrics. Newbury Park, CA: Sage Publications.

Borgman, C. L. 1992. National Electronic Library Workshop Report. In E. A. Fox, ed. 1993. Sourcebook on Digital Libraries: Report for the National Science Foundation, TR–93–35, VPI&SU Computer Science Department, December 1993, Blacksburg, VA, 439 pages. Available by anonymous FTP from directory pub/DigitalLibrary on fox.cs.vt.edu or at http://fox.cs.vt.edu/DLSB.html. pp. 126–147.

Borgman, C. L. 1993. Round in circles: The scholar as author and end-user in the electronic environment. In H. Woodward and S. Pilling, eds. The International Serials Industry. (pp. 45–59). London: Gower.

Borgman, C. L. 1995. The Global Information Infrastructure as a Digital Library. The Network Observer. Agre, P., ed. http://dlis.gseis.ucla.edu/people/pagre/tno/august-1995.html#borgman.

Borgman, C. L. 1996a. Will the Global Information Infrastructure be the Library of the Future? Central and Eastern Europe as a Case Example. IFLA (International Federation of Library Associations) Journal 22 (2): 121–127.

Borgman, C. L. 1996b. Why are online catalogs still hard to use? Journal of the American Society for Information Science. 47 (7): 493–503.

Borgman, C. L. 1996c. Automation is the answer, but what is the question? Progress and prospects for Central And Eastern European Libraries. Journal of Documentation 52 (3): 252–295.

Borgman, C. L. 1996d. Konyvtari automatizalas as halozatok. Reszlet a felsooktatasi vilagbanki projekt 1. 3 moduljaval kapcsolatos jelentesbol. (Final Report to the Hungarian Ministry of Culture and Education, World Bank Project, Module 1. 3: Library Automation and Networks.) Tudomanyos es Muszaki Tajekoztatas 43: 95-104. [Report submitted in English; published only in Hungarian translation].

Borgman, C. L. 1997a. From acting locally to thinking globally: A brief history of library automation. Library Quarterly 67 (3): 215–249. Also appeared in 1997, Library World, Journal of the Belarusian Library Association 3 (4): 10–14, translated into Russian by Petr Lapo.

Borgman, C. L. 1997b. Multi-Media, Multi-Cultural, and Multi-Lingual Digital Libraries, or How Do We Exchange Data in 400 Languages? D-Lib Magazine. Http://www.dlib.org/dlib/June97/06borgman.html.

Borgman, C. L. 1997c. Now that we have digital collections, why do we need libraries? In C. Schwartz and M. Rorvig, eds. Digital Collections: Implications for Users, Funders, Developers, and Maintainers; Proceedings of the American Society for Information Science Annual Meeting 34, November 1997, Washington, D. C. Medford, NJ: Information Today. pp. 27–33.

Borgman, C. L., Bates, M. J., Cloonan, M. V., Efthimiadis, E. N., Gilliland-Swetland, A., Kafai, Y., Leazer, G. L., Maddox, A. 1996. Social Aspects Of Digital Libraries. Final Report to the National Science Foundation; Computer, Information Science, and Engineering Directorate; Division of Information, Robotics, and Intelligent Systems; Information Technology and Organizations Program. Award number 95-28808. http://www-lis.gseis.ucla.edu/DL/Report.html.

Borgman, C. L., and Caidi, N. (1999). Developing National Information Infrastructures in Central and Eastern Europe: The Content vs. Conduit Debate. In A. Lass and R. E. Quandt, eds. Library Automation in Transitional Societies: Lessons from Eastern Europe. Oxford: Oxford University Press.

Borgman, C. L., Case, D. O., and Meadow, C. T. 1989. The design and evaluation of a front end user interface for energy researchers. Journal of the American Society for Information Science 40 (2): 86–98.

Borgman, C. L., Gallagher, A. L., Hirsh, S. G., and Walter, V. A. 1995. Children's Searching Behavior On Browsing And Keyword Online Catalogs: The Science Library Catalog Project. Journal of the American Society for Information Science 46 (9): 663–684.

Borgman, C. L., Hirsh, S. G., Hiller, J. 1996. Rethinking Online Monitoring Methods For Information Retrieval Systems: From Search Product To Search Process. Journal of the American Society for Information Science. 47 (7): 568–583.

Borgman, C. L., Moghdam, D., and Corbett, P. K. 1984. Effective Online Searching: A Basic Text. New York: Marcel Dekker, Inc.

Borgman, C. L., and Siegfried, S. L. 1992. Getty's Synoname and its cousins: A survey of applications of personal name matching algorithms. Journal of the American Society for Information Science 43 (7): 459–476.

Bot, M., Burgemeester, J., and Roes, H. 1998. The cost of publishing an electronic journal. A general model and a case study. D-Lib Magazine (November). http://www.dlib.org/dlib/november98/11roes.html.

Bowker, G., and Star, S. L. 1999. Sorting things out: Classification and practice. MIT Press.

Bowker, G., Star, S. L., Turner, W., and Gasser, L., eds. 1996. Social Science, Technical Systems, and Cooperative Work: Beyond the Great Divide. Hillsdale, NJ: Lawrence Erlbaum.

Boyle, J. 1996. Shamans, software, and spleens: Law and the construction of the information society. Cambridge, MA: Harvard University Press.

Branscomb, L. M., and Kahin, B. 1995. Standards processes and objectives for the national information infrastrucutre. In B. Kahin and J. Abbate, eds. Standards policy for information infrastructure. MIT Press, pp 3–31.

Bray, T., and Sperberg-McQueen, C. M., eds. 1997. XML: Extensible markup language. World-Wide Web Consortium. http://www.w3.org/pub/WWW/TR.

Brent, D. 1995. Stevan Harnad's "subversive proposal": Kick-starting electronic scholarship—a summary and analysis. The Information Society 11 (4): 275–283.

Brickell, A. 1997. Unicode/ISO 10646 and the CHASE project. In M. Segbert and P. Burnett, eds. Proceedings of the Conference on Library Automation in Central and Eastern Europe, Budapest, Hungary, April 10–13, 1996. Soros Foundation Open Society Institute Regional Library Program and Commission of the European Communities, Directorate General XIII, Telecommunications, Information Market and Exploitation of Research, Libraries Programme (DG XIII/E–4). Budapest: Open Society Institute.

Briet, S. 1951. Qu'est-ce que la documentation. Paris: Editions Techniques Industrielles et Techniques.

Brown, J. S. 1996. To dream the invisible dream. Communications of the ACM 39 (8): 30.

Brown, J. C., and Duguid, P. 1995. The social life of documents. First Monday. http://www.firstmonday.dk/issue1/documents/index.html#03.

Brown, R. H., Irving, L., Prabhakar, A., and Katzen, S. 1995. The Global Information Infrastructure: Agenda for Cooperation, March 1995. (http://www.iitf. nist.gov/documents/docs/gii/giiagend.html).

Bruce, B. C., and Sharples, M., eds. 1995. Special issue on Computer-Supported Collaborative Writing. Computer Supported Cooperative Work (CSCW). 3 (3–4): 225–404.

Buchinski, E. J., Avram, H. D., and McCallum, S. H. 1978. Initial considerations for a nationwide data base. Report of a study performed under the direction of the

Library of Congress Network Development Office. Network planning paper no. 3. 0160-9742 Washington: Library of Congress.

Buckland, M. K. 1988. Library services in theory and context, 2nd ed. Oxford: Pergamon.

Buckland, M. K. 1991. Information as thing. Journal of the American Society for Information Science 42 (5): 351–360.

Buckland, M. K. 1992. Redesigning Library Services: A Manifesto. Chicago: American Library Association. Available at http://sunsite.berkeley.edu/Literature/Library/Redesigning/html.html.

Buckland, M. K. 1997. What is a "document"? Journal of the American Society for Information Science 48 (9): 804–809.

Buckland, M. K. et al. 1999. Mapping entry vocabularies to unfamiliar metadata vocabularies. D-Lib Magazine 5 (1). Http://www.dlib.org/dlib/january99/buckland/01buckland.html.

Burkert, H. 1997. Privacy-enhancing technologies: Typology, critique, vision. In P. E. Agre and M. Rotenberg, eds. Technology and Privacy: The New Landscape. MIT Press. Pp. 125–142.

Caidi, N. (In progress). The information infrastructure as a discursive space: A case study of the library community in Central and Eastern Europe. PhD dissertation, Department of Information Studies, University of California, Los Angeles.

Carpenter, L., Shaw, S., and Prescott, A., eds. 1998. Towards the Digital Library: The British Library's Initiatives for Access Programme. London: The British Library.

Case, D. O. 1986. Collection and organization of written information by social scientists and humanists: A review and exploratory study. Journal of Information Science 12 (3): 97–104.

Case, D. O. 1991. Conceptual organization and retrieval of text by historians: The role of memory and metaphor. Journal of the American Society for Information Science 42 (9): 657–668.

Case, D. O., Borgman, C. L., and Meadow, C. T. 1986. End-user information-seeking in the energy field: implications for end-user access to DOE RECON databases. Information Processing and Management 22 (4): 299–308.

Chang, S-J., and Rice, R. E. 1993. Browsing: A multidimensional framework. In M. E. Williams, ed. Annual Review of Information Science and Technology 28. Medford, NJ: Learned Information, pp. 231–277.

Chapman, A. 1999. Availability of bibliographic records for the UK imprint. Journal of Documentation 55 (1): 6–15.

Chapman, G. (March 29, 1999). Digital nation: For entertainment firms, the choice may be to adapt to the Internet or die. Los Angeles Times, Business, pp. C1-C11.

Chen, H., and Dhar, V. 1990. User misconceptions of information retrieval systems. International Journal of Man-Machine Studies 32: 673–692.

Chen, S-S., and Wiederhold, G. 1999. National Science Foundation Workshop on Data Archival and Information Preservation, March 26–27,1999, Washington, D. C. Http://cecssrv1.cecs.missouri.edu/NSFWorkshop.

Cleverdon, C. W. 1964. Evaluation of operational information retrieval systems. Part 1: Identification of Criteria. Cranfield, Eng. : Cranfield College of Aeronautics.

Clinton Administration 1997. White Paper. The Clinton administration's policy on critical infrastructure protection: Presidential decision directive 63, May 22, 1998. http://www.pccip.gov. Reprinted in Electronic Privacy Information Center 1998. Critical infrastructure protection and the endangerment of civil liberties, pp. 36–49. Washington, DC: Electronic Privacy Information Center.

Clinton Administration 1998. President's commission on critical infrastructure protection: Executive Order 13010, July 15, 1997. http://www.pccip.gov.

Cohen, J. E. 1996. A Right to Read Anonymously: A Closer Look at Copyright Management in Cyberspace, 28 Connecticut Law Review 28: 981–1039.

Computer Science and Telecommunications Board; Commission on Physical Sciences, Mathematics, and Applications; National Research Council. 1997a. More than Screen Deep: Toward Every-Citizen Interfaces to the Nation's Information Infrastructure. Washington, D. C. : National Academy Press.

Computer Science and Telecommunications Board; Commission on Physical Sciences, Mathematics, and Applications; National Research Council. 1997b. For the Record: Protecting Electronic Health Information. Washington, D. C. : National Academy Press.

Conklin, J. 1987. Hypertext: An introduction and survey. IEEE Computer 29 (9): 17–41.

Cook, T. 1995. It's 10 o'clock: Do you know where your data are? (electronic data loss) Technology Review 98 (1): 48–53.

Cook, M. 1997. Access to archival holdings and unique library materials. World Information Report. UNESCO. Http://www.unesco.org/cii/wirerpt/vers-web.htm. Chapter 24, pp. 328–337.

Coyle, K. 1984. Consolidation of monograph records in the University of California online catalog. DLA Bulletin 4: 10–13.

Crane, D. 1971. Information needs and uses. In Cuadra, Carlos A. and Luke, Anne W., eds. Annual Review of Information Science and Technology 6. Chicago: Encyclopaedia Britannica, 3–39.

Crane, D. 1972. Invisible colleges; diffusion of knowledge in scientific communities. Chicago, IL: University of Chicago Press.

Crawford, J. C., Thom, L. C., and Powles, J. A. 1993. A survey of subject access to academic library catalogues in Great Britain. Journal of Librarianship and Information Science 25 (2): 85–93.

Croft, W. B. 1995. What do people want from information retrieval? (The Top 10 Research Issues for Companies that Use and Sell IR Systems). D-Lib Magazine. Http://www.dlib.org/November98/11croft.htm.

Cronin, B. 1996. Rates of return to citation. Journal of Documentation 52 (2): 188–197.

Cross-Language Information Retrieval. 1997. Third DELOS Workshop. Zurich, 5–7 March 1997. European Consortium for Informatics and Mathematics. Le Chesnay, France: ERCIM. Http://www-ercim.inria.fr.

Cummings, M. M. 1986. The Economics of Research Libraries. Washington, DC: Council on Library Resources.

Dam, K. W., and Lin, H. S., eds. 1996. Cryptography's Role in Securing the Information Society. Computer Science and Telecommunications Board; Commission on Physical Sciences, Mathematics, and Applications; National Research Council. Washington, D. C. : National Academy Press.

Daniels, P. J. 1986. Cognitive models in information retrieval—an evaluative review. Journal of Documentation 42 (4): 272–304.

David, P. A. 1995. Standardization policies for network technologies: the flux between freedom and order revisited. In R. Hawkins, R. Mansell, and J. Skea, eds. Standards, innovation and competitiveness: the politics and economics of standards in natural and technical envrionments. Aldershot, Hants, England: Gower. Pp 15–35.

Davies, R. 1992. Libraries in the former socialist countries: A new situation. The Liber Quarterly 2 (2): 215–226.

Davis-Brown, B., and Williamson, D. 1996. Cataloging at the Library of Congress in the digital age. Cataloging and Classification Quarterly 22 (3/4): 171–196.

Day, M., Heery, R., and Powell, A. 1999. National bibliographic records in the digital information environment: metadata, links, and standards. Journal of Documentation 55 (1): 16–32.

December, J. 1996. Units of analysis for Internet communication. Journal of Communication 46 (1): 14–38.

Dempsey, L. 1990. Bibliographic access: Patterns and developments. In L. Dempsey, ed. Bibliographic Access in Europe: First International Conference (pp. 1–29). Aldershot, England: Gower.

Dempsey, L. 1994. Network resource discovery: a European library perspective. In N. Smith, ed. Libraries, networks, and Europe: A European networking study. London: British Library Research and Development Department. (LIR series 101).

Dempsey, L., and Heery, R. 1998. Metadata: a current review of practice and issues. Journal of Documentation 54 (2): 145–172.

Dempsey, L., and Weibel, S. 1996. The Warwick metadata workshop: a framework for the deployment of resource description. D-Lib Magazine, July/August, http://www.dlib.org/dlib/July96/07weibel.html.

Dervin, B. 1977. Useful theory for librarianship: communication, not information. Drexel Library Quarterly 13 (3): 16–32.

Dervin, B. 1994. Information <--> Democracy: An examination of underlying assumptions. Journal of the American Society for Information Science 44 (8): 480–491.

Dervin, B., and Dewdney, P. 1986. Neutral questioning: a new approach to the reference interview. RQ 25 (4): 506–513.

Dervin, B., and Nilan, M. 1986. Information needs and uses. In M. E. Williams, ed. Annual Review of Information Science and Technology 21. White Plains, NY: Knowledge Industry Publications, 1–25.

Diffie, W., and Landau, S. 1998. Privacy on the Line: The Politics of Wiretapping and Encryption. MIT Press.

Dillon, A. 1994. Designing Usable Electronic Text: Ergonomic Aspects of Human Information Usage. London: Taylor and Francis.

Dillon, A. (in press). Spatial semantics and individual differences in the perception of shape in information space. Journal of the American Society for Information Science.

Dillon, A., and Gabbard, R. 1998. Hypermedia as an educational technology: A review of the quantitative research literature on learner comprehension, control, and style. Review of Educational Research. 68 (3): 322-349.

Dolby, J. L., Forsyth, V. J., and Resnikoff, H. L. 1969. Computerized Library Catalogs: Their Growth, Cost, and Utility. Cambridge: MIT Press.

Dosa, M. L. 1985. Information transfer as technical assistance for development. Journal of the American Society for Information Science 36 (3): 146–152.

Dozier, D. M., and Rice, R. E. 1984. Rival theories of electronic newsreading. In R. E. Rice, et al. The New Media: Communication, Research, and Technology. (pp. 103–128) Beverly Hills, CA: Sage.

Dowlin, K. E., and Shapiro, E. 1996. The centrality of communities to the future of major public libraries. In Books, Bricks, and Bytes, Daedalus, Journal of the American Academy of Arts and Sciences; Proceedings of the American Academy of Arts and Sciences 125 (4): 173–190. Republished in S. R. Graubard and P. LeClerc, eds. 1998. Books, Bricks, and Bytes: Libraries in the Twenty-First Century. New Brunswick, NJ: Transaction Publishers.

Dumais, S. T., and Landauer, T. K. 1982. Psychological Investigations of Natural Terminology for Command and Query Languages. In Badre, Albert; Shneiderman, B., eds. Directions in Human/Computer Interaction. Norwood, NJ: Ablex Publishing Co., 95–109.

Edge, D. O. 1977. Why I am not a co-citationist. Society for Social Studies of Science Newsletter 2: 13–19.

Edge, D. O. 1979. Quantitative measures of communication in science: A critical review. History of Science 17: 102–134.

Editors of WIRED. 1997. Kiss your browser goodbye: the radical future of media beyond the Web. WIRED 5.03, cover, 12–23.

Edwards, D. 1997. Internet legal research: What sites can you trust? Internet Legal Research, http://www.collegehill.com/ilp-news/edwards5.html.

Edwards, P. 1995. The closed world: computers and the politics of discourse. MIT Press.

Efthimiadis, E. N. 1992. Interactive Query Expansion and Relevance Feedback for Document Retrieval Systems. Unpublished doctoral dissertation, City University, London, U. K.

Efthimiadis, E. N. 1993. A user-centered evaluation of ranking algorithms for interactive query expansion. In: Korfhage, R., Rasmussen E., and Willett, P., eds. Proceedings of the 16th International Conference of the Association of Computing Machinery, Special Interest Group on Information Retrieval, June 1993, Pittsburgh, PA. pp. 146–159. New York: ACM Press.

Egan, D. E. 1988. Individual differences in human-computer interaction. In M. Helander, ed. Handbook of Human-Computer Interaction. Amsterdam: Elsevier, 543–568.

Egan, D. E., Remde, J. R., Landauer, T. K., Lochbaum, C. C., and Gomez, L. M. 1989. Behavioral evaluation and analysis of a hypertext browser. In Bice, K. and Lewis, C., eds. CHI'89: Human factors in computing systems conference proceedings. New York: Association for Computing Machinery, 205–210.

Ehn, P. 1988. Work-oriented design of computer artifacts. Stockholm: Arbetslivscentrum.

Eisenberg, D. 1989. Problems of the paperless book. Scholarly Publishing 21 (1): 11–26.

Ellis, D. 1989. A behavioural model for information retrieval system design. Journal of Information Science 15: 237–247.

Electronic Privacy Information Center. 1998. Critical infrastructure protection and the endangerment of civil liberties: An assessment of the President's Commission on Critical Infrastructure Protection (PCCIP). Washington, DC: Electronic Privacy Information Center. http://www.epic.org.

Eres, B. K. 1981. Transfer of information technology to less developed countries: A systems approach. Journal of the American Society for Information Science 32 (2): 97–102.

Eres, B. K. 1985. Socioeconomic conditions related to information activity in less developed countries. Journal of the American Society for Information Science 36 (3): 213–219.

Eres, B. K. 1989. International information issues. In M. E. Williams, ed. Annual Review of Information Science and Technology (Vol. 24, pp. 3–32). Amsterdam: Elsevier.

Ester, M. 1996. Digital image collections: Issues and practice. Washington, D. C. : Commission on Preservation and Access.

Europe and the Global Information Society. Recommendations to the European Council. 1994. Brussels: European Council. (Known as "The Bangemann Report.")

Federal Communications Commission. 1996. Universal Service. http://www.fcc.gov/ccb/universal_service/welcome.html.

Fidel, R. 1995. User-centered indexing. Journal of the American Society for Information Science 45 (8): 572–576.

Filtering and Collaborative Filtering. 1997. Fifth DELOS Workshop. Budapest, 10-12 November 1997. European Consortium for Informatics and Mathematics. Le Chesnay, France: ERCIM. Http://www-ercim.inria.fr.

Flynn, P. 1997. W[h]ither the web? The extension or replacement of HTML. Journal of the American Society for Information Science 48 (7): 614–621.

Foley, J. D., Van Dam, A., Feiner, S. K., and Hughes, J. F. 1990. Computer Graphics: Principles and Practice. 2nd ed. Reading, MA: Addison-Wesley.

Folkman, S. 1984. Personal control and stress and coping processes: a theoretical analysis. Journal of Personality and Social Psychology 46: 839–852.

Foskett, D. J. 1984. Pathways for Communication: Books and Libraries in the Information Age. London: Clive Bingley.

Foster, I., and Kesselman, C. 1999. The Grid: Blueprint for a New Computing Infrastructure. Los Altos, CA: Morgan Kaufmann.

Fox, E. A., ed. 1993. Sourcebook on Digital Libraries: Report for the National Science Foundation, TR–93–35, VPI&SU Computer Science Department, December 1993, Blacksburg, VA, 439 pages. http://fox.cs.vt.edu/DLSB.html.

Fox, E. A., Akscyn, R. M., Furuta, R. K., and Leggett, J. J. 1995. Digital Libraries [Special issue introduction]. Communications of the ACM 38 (4): 22–28.

Fox, E. A., and Marchionini, G., eds. 1996. Proceedings of the 1st ACM International Conference on Digital Libraries. New York: Association for Computing Machinery.

Fox, R. 1999. News track. Communications of the ACM 42 (4): 11–12.

Frederking, R., Mitamura, T., Nyberg, E., and Carbonell, J. 1997. Translingual information access. AAAI Spring Symposium on Cross-Language Text and Speech Retrieval. Http://www.cs.cmu.edu/~ref/aaai-ref.html.

Friedlander, A. 1995a. Emerging infrastructure: The growth of railroads. Reston, VA: Corporation for National Research Initiatives. http://www.cnri.reston.va.us/series.html.

Friedlander, A. 1995b. Natural monopoly and universal service: Telephones and telegraphs in the U. S. communications infrastructure, 1837–1940. Reston, VA: Corporation for National Research Initiatives. http://www.cnri.reston.va.us/series.html.

Friedlander, A. 1996a. Power and light: Electricity in the U. S. energy infrastructure, 1870–1940. Reston, VA: Corporation for National Research Initiatives. http://www.cnri.reston.va.us/series.html.

Friedlander, A. 1996b. "In God we trust": All others pay cash: Banking as an American infrastructure, 1800-1935. Reston, VA: Corporation for National Research Initiatives. http://www.cnri.reston.va.us/series.html.

Froomkin, M. 1998. Five critical issues relating to impacts of information technology. In Computer Science and Telecommunications Board; Commission on Physical Sciences, Mathematics, and Applications; National Research Council. 1998. Fostering Research on the Economic and Social Impacts of Information Technology: Report of a Workshop. Washington, D. C. : National Academy Press. Pp. 147–149.

Fuller, S. 1995a. Cyberplatonism: An inadequate constitution for the republic of science. The Information Society 11 (4): 293–304.

Fuller, S. 1995b. Cybermaterialism, or where there is no free lunch in cyberspace. The Information Society 11 (4): 325–332.

Furnas, G. W., Landauer, T. K., Gomez, L. M., Dumais, S. T. 1987. The vocabulary problem in human-system communication. Communications of the ACM 30 (11): 965–971.

G-7 Ministerial Conference on the Information Society. 1995a. Chair's conclusions. http://www.ispo.cec.be/g7/g7main.html.

G-7 Ministerial Conference on the Information Society. 1995b. Electronic libraries project. http://www.ispo.cec.be/g7/g7main.html or http://www.cec.lu.

Garvey, W. D., and Griffith, B. C. 1964. Scientific information exchange in psychology. Science 146: 1655–1659.

Geer, D. E. 1998. Risk management is where the money is. Forum on Risks to the Public in Computers and Related Systems, ACM Committee on Computers and Public Policy. Risks-Forum Digest, 12 November 1998, 20 (06), http://catless.ncl.ac.uk/Risks/20.06.html or ftp.sri.com/risks/.

Gifford, P. 1993. The libraries of eastern Europe: Information and democracy. Representations 42: 100–106.

Gilbreth, L. M. 1921. The psychology of management: the function of the mind in determining, teaching and installing methods of least waste. New York: Macmillan.

Gillespie, A., and Robins, K. 1989. Geographical inequalities: The spatial bias of new communications technologies. In M. Siefert, G. Gerbner, and J. Fisher, eds. The Information Gap: How Computers and Other New Communication Technologies Affect the Social Distribution of Power. Oxford: Oxford University Press, pp. 7–18.

Gilliland-Swetland, A. 1998. Defining Metadata. In M. Baca, ed. Introduction to Metadata: Pathways to Digital Information. Los Angeles: Getty Information Institute.

Ginsparg, P. 1994. First steps towards electronic research communication. Computers in Physics 8 (4): 390–396. http://xxx.lanl.gov/blurb/

Ginsparg, P. 1996. Winners and losers in the global research village. Invited talk, UNESCO, Paris, 21 February 1996. http://xxx.lanl.gov/blurb/pg96unesco.html.

Glass, A. L., Holyoak, K. J., and Santa, J. L. 1979. Cognition. Reading, MA: Addison-Wesley.

Gore, A. 1994a. Al Gore, Speech on U. S. Vision for the Global Information Infrastructure, World Telecommunication Development Conference, Buenos Aires, March 1994. Quoted in Brown, R. H., Irving, L., Prabhakar, A., Katzen, S. The Global Information Infrastructure: Agenda for Cooperation, March 1995. (http://www.iitf.nist.gov).

Gore, A. 1994b. The Information Superhighway. Speech, The Superhighway Summit, University of California, Los Angeles, January 11, 1994.

Gorman, M. 1969. Bibliographical Data in National Bibliography Entries; A Report on Descriptive Cataloging Made for UNESCO and IFLA, Provisional Abridged Text, 23 pp. (IFLA, International Meeting of Cataloging Experts, Copenhagen. Document for Examination No. 2).

Graubard, S. R., and LeClerc, P., eds. 1998. Books, Bricks, and Bytes: Libraries in the Twenty-First Century. New Brunswick, NJ: Transaction Publishers.

Green, S., Cunningham, P., Somers, F. 1998. Agent mediated collaborative Web page filtering. In Klusch, M., Weiss, G., eds. Cooperative Information Agents II. Learning, Mobility and Electronic Commerce for Information Discovery on the Internet. Second International Workshop, CIA'98. Proceedings, Paris, France, 4-7 July 1998. Berlin, Germany: Springer-Verlag, 1998. pp. 195-205.

Greenberg, D. 1998. Camel drivers and gatecrashers: Quality control in the digital research library. In B. L. Hawkins and P. Battin, eds. The Mirage of Continuity: Reconfiguring Academic Information Resources for the 21st Century. Washington, DC: Council on Library and Information Resources and the Association of American Universities. pp. 105–116.

Griffiths, J-M. 1998. Why the web is not a library. In B. L. Hawkins and P. Battin, eds. The Mirage of Continuity: Reconfiguring Academic Information Resources for the 21st Century. Washington, DC: Council on Library and Information Resources and the Association of American Universities. pp. 229–246.

Gross, R. A., and Borgman, C. L. 1995. The incredible vanishing library. American Libraries 26 (9): 900–904.

Haigh, R. 1997. What shall I wear to the computer revolution? Some thoughts on electronic researching in Law. Law Library Journal 89 (2): 245–264.

Hakala, J., Husby, O., Koch, T. 1996. Warwick framework and Dublin core set provide a comprehensive infrastructure for network resource description. Report form the Metadata Workshop II, Warwick, UK, April 1–3, 1996. http://www.ub2.lu.se/tk/warwick.html.

Halem, M., Shaffer, F., Palm, N., Salmon, E., Raghavan, S., and Kempster, L. 1999. Technology assessment of high capacity data storage systems: Can we avoid a data survivability crisis? Greenbelt, MD: NASA Goddard Space Flight Center. Paper presented at National Science Foundation Workshop on Data Archival and Information Preservation, March 26–27, 1999, Washington, D. C. Http://cecssrv1.cecs.missouri.edu/NSFWorkshop.

Hankiss, E. 1994. European paradigms: East and West, 1945–1994. Daedalus, Journal of the American Academy of Arts and Sciences. Proceedings of the American Academy of Arts and Sciences 123 (3): 115–126.

Harmon, A. 1998. Corporate delete keys busy as e-mail turns up in court. New York Times, November 11, A1, C2 (national edition).

Harnad, S. 1990. Scholarly skywriting and the prepublication continuum of scientific inquiry. Psychological Science 1: 342–344. ftp://ftp.princetonj.edu/pub/harnad/Harnad/harnad90.skywriting.

Harnad, S. 1995a. The PostGutenberg Galaxy: How to get there from here. The Information Society 11 (4): 285–292.

Harnad, S. 1995b. Sorting the esoterica from the exoterica: There's plenty of room in cyberspace—A response to Fuller. The Information Society 11 (4): 305–321.

Harter, S. P., and Hert, C. A. 1997. Evaluation of information retrieval systems: Approaches, issues, and methods. In M. E. Williams, ed. Annual Review of Information Science and Technology, Vol. 32, pp. 3–94. Medford, NJ: Information Today.

Havel, V. 1985. The power of the powerless. London: Hutchinson.

Hawkins, R. W. 1995. Standards making as technological diplomacy: assessing objectives and methodologies in standards institutions. In R. Hawkins, R. Mansell, and J. Skea, eds. Standards, innovation and competitiveness: the politics and economics of standards in natural and technical envrionments. Aldershot, Hants, England: Gower. Pp. 147–158.

Hawkins, B. L. 1998. The unsustainability of the traditional library and the threat to higher education. In B. L. Hawkins and P. Battin, eds. The Mirage of Continuity: Reconfiguring Academic Information Resources for the 21st Century. Washington, DC: Council on Library and Information Resources and the Association of American Universities. Pp. 129–153.

Hawkins, B. L., and Battin, P., eds. 1998. The Mirage of Continuity: Reconfiguring Academic Information Resources for the 21st Century. Washington, DC: Council on Library and Information Resources and the Association of American Universities.

Hawkins, R., Mansell, R., and Skea, J., eds. 1995. Standards, innovation and competitiveness: the politics and economics of standards in natural and technical environments. Aldershot, Hants, England: Gower. Pp. 147–158.

Hayes, R. M., and Becker, J. 1970. Handbook of Data Processing for Libraries. Los Angeles: Melville.

Hedstrom, M. 1991. Understanding electronic incunabula: A framework for research on electronic records. The American Archivist 54 (3): 334–354.

Hedstrom, M. 1993. Electronic records program strategies: An assessment. In M. Hedstrom, ed. Electronic Records Management Program Strategies. Archives and Museum Informatics Technical Report No. 18. Pittsburgh, PA: Archives and Museum Informatics.

Hedstrom, M. 1998. Digital preservation: A time bomb for digital libraries. Computers and the Humanities 31: 189–202.

Hein, M. 1991. Library cooperation based on information technology networks: A vision for a European library future. IFLA Journal 17: 39–44.

Heinz, J. 1991. U. S. Strategic Trade: An export control system for the 1990s. Boulder, CO: Westview Press.

Hert, C. A 1996. User Goals on an Online Public Access Catalog. Journal of the American Society for Information Science 47 (7): 504–518.

Hibbitts, B. 1996. Last writes? Reassessing the law review in the age of cyberspace. New York University Law Review 71 (3), (June 1996): 615–688.

Higginbotham, B. B., and Bowdoin, S. 1993. Access versus Assets. Chicago: American Library Association.

Hildreth, C. R. 1993. An evaluation of structured navigation for subject searching in online catalogues. London: City University, Department of Information Science. Doctoral dissertation.

Hill, L. L., Frew, J., and Zheng, Q. 1999. Geographic names: The implementation of a gazetteer in a georeferenced digital library. D-Lib Magazine 5 (1). http:www.dlib.org/dlib/january99.

Hillis, D. 1997. A time of transition. Communications of the ACM 40 (2): 37–39.

Hirsh, S. G. 1998. Relevance determinations in children's use of electronic resources: A case study. In R. Larson, K. Petersen, & C. M. Preston, eds. ASIS '98: Proceedings of the 61st American Society for Information Science Annual Meeting 35. October 24-29, 1998, Pittsburgh. Medford, NJ: Information Today. pp. 63-72.

Holley, R. P. 1993. Cooperative cataloging outside North America: Status report 1993. Cataloging and Classification Quarterly 17 (3/4): 201–236.

Horsnell, V., ed. 1988. Mechanisms for Library Cooperation: Getting our Act Together. Proceedings of the 13th Annual Seminar of the MARC Users' Group. Aldershot, Hants, England: Gower.

Hudson, T. 1996. The cost of keeping up. Hospitals and Health Networks 70 (23): 54–60.

Hyslop, C. 1996. From cataloging to gateway: The program for cooperative cataloging. ALCTS Newsletter 7 (4): 52A–52D.

Iacono, S., and Kling, R. 1995. Computerization movements and tales of technological utopianism. In R. Kling, ed. Computerization and Controversy: Value Conflicts and Social Choices. Academic Press.

IFLA. 1998. International Federation of Library Associations and Institutions. Http://www.ifla.org.

Information Freedom and Censorship. 1988. The Article 19 World Report 1988. Prepared by the staff of Article 19. Harlow: Longman.

Information Freedom and Censorship. 1991. The Article 19 World Report 1991. Prepared by the staff of Article 19. London: Library Association Publishing.

Information Infrastructure Program / IIF/ 1991–1994. 1992. Budapest: Hungarian Academy of Sciences, Computer Science Institute (Sztaki).

Information Technology Research: Investing in Our Future. 1999. President's Information Technology Advisory Committee, Report to the President. February 24. National Coordination Office for Computing, Information, and Communications. Http://www.ccic.gov.

Ingwersen, P. 1984. Psychological aspects of information retrieval. Social Science Information Studies 4: 83–95.

Ingwersen, P. 1996. Cognitive perspectives of informaton retrieval interaction: elements of a cognitive IR theory. Journal of Documentation 52 (1): 3–50.

Innis, H. A. 1951. The Bias of Communication. Toronto: University of Toronto Press.

Institute of Information Science (IZUM). 1993a. COBISS (Cooperative Online Bibliographic System and Services) conception, organization, and terms and conditions of co-operation. Maribor, Slovenia: IZUM.

Institute of Information Science (IZUM). 1993b. COBISS (Cooperative Online Bibliographic System and Services) COBISS/OPAC users' manual. Maribor, Slovenia: IZUM.

Janes, J. W., and Rosenfeld, L. B. 1996. Networked information retrieval and organization: Issues and questions. Journal of the American Society for Information Science 47 (9): 711–715.

Jehl, D. (March 18, 1999). Riyadh journal: The Internet's "open sesame" is answered warily. The New York Times International Edition.

Johnson, K. E., and Krzyminski, R. J. 1999. Searching the web has become a standard practice in legal research. Law Office Computing 9 (2): 59–66.

Kahin, B. 1995. The Internet and the National Information Infrastructure. In B. Kahin and J. Keller, eds. Public Access to the Internet. MIT Press. pp. 3–23.

Kahin, B., and Abbate, J., eds. 1995. Standards policy for information infrastructure. MIT Press.

Kahin, B., and Keller, J., eds. 1995. Public Access to the Internet. MIT Press.

Kahin, B., and Nesson, C., eds. 1997. Borders in Cyberspace: Information Policy and the Global Information Infrastructure. MIT Press.

Kahle, B. 1997. Preserving the Internet. Scientific American 276 (3): 82–83.

Kahn, R., and Wilensky, R. 1995. A framework for distributed digital object services. hdl:cnri.dlib/tn95–01. (http://WWW.CNRI.Reston.VA.US/home/cstr/arch/k-w.html)

Kando, N., and Aizawa, A. 1998. Cross-lingual information retrieval using automatically generated multilingual keyword clusters. IRAL '98, Singapore, 15–16 October 1998. Http://www.rd.nacsis.ac.jp/~kando.

Kando, N., Aizawa, A., Tsuji, K., Kageura, K., and Kuriyama, K. 1998. Cross-language information retrieval and automatic construction of multilingual lexicons. In R. Larson., K. Petersen, and C. M. Preston, eds. ASIS '98: Proceedings of the 61st American Society for Information Science Annual Meeting 35. October 24–29, 1998, Pittsburgh. Medford, NJ: Information Today. pp. 572.

Kang, J. 1998. Information privacy in cyberspace transactions. Stanford Law Review 50 (4): 1193–1294.

Karnitas, E. 1996. Latvian Information Infrastructure: The present stage and plans for development. Riga: Latvian Academy of Sciences.

Katz, J., and Aspden, P. 1997. Motives, hurdles, and dropouts. Communications of the ACM 40 (4): 97–102.

Kedzie, C. R. 1997. The third waves. In B. Kahin and C. Nesson, eds. Borders in Cyberspace: Information Policy and the Global Information Infrastructure. MIT Press. Pp. 106–128.

Keller, J. 1995. Public access issues: An introduction. In B. Kahin and J. Keller, eds. Public Access to the Internet. MIT Press, pp 34–45.

Keller, M. A. 1998. Libraries in the digital future. Science 281: 1461–1462.

Kelly, B. 1999. The evolution of web protocols. Journal of Documentation 55 (1): 71–81.

Kent, S. G. 1996. American public libraries: A long transformative moment. In Books, Bricks, and Bytes, Daedalus, Journal of the American Academy of Arts and Sciences; Proceedings of the American Academy of Arts and Sciences 125 (4): 207–220. Republished in S. R. Graubard and P. LeClerc, eds. 1998. Books, Bricks, and Bytes: Libraries in the Twenty-First Century. New Brunswick, NJ: Transaction Publishers.

Kessler, J. 1996. Internet Digital Libraries: The International Dimension. Boston: Artech House.

Kislovskaya, G. 1996. Preservation challenges in a changing political climate: A report from Russia. Washington, D. C. : Commission on Preservation and Access.

Kiss, J. 1972. Libraries in Hungary. Budapest: National Szechenyi Library.

Kleiber, C., Montgomery, L. A., and Craft-Rosenberg, M. 1995. Information needs of the siblings of critically ill children. Childrens Health Care 24: 47–60.

Kling, R., and Covi, L. 1995. Electronic journals and legitimate media in the systems of scholarly communication. The Information Society 11 (4): 261–272.

Koberg, D., and Bagnall, J. 1972. The Universal Traveler. A Soft-Systems Guidebook to Creativity, Problem-Solving and the Process of Design. Los Altos, CA: Morgan Kaufman.

Kochen, M. 1989. How well do we acknowledge intellectual debts? Current Contents: Social and Behavioral Sciences 21 (25): 7–14.

Kollock, P. 1999. The production of trust in online markets. In E. J. Lawler, M. Macy, S. Thyne, and H. A. Walker, eds. Advances in Group Processes 16.

Greenwich, CT: JAI Press. Http://www.sscnet.ucla.edu/soc/faculty/kollock/papers/online_trust.htm.

Korfhage, R. R. 1997. Information storage and retrieval. New York: Wiley.

Krohne, H. W. 1986. Coping with stress: dispositions, strategies, and the problem of measurement. In C. D. Spielberger and I. G. Sarason, eds. Dynamics of stress. New York: Plenum.

Krohne, H. W. 1989. The concept of coping modes: Relating cognitive person variables to actual coping behavior. Advances in Behaviour Research & Therapy 11 (4): 235-248.

Krohne, H. W. 1996. Individual differences in coping. In Handbook of coping: Theory, research, applications. Zeidner, M. et al., eds. Wiley. p. 381-409.

Krzys, R., Litton, G., and Hewitt, A. 1983. World Librarianship: A Comparative Study. New York: Marcel Dekker.

Kuhlthau, C. C. 1988a. Longitudinal case studies of the information search process in libraries. Library and Information Science Research 10 (3): 257–304.

Kuhlthau, C. C. 1988b. Developing a model of the library search process: Cognitive and affective aspects. RQ 28 (2): 232–242.

Kuhlthau, C. C. 1991. Inside the search process: Information seeking from the user's perspective. Journal of the American Society for Information Science 42 (5): 361–371.

Kwasnik, B. 1991. The importance of factors that are not document attributes in the organzation of personal documents. Journal of Documentation 47 (4): 389–398.

Lagoze, C. 1996. The Warwick framework: A container architecture for diverse sets of metadata. D-Lib Magazine, July/August, http://www.dlib.org/dlib/July96/lagoze/07lagoze.html.

Lamm, D. S. 1996. Libraries and publishers: A partnership at risk. Daedalus, Journal of the American Academy of Arts and Sciences; Books, Bricks, and Bytes: Proceedings of the American Academy of Arts and Sciences 125 (4): 127–146. Republished in S. R. Graubard and P. LeClerc, eds. 1998. Books, Bricks, and Bytes: Libraries in the Twenty-First Century. New Brunswick, NJ: Transaction Publishers.

Lancaster, F. W. 1968. Information Systems: Characteristics, Testing, and Evaluation. New York: Wiley.

Lancaster, F. W. 1978. Toward paperless information systems. San Diego: Academic Press.

Lancaster, F. W., ed. 1992. Artificial intelligence and expert systems: Will they change the library? Urbana-Champaign: Graduate School of Library and Information Science, University of Illinois.

Lancaster, F. W., Connell, T. H., Bishop, N., and McCowan, S. 1991. Identifying barriers to effective subject access in library catalogs. Library Resources and Technical Services 35 (2): 377–391.

Lancaster, F. W., and Fayen, E. G. 1973. Information Retrieval On-Line. Los Angeles: Melville.

Lancaster, F. W., and Smith, L. C. 1983. Compatibility Issues Affecting Information Systems and Services. General Information Programme and UNISIST. Paris, UNESCO.

Landauer, T. K. 1995. The Trouble with Computers: Usefulness, Usability and Productivity. MIT Press.

Larson, R. R. 1991a. Between Scylla and Charybdis: Subject searching in the online catalog. In Advances in Librarianship 15. San Diego: Academic Press, pp. 175-236.

Larson, R. R. 1991b. Classification clustering, probabilistic information retrieval and the online catalog. Library Quarterly 61 (2): 133–173.

Larson, R. R. 1991c. The decline of subject searching: Long-term trends and patterns of index use in an online catalog. Journal of the American Society for Information Science 42 (3): 197–215.

Larson, R. R. 1994. Design and development of a network-based electronic library. In Andersen, D. L., Galvin, T. J., and Giguere, M. D. Navigating the Networks: Proceedings of the American Society for Information Science Mid-Year Meeting, Portland, Oregon, May 21-25, 1994. Medford, NJ: Learned Information, 95-114.

Lass, A. 1999a. The cross currents of technology transfer: The Czech and Slovak library information network. In R. Ekman & R. E. Quandt, eds. Technology and Scholarly Communication. Berkeley: University of California Press.

Lass, A. 1999b. Portable worlds: On the limits of replication in the Czech and Slovak Republics. In. M. Buraway & K. Verdery, eds. Uncertain Transitions: Ethnographics of Change in the Former Socialist World. Denver: Rowman & Littlefield.

Lass, A. 1999c. Managing delay: The micropolitics of time in the Czech and Slovak automation projects. In A. Lass and R. E. Quandt, eds. Library Automation in Transitional Societies: Lessons from Eastern Europe. Oxford: Oxford University Press. pp. 345-359.

Lass, A., and Quandt, R. E. (1999a). Introduction. In A. Lass and R. E. Quandt, eds. Library Automation in Transitional Societies: Lessons from Eastern Europe. Oxford: Oxford University Press. pp. 3–27.

Lass, A., and Quandt, R. E., eds. (1999b). Library Automation in Transitional Societies: Lessons from Eastern Europe. Oxford: Oxford University Press.

Lavigne, M., ed. 1992. The Soviet Union and Eastern Europe in the Global Economy. Cambridge: Cambridge University Press.

Lawton, G. 1998. Multicasting: Will it transform the Internet? IEEE Computer 31 (7): 13–15.

Layne, S. S. 1994. Some issues in the indexing of images. Journal of the American Society for Information Science 45 (8): 583–588.

Leazer, G. H. 1994. A conceptual schema for the control of bibliographic works. In Andersen, D. L., Galvin, T. J., Giguere, M. D. Navigating the Networks: Proceedings of the American Society for Information Science Mid-Year Meeting, Portland, Oregon, May 21-25, 1994. Medford, NJ: Learned Information, pp 115-135.

Leazer, G. H., and Rohdy, M. 1994. The bibliographic control of foreign monographs: A review and baseline study. Library Resources and Technical Services 39 (1): 29–42.

Lehmann, K-D. 1996. Making the transitory permanent: The intellectual heritage in a digitized world of knowledge. In Books, Bricks, and Bytes, Daedalus, Journal of the American Academy of Arts and Sciences; Proceedings of the American Academy of Arts and Sciences 125 (4): 307–330. Republished in S. R. Graubard and P. LeClerc, eds. 1998. Books, Bricks, and Bytes: Libraries in the Twenty-First Century. New Brunswick, NJ: Transaction Publishers.

Lesk, M. E. 1990. Image formats for preservation access. Information Technology and Libraries 9 (4): 300–308.

Lesk, M. E. 1997a. Practical Digital Libraries: Books, Bytes, and Bucks. San Francisco: Morgan Kaufman.

Lesk, M. 1997b. Going digital. Scientific American 276 (3): 58–60.

Lesk, M., Fox, E., and McGill, M., eds. 1991. A National Electronic Science, Engineering, and Technology Library. Reprinted in Fox 1993, pp. 4–24.

Leventhal, L., Lancaster, A-M., Marcus, A., Nardi, B., Nielsen, J., Kurosu, M., and Heller, R. 1994. Designing for diverse users: Will just a better interface do? In C. Plaisant, ed. CHI '94, Human Factors in Computing Systems, Conference Companion. Boston, April 24–28, 1994. New York: ACM, 191–192.

Levy, D. M., and Marshall, C. C. 1995. Going Digital: A look at the assumptions underlying digital libraries. Communications of the ACM 38 (4): 77–84.

Libicki, M. C. 1995a. Standards: The rough road to the common byte. In B. Kahin and J. Abbate, eds. Standards policy for information infrastructure. MIT Press, pp. 35–78.

Libicki, M. C. 1995b. Information Technology Standards. Boston: Digital Press.

Library of Congress. 1995.organizing the Global Digital Library Conference. gopher://marvel.loc.gov/00/loc/conf.meet/gdl/

Library of Congress. 1996.organizing the Global Digital Library Conference II. http://lcweb.loc.gov/catdir/ogdl2/

Library of Congress. 1997. Dublin Core / MARC / GILS Crosswalk. Washington, DC: Library of Congress, Network Development and MARC Standards Office. http://lcweb.loc.gov/marc/dccross.html.

Library of Congress. 1998. MARC Document Type Definitions. Background and development. Washington, DC: Library of Congress, Network Development and MARC Standards Office. http://www.loc.gov/marc/marcdtd/marcdtdback.html.

Library of Congress Network Advisory Group. 1977a. The library bibliographic component of the National Library and Information Service Network. Avram, H. D. and Maruyama, L. S., eds. Preliminary edition. Washington: Library of Congress.

Library of Congress Network Advisory Group. 1977b. Toward a national library and information service network: the library bibliographic component. Avram, H. D. and Maruyama, L. S., eds. Prelim. ed. Washington: Library of Congress.

Licklider, J. C. R., and Vezza, A. 1978. Applications of information networks. IEEE Proceedings 66: 1330–1346.

Lievrouw, L. A. 1990. Reconciling structure and process in the study of scholarly communication. In C. L. Borgman, ed. 1990. Scholarly Communication and Bibliometrics. pp. 59–69. Newbury Park, CA: Sage.

Lievrouw, L. A., ed. 1994a. Special topic issue: Information resources and democracy. Journal of the American Society for Information Science 44 (8): 350–421.

Lievrouw, L. A. 1994b. Information resources and democracy: Understanding the paradox. Journal of the American Society for Information Science 44 (8): 350–357.

Lievrouw, L. A., Rogers, E. M., Lowe, C. U., and Nadel, E. 1987. Triangulation as a research strategy for identifying invisible colleges among biomedical sciences. Social Networks 9: 217–238.

Lohse, G. L., and Spiller, P. 1998. Electronic shopping. Communications of the ACM 41 (7): 81–87.

Losee, R. M. 1997. A discipline independent definition of information. Journal of the American Society for Information Science 48 (3): 254–269.

Lucier, R. E. 1995. Building a digital library for the health sciences: Information space complementing information place. Bulletin of the Medical Library Association 83 (3): 346–350.

Lundvall, B-A. 1995. Standards in an innovative world. In R. Hawkins, R. Mansell, and J. Skea, eds. Standards, innovation and competitiveness: the politics and economics of standards in natural and technical environments. Aldershot, Hants, England: Gower. Pp.7–12.

Lyman, P. 1996. What is a digital library? Technology, intellectual property, and the public interest. In Books, Bricks, and Bytes, Daedalus, Journal of the American Academy of Arts and Sciences; Proceedings of the American Academy of Arts and Sciences 125 (4): 1–33. Republished in S. R. Graubard and P. LeClerc, eds. 1998. Books, Bricks, and Bytes: Libraries in the Twenty-First Century. New Brunswick, NJ: Transaction Publishers.

Lyman, P. 1998 The UCC 2-B debate and the sociology of the information age. Berkeley Journal of Law and Technology. 13 (3): 1063-1087.

Lynch, C. A. 1991. Visions of electronic libraries. The Bowker Annual: Library and Book Trade Almanac Facts, Figures and Reports. pp. 75–82. New Providence, NJ: R. R. Bowker.

Lynch, C. A. 1993a. Accessibility and Integrity of Networked Information Collections (Background Paper No. BP-TCT–109). Washington: Office of Technology Assessment.

Lynch, C. 1993b. Interoperability: The standards challenge for the 90s. Wilson Library Bulletin, March: 38–42.

Lynch, C. 1998. The evolving Internet: Applications and network service infrastructure. Journal of the American Society for Information Science 49 (11): 961–972.

Lynch, C., Garcia-Molina, H. 1995. Interoperability, scaling, and the digital libraries research agenda. http://www.hpcc.gov/reports/reports-nco/iita-dlw/main.html.

Lynch, C., Michelson, A., Summerhill, C., Preston, C. 1995. Information Discovery and Retrieval. White paper. Washington, DC: Coalition for Networked Information. Available from ftp.cni.org.

Lynch, C. A., and Preston, C. M. 1990. Internet access to information resources. In M. E. Williams, ed. Annual Review of Information Science and Technology 25. Amsterdam: Elsevier, pp 263–312.

Lynch, C. A., and Preston, C. 1991 Evolution of networked information resources. In M. E. Williams, ed. National Online Meeting 1991: Proceedings of the 12th National Online Meeting, New York, May 7–9, 1991. Medford, New Jersey: Learned Information, 221–230.

Lynn, M. S., and the Technology Assessment Advisory Committee to the Commission on Preservation and Access. 1990. Preservation and Access technology: The relationship between digital and other media conversion processes: A structured glossary of technical terms. Information Technology and Libraries 9 (4): 309–336.

Maack, M. N. 1993. L'Heure Joyeuse, the first children's library in France: its contribution to a new paradigm for public libraries. The Library Quarterly 63 (3): 257–281.

Maciuszko, K. L. 1984. OCLC: A decade of development, 1967–1977. Littleton, CO: Libraries Unlimited.

Maes, P. 1994. Agents that reduce work and information overload. Communications of the ACM 37 (7): 30–40, 146.

Mann, C. C. 1998. Who will own your next good idea? Atlantic Monthly. http://www.theatlantic.com/issues/98sep/copy.htm.

Mansell, R. 1993. The new telecommunications: A political economy of network evolution. London: Sage.

Marchionini, G. 1995. Information seeking in electronic environments. NY: Cambridge University Press.

Marcoux, Y., and Sevigny, M. 1997. Why SGML? Why now? Journal of the American Society for Information Science 48 (7): 584–592.

Markey, K. 1984. Subject searching in library catalogs: Before and after the introduction of online catalogs. Dublin, OH: OCLC Online Computer Library Center.

Markey, K. 1986. Users and the online catalog: subject access problems. In J. R. Matthews, ed. The Impact of Online Catalogs, New York: Neal-Schuman Publishers, Inc., 35–69.

Markey, K., and Demeyer, A. N. 1986. Dewey Decimal Classification Online Project: Evaluation of a Library Schedule and Index Integrated into the Subject Searching Capabilities of an Online Catalog: Final Report to the Council on Library Resources. Dublin, OH: OCLC Online Computer Library Center, Inc.

Markus, M. L. 1994. Finding a happy medium: Explaining the negative effects of electronic communication on social life at work. ACM Transactions on Information Systems 12 (2): 119–149.

Mason, E. 1971a. The great gas bubble prick't; or, computers revealed—by a gentleman of quality. College and Research Libraries 32 (3): 183–195.

Mason, E. 1971b. Along the academic way. Library Journal 96 (May 15): 1675–1676.

Mason, E. 1972. Computers in libraries. Library Resources and Technical Services 16 (1): 5–10.

Mason, J. D. 1997. SGML and related standards: New directions as the second decade begins. Journal of the American Society for Information Science 48 (7): 593–596.

Mason, M. G. 1996. The yin and yang of knowing. In Books, Bricks, and Bytes, Daedalus, Journal of the American Academy of Arts and Sciences; Proceedings of the American Academy of Arts and Sciences 125 (4): 161–171. Republished in S. R. Graubard and P. LeClerc, eds. 1998. Books, Bricks, and Bytes: Libraries in the Twenty-First Century. New Brunswick, NJ: Transaction Publishers.

Mastanduno, M. 1992. Economic Containment: CoCom and the Politics of East-West Trade. Ithaca: Cornell University Press.

Matthews, J. R., Lawrence, G. S., and Ferguson, D. K. 1983. Using online catalogs: A nationwide survey. New York: Neal-Schuman.

Mayer-Schonberger, V., and Foster, T. E. 1997. A regulatory web: Free speech and the global information infrastructure. In B. Kahin and C. Nesson, eds. Borders in Cyberspace: Information Policy and the Global Information Infrastructure. MIT Press. Pp. 235–254.

McCallum, S. H. 1989. IFLA's role in international bibliographic data exchange—UNIMARC. IFLA Journal 15 (1): 50–56.

McChesney, R. W. 1996. The internet and U. S. communication policy-making in historical and critical perspective. Journal of communication 46 (1): 98–124.

McClung, P. A. 1996. Digital collections inventory report. Washington, D. C. : Council on Library Resources; Commission on Preservation and Access.

McCune, D. 1998. A scholarly publisher's view on electronic publishing. (Sage Publications.) Unpublished lecture, April 15, 1998, graduate seminar in electronic publishing, UCLA, C. L. Borgman, Professor.

McGarry, D., and Svenonius, E. 1991. More on improved browsable displays for online subject access. Information Technology And Libraries 10 (3): 185–191.

McKnight, C., Dillon, A., and Richardson, J. 1991. Hypertext in Context. Cambridge: Cambridge University Press.

McLean, I. 1989. Democracy and New Technology. Cambridge, Eng. : Polity Press.

McLuhan, M. 1964. Introduction. In H. A. Innis, The Bias of Communication, 2nd ed. Toronto: University of Toronto Press.

Meadow, C. T., Cerny, B. A., Borgman, C. L., and Case, D. O. 1989. Online access to knowledge: System design. Journal of the American Society for Information Science 40 (2): 99–109.

Meadows, A. J. 1974. Communication in Science. London: Butterworths.

Meadows, J. 1991. Electronic information and Eastern Europe. Aslib Proceedings 43 (7/8): 249–255.

Meadows, A. J. 1998. Communicating Research. San Diego: Academic Press.

Meeks, B. N. 1999. The privacy hoax. Communications of the ACM 42 (2): 17–19.

Melody, W. H., Salter, L., and Heyer, P., eds. 1981. Culture, Communication, and Dependency: The Tradition of H. A. Innis. Norwood, NJ: Ablex.

Menzel, H. 1966. Information needs and uses in science and technology. In C. A. Cuadra, ed. Annual Review of Information Science and Technology 1. New York: Wiley Interscience. pp. 41–69.

Merriam-Webster 1993. Merriam Webster's Collegiate Dictionary, 10th ed. Springfield, MA: Merriam-Webster.

Metadata and Interoperability in Digital Library Related Fields. 1996. Second DELOS Workshop. Bonn, 7-8 October 1996. European Consortium for Informatics and Mathematics. Le Chesnay, France: ERCIM. Http://www-ercim.inria.fr.

Metadata FAQ (Frequently Asked Questions). 1996. http://www.its.nbs.gov/nbs/meta/faqa.htm.

Metadata for Web Databases. 1998. 11th ERCIM Database Research Group Workshop. Sankt Augustin, Germany, 25-26 May 1998. European Consortium for Informatics and Mathematics. Le Chesnay, France: ERCIM. Http://www-ercim.inria.fr

Micco, M. 1991. The next generation of online public access catalogs: a new look at subject access using hypermedia. In D. A. Tyckoson, ed. Enhancing access to information: Designing catalogs for the 21st century. New York: Haworth Press, 103–132.

Miller, W. 1997. Troubling myths about on-line information. Chronicle of Higher Education 63 (47), A44.

Miller, S. M., and Mangan, C. E. 1983. Interesting effects of information and coping style in adapting to gynaecological stress: should a doctor tell all? Journal of Personality and Social Psychology 45: 223–236.

Miller, B. N., Riedl, J. T., Konstan, J. A. 1997. Experiences with GroupLens: making Usenet useful again. Proceedings of the USENIX 1997 Annual Technical Conference. Berkeley, CA: USENIX Association. Pp. 219-233.

Mitchell, W. J. 1995. City of Bits: Space, Place, and the Infobahn. MIT Press.

Moore, R., Baru, C., Gupta, A., Ludaescher, B., Marciano, R., and Rajasekar, A. 1999. Collection-Based Long-Term Preservation, GA Report GA-A23183 submitted to National Archives and Records Administration, June 1999.

Moravcsik, M. J., and Murugesan, P. 1975. Some results on the function and quality of citations. Social Studies of Science 5: 86–92.

More on Mason (other correspondence concerning Mason's article). 1971. College and Research Libraries 32 (Sept.): 388–392.

Morin, J.-H. 1998. HyperNews, a hypermedia electronic-newspaper environment based on agents. In R. H. Sprague, Jr., ed. 1998. Proceedings of the Thirty-First Hawaii International Conference on System Sciences. Volume II: Digital Documents Track. Los Alamitos, CA: IEEE Computer Society. pp. 58–67.

Morris, W., ed. 1981. The American Heritage Dictionary of the English Language. Boston: Houghton Mifflin.

Myers, B. A., and Rosson, M. B. 1992. Survey on user interface programming. In Proceedings of the ACM Computer-Human Interaction Conference, Monterey, CA May 3–7, 1992. New York: Association for Computing Machinery. pp. 195–202.

Namioka, A., and Schuler, D., eds. 1990. PDC '90: Participatory Design conference proceedings. March 31–April 1, 1990, Seattle, WA. Palo Alto, CA: Computer Professionals for Social Responsibility.

National Information Infrastructure: Agenda for Action. 1993. http://real.utk .edu/FINS/Information_Infrastructure/Fins-II–09.txt.

National Research Council; Commission on Physical Sciences, Mathematics, and Applications; Computer Science and Telecommunications Board; NRENAISSANCE Committee, L. Kleinrock, Chair. 1994. Realizing the Information Future: The Internet and Beyond. Washington, DC: National Academy Press.

National Science Foundation. 1993. Research On Digital Libraries, NSF 93–141, A Joint Initiative of: National Science Foundation Computer and Information Science and Engineering Directorate; Advanced Research Projects Agency, Computing Systems Technology Office and the Software And Intelligent Systems Technology Office; and the National Aeronautics and Space Administration. Washington, DC: National Science Foundation.

National Science Foundation. 1998. Digital Libraries Initiative - Phase II. Call for Proposals. Arlington, VA: National Science Foundation. http://www.nsf.gov/pubs/ 1998/nsf9863/nsf9863.htm

National Science and Technology Council; Committee on Technology; Subcommittee on Computing, Information, and Communications R and D. 1998. Networked Computing for the 21st Century. Supplement to the President's FY 1999 Budget. Washington, DC: Office of Science and Technology Policy.

Neelameghan, A. 1997. International cooperation and assistance. World Information Report. Paris: UNESCO. Http://www.unesco.org/cii/wirerpt/vers-web.htm. Chapter 27, pp. 361–380.

Neelameghan, A., and Tocatlian, J. 1985. International cooperation in information systems and services. Journal of the American Society for Information Science 36 (3): 153–163.

Nelson, T. H. 1987. Literary Machines: The Report on, and of, Project Xanadu Concerning Word Processing, Electronic Publishing, Hypertext, Thinkertoys, Tomorrow's Intellectual Revolution, and Certain other Topics Including Knowledge, Education, and Freedom. Swarthmore, PA: Theodore Holm Nelson.

Newhagen, J. E., and Rafaeli, S., eds. 1996. Symposium: The Net. Journal of Communication 46 (1): 4–124.

Newman, N. S. 1999. Evaluation criteria and quality control for legal knowledge systems on the Internet: A case study. Law Library Journal 91 (1): 9–27.

The next 50 years. 1997. Communications of the ACM 40 (2): 3–142, passim. Special 50th anniversary of ACM issue.

Nielsen, J. 1993. Usability Engineering. Boston: Academic Press.

Noam, E. 1992. Telecommunications in Europe. New York: Oxford University Press.

Norman, D. A. 1988. The psychology of everyday things. New York: Basic Books.

Nunberg, G. 1996. Introduction. In G. Nunberg, ed. The future of the book. Berkeley, CA: University of California Press, pp. 9–20.

O'Brien, A. 1994. Online catalogs: Enhancements and developments. In M. E. Williams, ed. Annual Review of Information Science and Technology, 29. Medford, NJ: Learned Information. Published on behalf of the American Society for Information Science. pp. 219–242.

OCLC Online Computer Library Center. 1998a. OCLC System Statistics. Dublin, OH: OCLC. Http://www.oclc.org.

OCLC Online Computer Library Center. 1998b. Personal communication, Richard Greene, Cataloging and Technical Services, OCLC, Dublin, OH.

Odlyzko, A. M. 1995. Tragic loss or good riddance? The impending demise of traditional scholarly journals. International Journal of Human-Computer Studies 42, 71–122. http://www.research.att.com/~amo.

Odlyzko, A. M. 1996. On the road to electronic publishing. Euromath Bulletin 2 (1): 49–60. http://www.research.att.com/~amo.

Odlyzko, A. M. 1997. Silicon dreams and silicon bricks: the continuing evolution of libraries. Library Trends 46 (1): 152–167.

Odlyzko, A. M. 1998. The economics of electronic journals. Journal of Electronic Publishing 4 (1). http://www.press.umich.edu/jep/04–01/odlyzko.htm. Also appeared in 1997 First Monday 2 (8), http://www.firstmonday.dk/ and in R. Ekman and R. Quandt, eds. Technology and Scholarly Communication. Berkeley: University of California Press. http://www.research.att.com/~amo.

Office of Science and Technology Policy; Federal Coordinating Council for Science, Engineering, and Technology; Committee on Physical, Mathematics, and Engineering Sciences. 1994. High Performance Computing and Communications:

Toward a National Information Infrastructure. Washington, DC: Executive Office of the President, Office of Science and Technology Policy.

Okerson, A. S. 1996a. When will we know it's a library? In G. Marchionini and E. A. Fox, eds. Proceedings of ACM Digital Libraries '96. New York: Association for Computing Machinery.

Okerson, A. S. 1996b. Buy or lease? Two models for scholarly information at the end (or the beginning) of an era. In Books, Bricks, and Bytes, Daedalus, Journal of the American Academy of Arts and Sciences; Proceedings of the American Academy of Arts and Sciences 125 (4): 55–76. Republished in S. R. Graubard and P. LeClerc, eds. 1998. Books, Bricks, and Bytes: Libraries in the Twenty-First Century. New Brunswick, NJ: Transaction Publishers.

Olsen, J. 1997. The gateway: point of entry to the electronic library. In L. Dowler, ed. Gateways to knowledge: The role of academic libraries in teaching, learning, and research. MIT Press. pp. 123–132.

Oppliger, R. 1997. Internet security: Firewalls and beyond. Communications of the ACM 40 (5): 92–102.

Otlet, P. 1934. Traite de documentation. Brussels: Editiones Mundaneum. (Reprinted 1989, Liege: Centre de Lecture Publique de al Communaute Francaise).

Otlet, P. 1990. International Organization and Dissemination of Knowledge: Selected Essays of Paul Otlet. W. B. Rayward, ed. and trans. Amsterdam: Elsevier.

Oudet, B. 1997. Multilingualism on the Internet. Scientific American 276 (3): 77–78.

Paepcke, A., Chang, C-C. K., Garcia-Molina, H., and Winograd, T. 1998. Interoperability for digital libraries worldwide. Communications of the ACM 41 (4): 33–43.

Pafford, J. H. P. 1935. Library co-operation in Europe. London: The Library Association.

Paisley, W. J. 1965. The flow of (behavioral) science information—a review of the literature. Palo Alto: Institute for Communication Research, Stanford University.

Paisley, W. J. 1980. Information and work. In B. Dervin and M. J. Voigt, eds. Progress in the Communication Sciences (Vol. 2, pp. 114–165). Norwood, NJ: Ablex.

Paisley, W. 1984. Communication in the communication sciences. In Dervin, B. and Voigt, M., eds. Progress in the Communication Sciences. Norwood, NJ: Ablex.

Paisley, W. 1989. Bibliometrics, scholarly communication, and communication research. Communication Research 16 (5): 701–717.

Paisley, W. 1990. The future of bibliometrics. In C. L. Borgman, ed. Scholarly Communication and Bibliometrics, pp. 281–299. Newbury Park, CA: Sage Publications.

Parks, M. R., and Floyd, K. 1996. Making friends in cyberspace. Journal of Communication 46 (1): 80–97.

Pentland, A. 1996. Smart rooms. Scientific American 274 (4): 54–62.

Pejtersen, A. M., Austin, A. 1984. Fiction retrieval: Experimental design and evaluation of a search system based on users' value criteria. Journal of Documentation 40 (1): 25–35.

Perry, J. W., Kent, A., and Berry, M. M. 1956. Machine Literature Searching. New York: Interscience.

Peters, C., and Picchi, E. 1997. Across Languages, Across Cultures: Issues in Multilinguality and Digital Libraries. D-Lib Magazine. http://www.dlib.org/dlib/may97/peters/05peters.html.

Pew Foundation. 1998. To publish and perish. http://www.arl.org/scomm/pew/pewrept.html.

Phillips, D. J. 1998. Cryptography, secrets, and the structuring of trust. In P. E. Agre and M. Rotenberg, eds. Technology and Privacy: The New Landscape. MIT Press. Pp. 125–142.

Plowman, L. 1995. The interfunctionality of talk and text. Computer Supported Cooperative Work (CSCW) 3 (3–4): 229–246.

Polya, G. 1957. How to Solve It. Garden City, NJ: Doubleday/Anchor.

Pontin, J. 1998. The post-PC world. The new era of ubiquitous computing. Red Herring 61 (December): 50–66, passim.

Porck, H. J. 1996. Mass deacidification: An update on possibilities and limitations. Amsterdam: European Commission on Preservation and Access, and Washington, D. C. : Commission on Preservation and Access.

Preservation of Digital Information. 1998. Sixth DELOS Workshop. Tomar, Portugal, 17-19 June 1998. European Consortium for Informatics and Mathematics. Le Chesnay, France: ERCIM. Http://www-ercim.inria.fr.

Price, J. W., and Price, M. S. 1985. International Librarianship Today and Tomorrow: A Festschrift for William J. Welsh. New York: K. G. Saur.

Priss, U., and Old, J. 1998. Information access through conceptual structures and GIS. In R. Larson, K. Petersen, and C. M. Preston, eds. ASIS '98: Proceedings of the 61st American Society for Information Science Annual Meeting 35. October 24–29, 1998, Pittsburgh. Medford, NJ: Information Today. pp. 91–99.

Proceedings of the IEEE International Forum on Research and Technology Advances in Digital Libraries (ADL '98). 1998. April 22–24, Santa Barbara, CA. Los Alamitos, CA: IEEE Computer Society.

Quarterman, J. S. 1990. The Matrix: Computer Networks and Conferencing Systems Worldwide. Bedford, MA: Digital Press.

Rajasekar, A., Marciano, R., and Moore, R. 1999. Collection Based Persistent Archives, Proceedings of the 16th IEEE Symposium on Mass Storage Systems, March 1999.

Rastl, P. 1994. Coordinating networks in Central and Eastern Europe: CEEnet. Proceedings of INET '94 / JENC5. June 1994, Prague.

Rau, P. 1990. Council of Europe working party on retrospective cataloguing, Text of recommendations (R (89)11, 19 September 1989). ZU 16 (1): 29–31.

Rawlins, G. J. E. 1991. The new publishing: Technology's impact on the publishing industry over the next decade. Technical report. Department of Computer Science, Indiana University, Bloomington, IN 47405. Available via ftp from iuvax .cs.indiana.edu: /usr/ftp/pub/techreports/tr340.ps.z.

Rayward, W. B. 1993. Electronic information and the functional integration of libraries, museums and archives. In S. Ross and E. Higgs, eds. Electronic Information Resources and Historians: European Perspectives. St. Katharinen: Scripta Mercaturae Verlag, pp. 227–243.

RECON Working Task Force. 1969. Conversion of retrospective catalog records to machine-readable form; a study of the feasibility of a national bibliographic service. Rather, J. C., ed. Washington: Library of Congress.

RECON Working Task Force. 1973. National aspects of creating and using MARC/RECON records. Rather, J. C., and Avram, H. D., eds. Washington: Library of Congress.

Reich, R. B. 1992. The Work of Nations. New York: Vintage.

Reitman, W. 1964. Heuristic decision procedures, open constraints, and the structure of ill-defined problems. In M. W. Shelley and G. L. Bryan, eds. Human Judgements and Optimality. New York: Wiley.

Rice, R. E., et al. 1984. The New Media: Communication, Research, and Technology. Beverly Hills, CA: Sage.

Rice, R. E., Borgman, C. L., Bednarski, D., and Hart, P. J. 1989. Journal-to-journal citation data: Issues of validity and reliability. Scientometrics 15 (3–4): 257–282.

Richardson, J. V. 1995. Knowledge-based systems for general reference work: applications, problems, and progress. San Diego: Academic Press.

Ritchie, L. D. 1991. Communication Concepts 2: Information. Newbury Park, CA: Sage.

Roberts, G. F. 1998. The home page as genre: a narrative approach. In R. H. Sprague, Jr., ed. 1998. Proceedings of the Thirty-First Hawaii International Conference on System Sciences. Volume II: Digital Documents Track. Los Alamitos, CA: IEEE Computer Society. pp. 78–86.

Roberts, R., comp. 1994. Library development in Central and Eastern Europe: From assistance to cooperation; an investment for the future. Proceedings of a workshop held in Strasbourg, 3–4 February 1994. Final Report. Directorate-General XIII, Telecommunications, Information Market and Exploitation of Research. Luxembourg: Office for Official Publications of the European Communities. EUR 15660 EN.

Robertson, S. E., and Hancock-Beaulieu, M. M. 1992. On the evaluation of IR systems. Information Processing and Management 28 (4): 457–466.

Rogers, E. M. 1983. Diffusion of Innovations, 3rd ed. New York: Free Press.

Rogers, E. M. 1986. Communication technology: The New Media in Society. New York: Free Press.

Rogers, E. M. 1995. Diffusion of Innovations, 4th ed. New York: Free Press.

Rogers, E. M., and Cottrill, C. A. 1990. An author co-citation analysis of two research traditions: Technology transfer and the diffusion of innovations. In C. L. Borgman, ed. Scholarly Communication and Bibliometrics. Newbury Park, CA: Sage Publications. pp. 157–165.

Roget's II, The new thesaurus. 1980. Boston: Houghton Mifflin.

Ropers, N. 1989. Information and communication between east and west with the CSCE (Conference on Security and Co-operation in Europe). In J. Becker and T. Szecsko, eds. 1989. Europe Speaks to Europe. International Information Flows between Eastern and Western Europe. London: Pergamon Press. pp. 363–384.

Rosenberg, J. B., and Borgman, C. L. 1992. Extending the Dewey Decimal Classification via keyword clustering: The Science Library Catalog project. Proceedings of the 54th American Society for Information Science Annual Meeting 29. October 26–29, 1992, Pittsburgh. pp. 171–184. Medford, NJ: Learned Information.

Rotenberg, M. 1998. The privacy law sourcebook: United States Law, international law, and recent developments. Washington, DC: Electronic Privacy Information Center. http://www.epic.org.

Rothenberg, J. 1995. Ensuring the longevity of digital documents. Scientific American 272 (1): 24–29.

Rothenberg, J. 1996. Metadata to support data quality and longevity. First IEEE Metadata Conference, April 16–18, 1996, Silver Spring, MD. http://computer.org/conferen/meta96/rothenberg_paper/ieee.data-quality.html.

Rothenberg, J. 1997. Digital information lasts forever—or five years, whichever comes first. RAND Video V–079.

Rozsa, G. 1992. Hungarian research libraries: Their contribution to the European culture and cultural heritage. The Liber Quarterly 2 (2): 33–40.

Ruhleder, K. 1995. "Pulling down" books vs. "pulling up" files: Textual databanks and the changing culture of classical scholarship. In S. L. Star, ed. The Cultures of Computing. Oxford, UK: Blackwell, pp. 181–195.

Rupnik, J. 1991. Central Europe or Mitteleuropa? In S. R. Graubard, ed. Eastern Europe . . . Central Europe . . . Europe. Boulder: Westview Press. Pp. 233–266.

Rusbridge, C. 1998. Electronic Libraries Programme. Talk presented at IEEE International Forum on Research and Technology Advances in Digital Libraries (ADL '98). 1998. April 22–24, Santa Barbara, CA. Los Alamitos, CA: IEEE Computer Society.

Saint-Georges, I. de. 1998. Click here if you want to know who I am: Deixis in personal home pages. In R. H. Sprague, Jr., ed. 1998. Proceedings of the Thirty-First Hawaii International Conference on System Sciences. Volume II: Digital Documents Track. Los Alamitos, CA: IEEE Computer Society. pp. 68–77.

Salton, G. 1992. The state of retrieval system evaluation. Information Processing and Management 29 (7): 646–656.

Samuelson, P. 1995. Copyright and digital libraries. Communications of the ACM 38 (4): 15–21, 110.

Samuelson, P. 1996. Intellectual property rights and the global information economy. Communications of the ACM 39 (1): 23–28.

Samuelson, P. 1998. Encoding the law into digital libraries. Communications of the ACM 41 (4): 13–18.

Sanders, T. 1987. Slow Fires. Video/film, American Film Foundation and Council on Library and Information Resources.

Sanders, T. 1997. Into the Future: On the Preservation of Knowledge in the Digital Age. Video/film, American Film Foundation and Council on Library and Information Resources.

Saracevic, T. 1975. Relevance: A review of and a framework for the thinking on the notion in information science. Journal of the American Society for Information Science 26: 321–343.

Sawyer, P., Flanders, A., and Wixon, D. 1996. Making a difference—the impact of inspections. Proceedings of the Conference on Human Factors in Computing Systems, Association for Computing Machinery. New York: ACM, pp. 375–382.

Schamber, L. 1994. Relevance and information behavior. In M. E. Williams, ed. Annual Review of Information Science and Technology 29. Medford, NJ: Learned Information, 3–48.

Schatz, B. R. 1997. Information retrieval in digital libraries: Bringing search to the Internet. Science 275 (N5298): 327–334.

Schauble, P., & Smeaton, A. F., eds. 1998. An International Research Agenda for Digital Libraries. Summary Report of the Joint NSF-EU Working Groups on Future Developments for Digital Libraries Research. DELOS Workshop on Emerging Technologies in the Digital Libraries Domain. Brussels, Belgium, 12 October 1998. European Consortium for Informatics and Mathematics. Le Chesnay, France: ERCIM. Http://www-ercim.inria.fr.

Schiller, D. 1994. From culture to information and back again: commoditization as a route to knowledge. Critical Studies in Mass Communication 11 (1): 93–115.

Schneier, B., and Banisar, D. 1997. The electronic privacy papers: documents on the battle for privacy in the age of surveillance. New York: Wiley.

Schopflin, G. 1994. Postcommunism: The Problems of democratic construction. Daedalus, Journal of the American Academy of Arts and Sciences. Proceedings of the American Academy of Arts and Sciences 123 (3): 127–142.

Schottlaender, B., ed. 1992. Retrospective Conversion: History, Approaches, Considerations. New York: Haworth Press.

Segbert, M. 1996. Library co-operation with Central and Eastern Europe. Reports of Country Visits, Version 2.0. Luxembourg: Commission of the European Communities, Directorate General XIII, Telecommunications, Information Market and Exploitation of Resarch, Libraries Programme (DG XIII/E–4).

Segbert, M., and Burnett, P., eds. 1997. Proceedings of the Conference on Library Automation in Central and Eastern Europe, Budapest, Hungary, April 10–13, 1996. Soros Foundation Open Society Institute Regional Library Program and Commission of the European Communities, Directorate General XIII, Telecommunications, Information Market and Exploitation of Research, Libraries Programme (DG XIII/E–4). Budapest: Open Society Institute.

Shane, S. 1994. Dismantling Utopia: How Information Ended the Soviet Union. Chicago: Ivan R. Dee.

Shannon, C., and Weaver, W. 1949. The mathematical theory of communication. Urbana: University of Illinois Press.

Shapiro, C., and Varian, H. R. 1999. Information Rules: A Strategic Guide to the Network Economy. Cambridge, MA: Harvard Business School Press.

Shepherd, M., and Watters, C. 1998. The evolution of cybergenres. In R. H. Sprague, Jr., ed. 1998. Proceedings of the Thirty-First Hawaii International Conference on System Sciences. Volume II: Digital Documents Track. Los Alamitos, CA: IEEE Computer Society. pp. 97–109.

Shneiderman, B. 1980. Software Psychology: Human Factors in Computer and Information Systems. Boston: Little, Brown.

Shneiderman, B. 1987. Designing the User Interface: Strategies for Effective Human-Computer Interaction, 1st ed. Reading, MA: Addison-Wesley.

Shneiderman, B. 1992. Designing the User Interface: Strategies for Effective Human-Computer Interaction, 2nd ed. Reading, MA: Addison-Wesley.

Shneiderman, B. 1998. Designing the User Interface: Strategies for Effective Human-Computer Interaction, 3rd ed. Reading, MA: Addison-Wesley.

Shneiderman, B., Byrd, D., and Croft, W. B. 1997. Clarifying search: A user-interface framework for text searches. D-Lib Magazine 3 (1). http:///www.dlib.org/dlib/january97/retrieval.

Shute, S. J., and Smith, P. J. 1993. Knowledge-based search tactics. Information Processing and Management 29 (1): 29–45.

Silberman, S. 1998. Ex Libris: The joys of curling up with a good digital reading device. WIRED 6 (07): 98–104.

Simon, H. 1973. The structure of ill structured problems. Artificial Intelligence 4: 181–201.

Simsova, S. 1968. Lenin, Krupskaia, and libraries. G. Peacock and L. Prescott, trans. London: Clive Bingley.

Skelton, B. 1973. Scientists and social scientists as information users: A comparison of results of science user studies with the investigation into information requirements of the social sciences. Journal of Librarianship 5: 138–155.

Skvorecky, J. 1991. Bohemia of the soul. In S. R. Graubard, ed. Eastern Europe . . . Central Europe . . . Europe. Boulder: Westview Press. Pp 115–143.

Slangen, K., Kleemann, P. P., and Krohne, H. W. 1993. Coping with surgical stress. In Attention and avoidance: Strategies in coping with aversiveness, Krohne, H. W., ed. Hogrefe & Huber Publishers: Goettingen, Germany. pp. 321–346.

Slater, D. 1997. What have you done with IT lately? CIO 10 (21): 114–120.

Sloan, B. G. 1991. Linked Systems For Resource Sharing. Boston: G. K. Hall.

Small, H. G. 1978. Cited documents as concept symbols. Social Studies of Science 8: 327–340.

Small, H. G. 1982. Citation context analysis. In B. J. Dervin and M. J. Voigt, eds. Progress in communication science 3. Norwood, NJ: Ablex. pp. 287–310.

Small, H. G., and Greenlee, E. 1990. A co-citation analysis of AIDS research. In C. L. Borgman, ed. Scholarly Communication and Bibliometrics. Newbury Park, CA: Sage Publications. pp. 166–193.

Smiraglia, R. P., and Leazer, G. H. 1999. Derivative bibliographic relationships: The work relationship in a global bibliographic database. Journal of the American Society for Information Science 50 (6): 493-504.

Smith, A. 1999. Why digitize? Washington, DC: Council on Library and Information Resources.

Smith, J. W. T., ed. 1992. Networking and the Future of Libraries. Proceedings of the UK Office for Library Networking Conference, April 2–5, 1992. Westport: Meckler.

Smith, T. R., Andresen, D, Carver, L., Donlil, R., Fischer, C., Frew, J., Goodchild, M., Ibarra, O., Kemp, R. B., Kothuri, R., Larsgaard, M., Manjunath, B. S., Nebert, D., Simpson, J, Wells, A., Yang, T., and Zheng, Q. 1996. A digital library for geographically referenced materials. IEEE Computer 29 (5): 54–60.

Society of American Archivists. 1995. Position Statement: Archival issues raised by information stored in electronic form. Archives@miamiu.acs.muohio.edu. Reprinted in The CPSR Newsletter 13 (2): 11–12.

Soergel, D. 1998. Large multilingual vocabularies: Structure and software requirements. In R. Larson, K. Petersen, and C. M. Preston, eds. ASIS '98: Proceedings of the 61st American Society for Information Science Annual Meeting 35. October 24–29, 1998, Pittsburgh. Medford, NJ: Information Today. pp. 572.

Soros Foundations. 1995. Building Open Societies: Soros Foundations 1995 Report of Activities. New York: Open Society Institute.

Sprague, R. H., Jr., ed. 1998. Proceedings of the Thirty-First Hawaii International Conference on System Sciences. Volume II: Digital Documents Track. Los Alamitos, CA: IEEE Computer Society.

Sproull, L., and Kiesler, S. 1991. Connections: New Ways of Working in the Networked Organization. MIT Press.

Stam, D. C. 1984. How art historians look for information. Art Documentation 3 (1): 117–119.

Star, S. L., and Ruhleder, K. 1996. Steps toward an ecology of infrastructure: Design and access for large information spaces. Information Systems Research,

Special issue on Organizational Transformation, J. Yates and J. Van Maanen, eds. 7 (1): 111–134.

Stefik, M. 1997. Shifting the possible: How trusted systems and digital property rights challenge us to rethink digital publishing. Berkeley Technology Law Journal 12 (1): 137–160.

Stewart, L. 1996. User acceptance of electronic journals: Interviews with chemists at Cornell University. College and Research Libraries 57: 339–349.

Stone, S. 1982. Humanities scholars: information needs and uses. Journal of Documentation 38 (4): 292–312.

Strassmann, P. A. 1997. Will big spending on computers guarantee profitability? Datamation 43 (2): 75–85.

Sussman, G., and Lent, J. A., eds. 1991. Transnational Communications: Wiring the Third World. Newbury Park: Sage.

Svenonius, E. 1994. Access to nonbook materials: The limits of subject indexing for visual and aural languages. Journal of the American Society for Information Science 45 (8): 589–599.

Tagliacozzo, R., Kochen, M., and Rosenberg, L. 1970. Orthographic error patterns of author names in catalog searches. Journal of Library Automation 3 (2): 93–101.

Tague-Sutcliffe, J. M., ed. 1996. Special topic issue: Evaluation of information retrieval systems. Journal of the American Society for Information Science 47 (1): 1–105.

Tan, Z., Mueller, M., and Foster, W. 1997. China's new Internet regulations: Two steps forward, one step back. Communications of the ACM 40 (12): 11–16.

Taylor, A. G. 1984. Authority files in online catalogs: An investigation of their value. Cataloging and Classification Quarterly 4 (3): 1–17.

Taylor, R. S. 1968. Question-negotiation and information seeking in libraries. College and Research Libraries 29 (3): 178–194.

Tedd, L. A. 1993. An Introduction to Computer-Based Library Systems, 3rd ed. Chichester, England: John Wiley and Sons.

Tillett, B. B. 1991. A taxonomy of bibliographic relationships. Library Resources and Technical Services 35: 150–159.

Tillett, B. B. 1992. Bibliographic relationships: An empirical study of the LC machine-readable records. Library Resources and Technical Services 36: 162–188.

Tillett, B. B. (March 28, 1999). Director, Integrated Library Systems Program, Library of Congress, Washington, D. C. [Personal communication.]

Toffler, A. 1981. The Third Wave. London: Pan.

Trybula, W. J. 1997. Data mining and knowledge discovery. In M. E. Williams, ed. Annual Review of Information Science and Technology 32. New York: Knowledge Industry for American Society for Information Science, pp. 197–230.

Turkle, S. 1995. Life on the Screen. New York: Simon and Schuster.

Turtle, H. R., and Croft, W. B. 1991. Evaluation of an inference network-based retrieval model. ACM Transactions on information systems 9 (3): 187–222.

Turtle, H. R., and Croft, W. B. 1992. A comparison of text retrieval models. Computer Journal 35 (3): 279–290.

Unesco. 1981. Intergovernmental Council for the General Information Programme (Third Session). Paris, October 26–30, 1981. Science and Technology Information: Analytical Case Studies. Executive Summary Report. Paris: Unesco. PGI–81/CONF. 201/COL–4.

The Unicode Standard: A Technical Introduction, 1998. Http://www.unicode.org.

The Unicode Standard, Version 2.0. 1996. Reading, MA: Addison-Wesley.

United Nations. 1982. Administrative Committee on Coordination. Task Force on Science and Technology for Development. Technical Working Group 1. Second Session; October 4–7, 1982. New York: United Nations. ACC 1982 Conference Room Papers.

United Nations. 1998. Universal Declaration of Human Rights. Fiftieth Anniversary. Adopted and proclaimed by General Assembly Resolution 217 A (III) of 10 December 1948. High Commissioner for Human Rights. http://www.unhchr.ch/html/menu3/b/a_udhr.htm.

Van Bogart, J. W. C. 1995. Magnetic tape storage and handling: A guide for libraries and archives. Washington, D. C. : Commission on Preservation and Access, and St. Paul, MN: National Media Laboratory.

van Zuuren, F. J., and Wolfs, H. M. 1991. Styles of information seeking under threat: personal and situational aspects of monitoring and blunting. Personality and Individual Differences 12: 141–149.

Volkmer, I. 1997. Universalism and particularism: The problem of cultural sovereignty and global information flow. In B. Kahin and C. Nesson, eds. Borders in Cyberspace: Information Policy and the Global Information Infrastructure. MIT Press. Pp. 48–83.

Vosper, R. 1989. International Library Horizons: Some Personal Observations. Washington, DC: Library of Congress.

Wactlar, H. D., Christel, M. G., Yihong Gong, and Hauptmann, A. G. 1999. Lessons learned from building a terabyte digital video library. IEEE Computer 32 (2): 66–73.

Wagner, C. S., Cargill, C. F., and Slomovic, A. 1995. Open systems standards in manufacturing: implications for the national information infrastructure. In B. Kahin and J. Abbate, eds. Standards policy for information infrastructure. MIT Press, pp. 178–197.

Walker, S. 1988. Improving subject access painlessly: recent work on the Okapi online catalogue projects. Program 22 (1): 21–31.

Walker, S., and Hancock-Beaulieu, M. M. 1991. OKAPI at City: An evaluation facility for interactive IR. London: British Library. (British Library Research Report no. 6056).

Walsh, J. P., and Bayma, T. 1996. The virtual college: Computer-mediated communication and scientific work. The Information Society 12 (4): 343–363.

Wanting, B. 1984. How do children ask questions in children's libraries? Concepts of visual and auditory perception and language expression. Social Science Information Studies 4: 217–234.

Waters, D. J. 1998a. What are digital libraries? CLIR (Council on Library and Information Resources) Issues, No. 4. http://www.clir.org/pubs/issues/issues04.html.

Waters, D. J. 1998b. Steps toward a system of digital preservation: Some technological, political, and economic considerations. In B. L. Hawkins and P. Battin, eds. The Mirage of Continuity: Reconfiguring Academic Information Resources for the 21st Century. Washington, DC: Council on Library and Information Resources and the Association of American Universities. pp. 193–206.

Weber, H., and Dorr, M. 1997. Digitization as a method of preservation? Washington, DC: Commission on Preservation and Access, and Amsterdam: European Commission on Preservation and Access.

Weibel, S. 1995. Metadata: The foundations of resource description. D-Lib Magazine. http://www.dlib.org/dlib/July95/07weibel.html.

Weibel, S., Iannella, R., and Cathro, W. 1997. The 4th Dublin Core Metadata Workshop Report. DC-4, March 3-5, 1997, National Library of Australia, Canberra. D-Lib Magazine. http://www.dlib.org/dlib/june97/metadata/06weibel.html.

Weibel, S., and Miller, E. 1997. Image description on the Internet. A summary of the CNI/OCLC Image Metadata Workshop, September 24-25, 1996, Dublin, Ohio. D-Lib Magazine. http://www.dlib.org/dlib/January97/oclc/01weibel.html.

Wellman, B. 1998. Networks in the Global Village. Boulder, CO: Westview Press.

Weschler, L. 1995. Mr. Wilson's Cabinet of Wonder. New York: Vintage Books.

White, A. S. 1995. The Internet: Is it curtains for Lexis-Nexis and Westlaw? Legal Information Alert 14 (4): 1–3.

White, H. D. 1990. Author co-citation analysis: Overview and defense. In C. L. Borgman, ed. Scholarly Communication and Bibliometrics, pp. 84–106. Newbury Park, CA: Sage Publications.

White, H. D., and McCain, K. W. 1997. Visualization of literatures. In M. E. Williams, ed. Annual Review of Information Science and Technology 32. New York: Knowledge Industry for American Society for Information Science, pp. 99–168.

Wilson, T. D. 1981. On user studies and information needs. Journal of Documentation 37 (1): 3–15.

Wilson, T. D. 1988. The cognitive approach to information seeking behavior and information use. Social Science Information Studies 4 (2): 197–204.

Wilson, T. D. 1994. Information needs and uses: fifty years of progress? In B. C. Vickery, ed. Fifty Years of Information Progress: A Journal of Documentation Review. London: Aslib. Pp. 15–51.

Wilson, T. D. 1996. Information behaviour: An inter-disciplinary perspective. British Library Research and Innovation Report, 10. London: British library Research and Innovation Centre.

Wilson, T. D. 1997. Information behaviour: an interdisciplinary perspective. Information Processing and Management 33 (4): 551–572.

Winograd, T. 1997. The Design of Interaction. In Peter Denning and Bob Metcalfe, eds. Beyond Calculation, The Next 50 Years of Computing, Springer-Verlag, 1997.

Winograd, T., Bennett, J., De Young, L., and Hartfield, B., eds. 1996. Bringing Design to Software. Reading, MA: Addison-Wesley.

Yates, J., and Orlikowski, W. 1992. Genres of organizational communication: A structurational approach to studying communication and media. Academy of Management Review 17 (2): 299–326.

Young, P. R. 1996. Librarianship: A changing profession. In Books, Bricks, and Bytes, Daedalus, Journal of the American Academy of Arts and Sciences; Proceedings of the American Academy of Arts and Sciences 125 (4): 103–125. Republished in S. R. Graubard and P. LeClerc, eds. 1998. Books, Bricks, and Bytes: Libraries in the Twenty-First Century. New Brunswick, NJ: Transaction Publishers.

Z. 1991. To the Stalin Mausoleum. In S. R. Graubard, ed. Eastern Europe . . . Central Europe . . . Europe. Boulder: Westview Press. Pp 283–338.

Zhao, D. G., and Ramsden, A. 1995. Report on the ELINOR electronic library pilot. Information Services and Use 15: 199–212.

Zonis, M., and Semler, D. 1992. The East European Opportunity: The Complete Business Guide and Sourcebook. New York: John Wiley and Sons.

Index